An Attacking Repertoire for White

Sam Collins

BATSFORD

First Published 2004

Copyright © Sam Collins 2004

The right of Sam Collins to be identified as Author of this work has been
asserted by him in accordance with the Copyright, Designs and Patents Act 1988.

ISBN 0 7134 8910 3

A CIP catalogue record for this book is available from the British Library.

Printed in Great Britain by
Creative Print and Design (Wales), Ebbw Vale

for the publishers

B T Batsford
Chrysalis Books Group
The Chrysalis Building
Bramley Road
London W10 6SP

www.chrysalisbooks.co.uk

An imprint of Chrysalis Books Group plc

Distributed in the United States and Canada by Sterling Publishing Co.,
387 Park Avenue South, New York, NY 10016, USA

Contents

Bibliography

Books

Anti-Sicilians: A Guide for Black, Rogozenko (Gambit 2003)

Attacking with 1 e4, Emms (Everyman 2001)

Easy Guide to the Panov-Botvinnik Attack, Aagaard (Cadogan 1998)

Learn from the Chess Grandmasters, Keene (Batsford 1998)

Mastering the French, McDonald & Harley (Batsford 1997)

My Best Games of Chess, Anand (Gambit 1998)

NCO, Nunn, Burgess, Emms & Gallagher (Gambit 1998)

An Opening Repertoire for the Attacking Player, Keene & Levy (Batsford 1994)

Play the 2 c3 Sicilian, Rozentalis & Harley (Gambit 2002)

Soft Pawn, Hartston (Cadogan 1995)

The Scotch Game, Wells (Batsford 1998)

Periodicals

New in Chess

NIC Yearbook

Databases

MegaBase 2004

TWIC

Programs

Chessbase 8

Fritz 5

THIS BOOK IS DEDICATED TO
GERRY MURPHY

Acknowledgements

To my parents, David and Jackie, for love and support in this and everything else;

To my friends, especially David and Kevin, for everything;

To Alex Baburin, John Shaw, Brian Kelly and Richard Palliser for playing better chess than I do and sharing some insights;

To Jimmy Adams, Malcolm Pein and Roger Huggins at Batsford for opportunities and advice;

To Herbert Scarry and the whole Irish Chess Union for tireless work and inestimable help.

Introduction

Writing an opening repertoire manual is a daunting task. I'm under no illusions as to the saturation of the genre, the endless collections of good and bad texts with which hapless club players are faced at every tournament bookstall. It was a thought which troubled me during the preparation of this book – among so many, it's difficult to stand out.

Yet with the realisation that too many repertoire books exist comes the epiphany that there's a reason for this – done properly, an opening repertoire work could serve its reader to an incredible degree for the rest of his chess career. To select interesting, promising variations, present them in an accessible fashion and communicate something of how to handle the resulting positions is a challenge worth facing. Conversely, such a book should be read before perhaps any others, since what I'm about to discuss will have a huge impact on half of your games, if you like the lines and the analysis and, of course, actually read the thing.

I took on this project in order to better learn the lines contained here. Having played competitive chess for nearly half my life and in a wide range of countries and tournaments, I've never seen the romance in losing games through lack of preparation. Too many times I've found myself thinking endlessly in positions perfectly familiar to my opponent, unaware of the plethora of games on my database illustrating just how to handle the position in front of me. Opening theory may seem like a chore but, irrespective of my claim that it is not so, it's one which must be tackled before we can know that we've played to our potential.

A word on the selection of lines. My initial instinct was to ensure quality by selecting the absolute main line of each opening – Ruy Lopez, Open Sicilians, 3 ♘c3 against the French and so on – before it became clear that such a repertoire couldn't be adequately covered in a single volume. That said, I was still very resistant to a failing which seems to be common amongst repertoire books, namely the selection of markedly inferior lines since they have less theory and are easier to cover. In the end, I plumped for a repertoire which is pretty topical (all of its branches are regularly essayed by strong players) and within the openings themselves I've tried to select the critical lines. While this text's primary purpose must be to equip the reader with good opening positions, it is pleasing that the repertoire touches on a broad range of setups which, when mastered, will enable the reader to handle a full spectrum of positions where he's nursing an initiative. The naturally-attacking Isolated Queen's Pawn (IQP) and e5-spearhead pawn structures are here, where attacks are often built up gradually, but so are lines with pawn free centres where every move is vital. Material equality abounds, but occasionally we've given the opponent a pawn in exchange for some play. The queens are on for most of it, but sometimes we have endgames where the black king floats around in the middle of the board. In short, I guess everyone has to put certain filters on the chess information they choose to engage with and assimilate, and I think looking through the glasses of this repertoire, studying the variations and the games of their exponents, will prove of immense benefit.

I'd prefer to leave the chess to the chapters, and will close here with the hope that you find this work of some use.

Sam Collins
Dublin 2004

CHAPTER ONE
The Sicilian Defence

"It is generally thought that the sharpest and most active defence to 1 e4 is the Sicilian. However, is there not a resemblence between the Sicilian defender and the wrestler who begins the fight before he has climbed into the ring?"

GM Viktor Korchnoi

1 e4 c5 2 c3

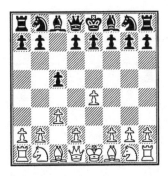

Your success against the Sicilian determines your success with 1 e4. You could have devastating novelties lined up against the French, the Pirc and the Caro – if you can't handle the position after 1 ... c5 then all your hard work doesn't matter. This line comes up in about a third of my White games, it's the most popular opening in the game today, and I've put this chapter first because knowing how to beat this stuff is as vital as knowing how to move the pieces.

My recommendation is the c3-Sicilian. For those of you whose eyes are glazing over at the very thought of this line, a confession: As a lifelong Sicilian player, I used to regard it somewhat contemptuously, as a boring and innocuous attempt at equality. White's play seemed devoid of ambition. Then this happened:

McShane – Collins
Kilkenny Masters 2002

1 e4 c5 2 ♘f3 e6 3 c3 ♘f6 4 e5 ♘d5 5 d4 cxd4 6 cxd4 d6 7 ♗d3 ♘b4 8 ♗b5+ ♗d7 9 ♗c4 ♗c6 10 0-0 ♘d7 11 ♘c3! ♗xf3 12 ♕xf3 ♘c2? 13 d5!!

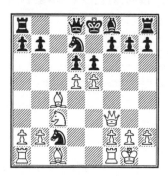

13 ... ♘d4 14 ♕g4 dxe5 15 dxe6 fxe6 16 ♗e3! ♘f6 17 ♕h3 ♕b6 18 ♗xd4 exd4 19 ♖fe1 ♗e7 20 ♖xe6 ♕c5 21 ♖ae1!

21 ... dxc3 22 ♖xe7+ ♕xe7 23 ♖xe7+ ♔xe7 24 ♕e6+ ♔d8 25 ♕d6+ ♔e8 26 ♗b5+ ♔f7 27 ♕c7+ 1-0

Oh, and this:

Motwani – Collins
British Championship 2003

1 e4 c5 2 c3 ♘f6 3 e5 ♘d5 4 ♘f3 e6 5 d4 cxd4 6 ♗c4 d6 7 cxd4 ♗e7 8 0-0 0-0 9 ♕e2 ♘c6 10 ♕e4 ♖e8 11 ♖e1 ♘b6 12 ♗d3 g6 13 ♘c3 ♘b4 14 ♗b1 ♘4d5 15 ♕g4! ♘xc3 16 bxc3 ♕c7 17 h4! ♘d7 18 h5 f5 19 ♕g3 ♔g7 20 hxg6 hxg6

21 ♗xf5!! exf5 22 exd6 ♗xd6 23 ♗h6+! ♔xh6 24 ♕h4+ ♔g7 25 ♖xe8 ♘f8 26 ♖ae1 1-0

So now I'm defecting to the dark side. White's idea is simple – he wants to get a pawn on d4 without conceding a central majority. Black can't stop this directly (2 ... e5 doesn't quite equalise, as we'll see), and his two main defences both focus on the e4-pawn (which can no longer be defended by a knight on c3).

That's about it. This line is solid, dangerous, and a great choice for club players. Personally, I certainly intend to keep it in my repertoire for a while to come.

The Typical 2 ... ♘f6 Structure

This is the most common pawn formation in the 2 ... ♘f6 variation. I just want to say three things.

NUMBER ONE: White's pawn structure, statically, is worse. This means that if Black can get into an endgame, or even just fully mobilise, he'll have the better chances.

NUMBER TWO: White has more space. This means that he can develop his pieces quickly to good squares.

NUMBER THREE: A black knight can't use f6. This means that Black's kingside is denied on of its most natural defenders.

ONE + TWO + THREE Necessity to act quickly + Active pieces + Insufficiently defended black king = What?

That's right. Checkmate the guy. You absolutely have to play actively and aggressively here, the above equation not only permits but demands it. If you're not comfortable with this obligation than play something else.

Game One
Pavasovic – Halkias
Vidmar Memorial 2003

1 e4 c5 2 c3 ♘f6 3 e5 ♘d5 4 d4 cxd4 5 ♘f3 ♘c6

This is one of Black's more popular defences in top-level c3-Sicilian encounters. In my opinion, it is Black's best attempt to equalise, though with the disadvantage that White has several boring and drawish options (not that I'd recommend these lines for a second, but if you're up against someone who is both higher-rated and a caveman you might wish to check them out). The main continuation here is 6 ♗c4, after which 6 ... ♘b6 7 ♗b3 d5! gives Black excellent prospects of equalising in a well-explored position. I've examined several attempts here and they're all just draws. So I've opted for a slightly more offbeat continuation based on a pawn sacrifice, which is objectively as good as 6 ♗c4 with the added bonus of being nice and trappy. It's main exponent seems to be Pavasovic, who has a very impressive score even against GMs in this line.

6 cxd4 d6 7 ♗c4 ♘b6 8 ♗b3!?

This is the fun line. 8 ♗b5 is safe for both sides after 8 ... dxe5 9 ♘xe5 ♗d7.

8 ... dxe5

8 ... d5 is actually a very tricky move, since the only way to a white advantage is the unlikely 9 ♘h4!. White can't allow ... ♗g4 and ... e6 (Note that 9 h3 isn't great: after 9 ... ♗f5 10 ♘c3 e6 11 0-0 ♗e7 12 ♗c2 ♗g6 13 a3 0-0 14 ♘e2 ♗xc2 15 ♕xc2 ♖c8 16 ♕d3 f6 17 exf6 ♗xf6 18 ♖e1 e5! Black was better, despite somehow losing very quickly in Khamrakulov-Teran Alvarez, Malaga Open 2004). Recent experience in this variation has been limited but quite favourable for White – I don't see how Black can pressurise the centre. 9 ... ♘c4 10 ♘c3 a6 11 0-0 b5 12 ♗c2 ♖a7 (Notkin gives 12 ... e6 13 g3 ♕b6 14 ♘e2 b4 as slightly better for White) 13 a4 b4 14 ♘e2 ♗g4 15 f3 ♗d7 16 b3 ♘b6 17 ♗e3 and the centre was rock-solid in Filipovic-Ilincic, Podgorica 1996.

9 d5!

This is the idea – the black knight is sidelined, while its white counterpart will dominate matters on e5. Of course this line involves sacrificing a pawn, but you can't have everything.

9 ... ♘a5

9 ... ♘b4 10 ♘c3 e6 11 ♗g5! is dangerous, for instance 11 ... f6 12 ♘xe5!! fxg5 13 ♕h5+ g6 14 ♘xg6 hxg6 15 ♕xh8 ♘d3+ 16 ♔f1 exd5 17 ♕d4 ♘f4 18 h4 ♗e6 19 ♖e1 ♕c7 20 hxg5 0-0-0 21 ♖h4 ♗f5 22 ♕xf4 ♗d6 23 ♕d2 ♗c5 24 ♘b5 ♘c4 25 ♗xc4 dxc4 26 ♖e8 ♕b6 27 ♘xa7+ 1-0 in Pavasovic-Kurnosov, Istanbul 2003.

10 ♘c3 ♘xb3

10 ... f6!? was the choice of the superbly-prepared Boris Gelfand when he faced Pavasovic at the Milan Vidmar Memorial in 2001. After 11 0-0 g6 12 ♗e3 ♗g7 13 ♗c5! ♗g4 14 h3 ♗xf3 15 ♕xf3 ♘xb3 16 axb3 0-0 17 ♖fd1 ♕d7 18 d6 exd6 the players agreed a draw, though I like White after 19

♗xd6 when he either gains an exchange or recoups his material with a better bishop.

11 ♕xb3 e6 12 ♘xe5 exd5

Van der Wiel essayed the interesting 12 ... ♘xd5 against Fressinet in Wijk aan Zee 2004. After 13 ♕b5+ ♗d7 14 ♕xb7 ♗b4, Fressinet opted for 15 ♗d2 (15 ♘xd7!? is very forcing but looks quite appealing. Black is forced to resort to tactics to maintain material equality: 15 ... ♕c8! [15 ... ♘xc3?? 16 ♕xb4 is hopeless] when the paradoxical 16 ♘c5!! [blocking the c-file!] 16 ... ♕xb7 [16 ... ♗xc5 17 ♕b5+ ♔f8 18 ♘xd5 ♖b8 19 ♕d3 exd5 20 0-0] 17 ♘xb7 ♖b8 [17 ... ♘xc3?? 18 a3 wins a piece] 18 ♗d2 ♖xb7 19 ♘xd5 exd5 is an endgame which would be good for Black if he had time to fully co-ordinate but 20 0-0-0! seems to give White a clear advantage due to the vulnerability of the d5-pawn. After 20 ... ♗d6 21 ♗c3 Black is in trouble) and after 15 ... ♗xc3 16 bxc3 ♕c8 17 ♖b1 ♘b6 18 ♕f3 0-0 19 ♕g3 ♘d5 20 c4 ♘e7 21 ♗b4 ♖e8 22 ♕f3 f6 23 ♘xd7 ♕xd7 24 0-0 I'd take White. If this isn't to your taste, have a look at the alternative to White's 15th, which is untested but looks pretty strong.

13 ♗e3!

Much more important than castling at this stage – having the option of ♗xb6 is very handy in the forthcoming complications.

13 ... ♗d6 14 ♕b5+

14 ... ♔f8!

This is clearly Black's best move, but of course such a move requires either good preparation or exceptional ability from the Black player.

The plausible 14 ... ♗d7?! led to a rout in Pavasovic-Panchenko, Pula Open 2001 after 15 ♘xd7 ♕xd7 16 0-0-0! ♕xb5 17 ♘xb5 ♔d7 18 ♗xb6 axb6 19 ♖xd5 ♔c6 20 ♖hd1 ♗c5 21 ♘c3 ♖he8 22 a3 ♖e7 23 ♔c2 and Black resigned due to the threat of 23 b4.

15 ♘f3

This calm retreat causes Black the most problems.

15 0-0-0 ♗e6 16 ♘f3 ♕c7 17 ♔b1 ♖d8 18 ♖he1 h6 19 ♘d4 ♗e5 20 ♕b4+ ♗d6 21 ♘xe6+ fxe6 22 ♕g4 ♗c5 23 ♕xe6 h5 24 ♗xc5+ ♕xc5 25 ♖d3 was yet another win in Pavasovic-Bergez,Mitropa Cup 1999, but Black can improve and I prefer the text.

15 ... ♗d7

15 ... ♗e6 16 0-0 ♘c4!?

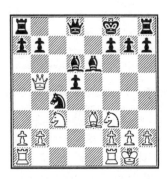

is the recommendation of most recent literature on this line. Seeing how strong White's initiative is when Black hangs on to the pawn, theoreticians have recommended this move as a clean equaliser. I think they have underestimated White's resources however.

a) 16 ... h6 is probably a little too slow: after 17 ♖fd1! ♔g8 18 a4! ♔h7 19 a5 ♘c8 20 ♘xd5 White was much more active in Pavasovic-Tratar, Graz 2001, and after 20 ... ♕d7 21 ♕d3+ ♗f5 22 ♕c4 ♕e6 23 ♘d4 ♕g6 24 ♘xf5 ♕xf5 25 ♘c7! ♖b8 26 ♖d5! ♕g6 27 ♖ad1 a6 28 h4! his advantage was decisive.

b) 16 ... ♕e8 soon equalised in Fressinet-Atarov, ACP Blitz 2004, but after 17 ♖fd1 ♕xb5 18 ♘xb5 ♘c4, instead of Fressinet's 19 ♗d4, I quite like 19 ♗xa7!?, when I prefer White after 19 ... ♘xb2 20 ♖db1 ♘c4 21 ♘xd6 ♖xa7 (21 ... ♘xd6? 22 ♗c5 followed by 23 ♖xb7) 22 ♘xb7, with interesting play after ♘c5 and ♘d4; 17 ♕xb7 ♕c8 18 ♕xc8+ ♖xc8 19 ♗d4 ♗c5 (19 ... a6 20 b3 ♘a5 21 ♘a4 ♘c6 is given as equal by Rozentalis and Harley, but 22 ♗c5! is pleasant for White) 20 ♗xc5+ (20 ♖ac1! ♔e7 21 b3 [Rogozenko only considered 21 ♗xg7] seems to give White good chances of a bind, for instance 21 ... ♗xd4 22 ♘xd4 ♘b2 [22 ... ♘e5 23 ♖fd1] 23 ♘ce2 ♘d3 24 ♖cd1 ♘c5 25 ♖fe1) 20 ... ♖xc5 21 ♘a4 ♖c8 22 b3 ♘a3 23 ♘d4 ♔e7 (23 ... ♘c2! 24 ♘xc2 ♖xc2 25 ♖fc1 ♖xc1+ 26 ♖xc1 ♔e7 is Rogozenko's suggestion. White has nothing here, especially since 27 ♖c7+? ♔d6 28 ♖xa7 ♖c8 is good for Black) 24 ♖ac1 ♔d6 was a slightly better endgame for White in Pavasovic-Jelen, Ljubljana 2002.

16 ♕b3 ♗e6 17 ♘d4 ♔g8 18 0-0 ♖c8 19 ♖fe1

This position is a perfect illustration of why Black generally prefers to ditch a pawn and bail out to an endgame. He has retained his extra pawn, but is effectively a rook down. Hanging on to the pawn will be a tough job too – the pressure on the queenside is enormous.

19 ... ♕d7 20 ♘cb5 ♗b8 21 ♘xe6 ♕xe6 22 ♗xb6 ♕xb6 23 ♕xd5

A transformation. White grabs back his pawn and maintains a ridiculous advantage in activity. Black's next fatally weakens his pawn structure, but I've no idea what to suggest instead.

23 ... ♕c6 24 ♕xc6 bxc6 25 ♖ac1! g6 26 ♖e7! ♔g7 27 ♘xa7 ♗xa7 28 ♖xa7 ♖he8 29 ♔f1 ♖cd8

This position offers excellent winning chances to White, and Pavasovic's technique is exquisite.

30 ♖e1! ♖f8 31 g3 ♖d2 32 ♖e2 ♖fd8 33 ♖ee7! ♖f8 34 b3 ♔h6 35 h4 g5 36 hxg5+ ♔xg5 37 ♖ec7 h5

Virtual resignation. The rest doesn't need any comment.

38 ⌐xc6 h4 39 gxh4+ ⌐xh4 40 ⌐f6 ⌐g5 41 ⌐fxf7 ⌐xf7 42 ⌐xf7 ⌐xa2
43 ⌐f3 ⌐b2 44 ⌐d3 ⌐f4 45 f3 ⌐a2 46 ⌐e1 ⌐e5 47 ⌐d1 ⌐b2 48 ⌐c1 ⌐h2
49 ⌐b1 ⌐e6 50 b4 ⌐h4 51 ⌐b3 ⌐d6 52 b5 ⌐c7 53 ⌐c2 ⌐d4 54 ⌐c3 ⌐d6
55 b6+ ⌐b7 56 ⌐c4 ⌐d1 57 ⌐c5 ⌐d2 58 f4 ⌐f2 59 ⌐b4 ⌐d2 60 ⌐d4
⌐c2+ 61 ⌐d6 ⌐xb6 62 ⌐b4+ ⌐a5 63 ⌐b8 ⌐f2 64 ⌐e5 1-0

Game Two
Sermek – Fercec
Croatian Cup 2002

1 e4 c5 2 c3 ⌐f6 3 e5 ⌐d5 4 ⌐f3 e6 5 d4 cxd4 6 cxd4 d6

This has become very popular nowadays. I think the main reason is that
there is no easy way for White to simplify the game, and so it makes sense
to learn this defence with Black which can then be used against both strong
and weak players. Nonetheless, it's quite tough to handle with Black – just
have a look at what McShane and Motwani did to me in the introduction.

7 ⌐c4

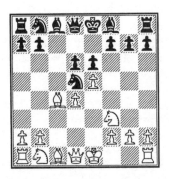

7 ... ⌐c6

This is the most popular approach – Black leaves his knight on d5. Since
⌐xd5 is rarely a good idea, this is perfectly logical.

7 ... ⌐b6 is okay, but has the defect of moving the knight even further
away from the kingside. Pavasovic-Ruck from the European Team
Championship 2003 continued 8 ⌐b3 (I prefer this to 8 ⌐d3 ⌐c6, when in
Howell-Poluljahov, Gibraltar Masters 2004 Black had already equalised
after 9 0-0 ⌐b4) 8 ... ⌐d7 (8 ... ⌐c6 should probably be met by 9 exd6
⌐xd6 10 ⌐c3 ⌐d5 11 0-0 0-0 12 ⌐e1 as in Har Zvi-Stisis, Israeli League
1999, when White was much better after 12 ... b6?! 13 ⌐xd5 exd5 14 ⌐g5
⌐e7 15 ⌐a4!) 9 0-0 ⌐c6 10 ⌐c3 ⌐e7 11 exd6 ⌐xd6 12 ⌐e5 0-0 13 ⌐f4
⌐d8 14 ⌐g4! ⌐8d7 15 ⌐h6 ⌐f6 16 ⌐xc6 bxc6 17 ⌐c2 ⌐e8 18 ⌐e4 g6

19 ♘d6 ♖e7 20 ♖fd1 when White's somewhat primitive handling gave him an excellent game.

8 0-0 ♗e7 9 ♕e2!

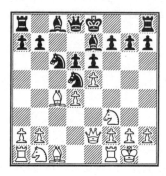

By far the best square for the queen – the e5-pawn is fortified, d1 is vacated for a rook, and ♕e4 is prepared. Note that in this position White is best advised to delay the development of his last two minor pieces, instead trying to force the d5-knight to move, when ♘c3 becomes more appealing.

9 ... 0-0

9 ... ♘b6 10 ♗b3 d5 looks and is time-wasting – White can secure good chances with 11 ♘c3 a6 12 ♖d1 ♗d7 13 ♕e3! ♖c8 14 ♕f4 h6 15 h4! (the past 3 moves have set up some nice kingside pressure, while Black's queenside counterplay is yet to get off the ground) 15 ... ♘a5 (15 ... ♘b4 16 a3 ♘c6 17 h5 ♗f8 18 ♕g4 ♘e7 19 ♘h4 ♘f5 20 ♘xf5 exf5 21 ♕g3 ♗e6 22 ♘a4 ♘xa4 23 ♗xa4+ b5 24 ♗b3 was much better for White in Sermek-Orel, Bled Open 2001, even before Black hung some material with 24 ... ♖g8? 25 ♗xh6) 16 ♕g3 ♔f8 17 ♘e2 ♘xb3 18 axb3 ♗b5 19 ♘f4, when 19 ... g5 20 ♘h5 ♗e2 21 ♖e1 ♗xf3 22 ♕xf3 ♘d7 23 ♗d2 ♕b6 24 ♖ec1 ♖c6 25 ♖xc6 bxc6 26 ♕d3 ♘b8 27 ♘f6 ♗xf6 28 exf6 ♔e8 29 ♗a5 ♕b7 30 hxg5 hxg5 31 ♕g3 ♔d7 32 ♕xg5 ♕c8 33 ♖e1 ♖g8 34 ♕h5 ♕f8 35 ♕h2 ♕c8 36 ♖xe6!! fxe6 37 ♕h7+ ♔d6 38 ♕e7 mate was the pretty conclusion of Sermek-Crisan, Vidmar Memorial 2001.

10 ♕e4 ♕c7

10 ... ♗d7 is Rogozenko's recommendation in his excellent book on Anti-Sicilians and so will undoubtedly be played more in the future. He considers several White moves here, but for some reason omits 11 ♖d1! which looks very logical to me, fortifying the centre and remaining flexible with the development of the minor pieces. Godena-Belotti, Italian Championship 1999 continued 11 ... ♖c8 (also 11 ... ♕c7 12 ♘a3 ♘a5 13 ♗d3 f5 14 exf6 ♘xf6 15 ♕h4 ♕d8 16 ♗g5 g6 17 ♖e1 ♖f7 18 ♘c2! ♖c8 19 ♘e3! ♘c6 20 a3 ♘h5 21 ♘g4 ♗xg5 22 ♘xg5 ♖f4 23 ♖e4! gave White

a huge attack in Handoko-Van Meter, US Open 2003) 12 ♗b3 ♔h8 13 ♘c3 f5 14 exf6 ♘xf6 15 ♕e2 d5 16 ♘e5! ♗xe5 17 dxe5 ♘g8 18 ♗e3 ♗c5 19 ♗xc5 ♖xc5 20 ♕e3 b6 21 ♗c2 ♘h6 22 ♖d4 ♕e7 23 ♖ad1 ♗e8 24 ♕g3 and White had more space, more active pieces and good attacking chances.

11 ♖e1

This has been Sermek's recent choice – previously he tried 11 ♘bd2. Putting the rook on e1 maintains the option of developing the knight on c3 or the bishop on g5.

11 ... ♗d7

11 ... a6 12 ♘g5 ♗xg5 13 ♗xg5 dxe5 (13 ... ♕b6 14 ♗d3 g6 15 ♘d2 dxe5 16 dxe5 ♕xb2 17 ♘f3 ♕a3 18 ♗c4 ♘ce7 19 ♘d4 b5 20 ♗b3 ♗b7 21 ♕h4 ♖fe8 22 ♖ad1 ♘c6 23 ♗xd5 exd5 24 ♘xc6 ♗xc6 25 ♖e3 ♕f8 26 ♗f6 ♗d7 27 ♖xd5 and White dominated in Kosintseva-Kursova, North Ural Cup 2003) 14 dxe5 ♘de7 15 ♘d2 ♘g6 16 ♘f3 b5 17 ♗b3 ♗b7 18 ♖ac1 ♖ac8 19 h4 ♕b8 occurred in Sermek-Stevic, Croatian Ch. 2002, and now instead of 20 ♕e3? ♘cxe5, 20 ♕e2! keeps a nice attacking position.

12 ♘g5

The positional approach, gaining the two bishops in return for relinquishing most of his kingside attacking chances.

12 ♗d3 would be tempting in the event of 12 ... g6?! 13 ♗h6 and 14 h4, but unfortunately Black can exploit the lack of pressure on the a2-g8 diagonal with 12 ... f5! 13 exf6 ♘xf6 when he stands very well.

12 ... ♗xg5

If he's going to chop it off he should do so now.

12 ... g6 is the alternative, but the attacking chances offered by the g5-knight are obvious. Fritz suggests the elegant 13 ♗b3!, preparing ♘c3, with excellent play.

13 ♗xg5 dxe5 14 dxe5 ♘de7 15 ♗d2!

White wants to put the bishop on c3, then probably build on the queenside – transferring either a knight (♘d2-f3-g5) or a rook (♖e3-g3/h3) to the kingside looks unconvincing. White has rather good long term chances in view of his better minor pieces, but Black would have remained solid. We are unfortunately denied the instruction of how Sermek would increase the pressure, since Black now blundered with:

15 ... ♘xe5?

This is just an oversight.

After 15 ... ♘g6 I think Sermek intended 16 f4 with more space and good attacking chances (16 ♗c3 ♘cxe5 17 ♗b3 gives reasonable compensation for the pawn).

16 ♕xe5 ♕xc4 17 ♕d6

I don't know if Black missed this move or simply thought he could force a perpetual attack on the white queen.

17 ... ♘d5 18 ♕xd7 ♖fd8 19 ♕xb7 ♖db8 20 ♕d7 ♖d8 21 ♕b7 ♖db8 22 ♕d7 ♖d8 23 b3! ♕d4 24 ♗c3 ♕d3 25 ♕c6 ♖ac8 26 ♕a4 ♘xc3 27 ♘xc3 ♖xc3 28 ♕xa7 ♖c2 29 h3!

Black has recovered his piece but is still dead lost – the connected queenside passers must decide, as long as White doesn't allow any sacrifices on f2.

29 ... h6 30 b4 ♖d7 31 ♕b6 ♖d6 32 ♕b8+ ♖d8 33 ♕a7 ♖d7 34 ♕e3 ♕c4 35 ♖ec1 ♖d3 36 ♖xc2 ♕xc2 37 ♕c1 ♕a4 38 ♕b2 ♕d7 39 b5 ♖d2 40 ♕e5 f6 41 ♕e1 e5 42 a4 ♕d4 43 ♖b1 ♕d3 44 b6 ♖e2 45 ♕f1 1-0

Game Three
Brynell – Hoerstmann
KB Czech Open 2002

1 e4 c5 2 c3 ♘f6 3 e5 ♘d5 4 d4 cxd4 5 ♘f3 e6 6 cxd4 b6

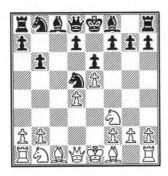

This line has been a big favourite of club players ever since it was recommended in Gallagher's seminal *Beating the Anti-Sicilians*. I used to play it all the time as a kid, with abysmal results. Despite a very clear and logical plan (after a knight exchange on c3 Black plans to exert pressure on the white pawns), I found that I lost game after game in this line because White's space advantage, left largely unchecked, could lead to a very natural kingside attack which I'd have to suffer before even thinking of working against backward pawns. It's notable that one of the most well respected lines for Black against the c3-Sicilian involves getting rid of the e5-pawn almost immediately, after which White has to work up a lot more piece activity to justify his position. This is all rather abstract but what I'm trying to say is that, when examining the material in the ... e6 and ... b6 line, you should note how often White manages to strike before Black gets round to attacking the weak c3-pawn.

7 ♗d3

For years 7 ♘c3 was 'the main line', with play proceeding 7 ... ♘xc3 8 bxc3 ♕c7 9 ♗d2.

7 ♗d3 was given the nod by Rozentalis and Harley, and as far as I can see is just a natural developing move which, by getting the king out of the centre, increases White's aggressive options.

7 ... ♗a6

7 ... ♗b7 8 0-0 ♗e7 (8 ... ♘b4 9 ♗e2 ♗e7 10 ♘c3 0-0 11 a3 ♘d5 12 ♘e4 f5 13 exf6 ♘xf6 14 ♘xf6+ ♗xf6 15 ♗d3 ♗d5 16 ♘e5 ♗xe5 17 dxe5 ♕h4 was slightly better for White after 18 f4! in Almasi-Polgar, Groningen 1997) 9 ♘bd2 0-0 is a natural developing approach for Black. The problem is that it does nothing to combat White's kingside build-up – both the d3-bishop and e5-pawn are left at large. Sermek-Pilz, Austria 1998 continued 10 ♘e4 f5 11 exf6 gxf6 12 ♗h6 ♖f7 13 ♘c3! (hitting Black's best minor piece while opening the b1-h7 diagonal) 13 ... ♗f8 14 ♗d2 ♖g7 15 ♗c4 ♘e7, when 16 d5! exd5 17 ♗b3 ♘a6 18 ♗h6 ♖f7 19 ♗xf8 ♕xf8

20 ♘xd5 ♘xd5 21 ♗xd5 ♗xd5 22 ♕xd5 was an excellent reward for a typical pawn sacrifice, with a clear advantage for White.

7 ... ♗b4+ 8 ♗d2 ♗xd2+ 9 ♕xd2 eases Black's development but trades off an important guardian of d6. Analysis of this variation is somewhat hampered by the dearth of high-level encounters – it seems that no-one plays like this with Black anymore. Rozentalis and Harley have suggested 9 ... ♗a6 10 ♗e4 ♘c6 11 ♗xd5 exd5 12 ♘c3 ♘b4 (12 ... ♘e7 is more compliant: the position after 13 0-0-0 is simply good for White) 13 a3!?, after which 13 ... ♘d3+ 14 ♔d1 d6 (otherwise White will mobilise fully with ♔c2, ♘e1 and ♖axe1) 15 ♘e1 ♘xe1 16 ♖xe1 0-0 17 ♕f4 looks promising for White.

8 0-0 ♗e7 9 ♘c3!

Compared to the 7 ... ♗b7 line, here White has no easy way to manoeuvre the knight to e4 via d2, so he goes for the other approach. While this statically weakens his pawns, the extra defence of d4 and elimination of the d5-knight improves his middlegame chances.

9 ... ♘xc3 10 bxc3 ♗xd3 11 ♕xd3 0-0

12 d5!

Again we see this move, trying to unsettle Black before he gets all his bits out. Both sides will have weaknesses but only White will be active enough to exploit them.

12 ... exd5 13 ♕xd5 ♘c6 14 ♖d1 ♕c7

14 ... ♕b8 15 ♗f4 ♖d8 16 ♕e4! ♕c8 was the similar continuation of Brynell-Kaimer from another round of the same tournament. White's activity is very hard to extinguish: 17 ♖d3 ♕a6 18 ♗g5 ♖ac8 19 h4 b5 20 ♖ad1 ♕xa2 21 ♗xe7 ♘xe7 22 ♘g5 g6 23 ♖xd7 ♖xd7 24 ♖xd7 h6 25 ♖xe7 hxg5 26 e6 ♖f8 27 exf7+ ♖xf7 28 ♖e8+ ♔h7 29 ♕d4 ♖g7 30 hxg5 ♕a4 31 ♕d8 and through simple means Brynell forced mate.

15 ♗f4 ♖fd8 16 ♕e4 ♕b7 17 ♗g5! ♖ab8 18 ♖d3 h6 19 ♗f4 ♘a5 20 ♕e2 ♖bc8 21 ♘d4 ♗f8 22 ♗xh6!

Simple chess has resulted in a decisive attack and the next few moves represent the beginning of the end.

22 ... d6 23 ♖g3 dxe5 24 ♗xg7 ♗xg7 25 ♘f5 f6 26 ♖xg7+ ♕xg7 27 ♘xg7 ♔xg7 28 ♖d1 ♖xd1+ 29 ♕xd1 ♖xc3 30 ♕d7+ ♔g6 31 h4!

Counting the material Black is a pawn down, but the main factor is that this extra pawn is the h-file passer. There is no way that Black can construct a fortress while trying to handle this.

31 ... ♘c6 32 ♕g4+ ♔f7 33 h5 ♘d4 34 ♕d7+ 1-0

35 h6 will be decisive.

The Isolated Queen's Pawn

One of the main characteristics of the 2 ... d5 variation is its tendency to give rise to Isolated Queen's Pawn positions. Since similar structures also arise from my recommendation against the Caro-Kann, its clear that you need to be able to handle this kind of pawn formation with White. I'll only be dealing in the briefest detail with this structure – readers are directed to some of the excellent middlegame books on this issue, above all Baburin's seminal *Winning Pawn Structures*.

The d4-pawn gives White an advantage in space. What this means is that he can develop his pieces more quickly and effectively than can Black. The knights lead happy and fulfilling lives on c3 and f3, the light-squared bishop tends to find the b1-h7 diagonal (as does the queen), the rooks belong on the d- and e-files, and the dark-squared bishop can be effective on g5 or (after ... g7-g6) h6. This means that White is invariably more actively developed than Black, thus a large number of games feature the advance d5. When the d- and e-pawns are swapped, a pawn-free centre is created which favours the more active side. This explains why Black plays with such care to prevent this advance, often simply blocking the square with a knight. This brings up a downside of the IQP. The square in front of the pawn can no longer be hit by a white pawn and so makes a perfect home for a black piece. Moreover, the pawn itself lacks long term pawn support and so, if Black mobilises and starts exerting pressure, demands defence by the white pieces. This spreads inactivity like a cancer through the white position as first one piece and then another play nursemaid to the d4-weakling.

To avoid such a situation, White has to generate play. The d5-advance has already been mentioned. Black's pieces must attend to it, and thus be diverted from their defensive duties (a knight on d5, for instance, can't also be on f6, holding the kingside). So White has quite a natural attack on the kingside – a queen and bishop battery on the b1-h7 diagonal can be effective, as can a rook lift (swinging a rook along the third rank to put some more pressure on the black fortress) or a h-pawn push (both to gain control of g5 and to threaten further damage with h5 and a pawn exchange). All the while White should be attentive to sacrifices on e6 and f7, which can prove very tasty indeed. After Black plays ... g6, the white light-squared bishop can be biting on granite and often seeks employment on the a2-g8 diagonal, when these sacrifices become real possibilities. Finally (especially when Black opts for a formation with ... a6 and ... b5) White can play a little on the queenside, for instance by plonking a knight on c5. There are numerous examples of perfect handling of the IQP in this book, this has just been an overview.

Yusupov – Lobron
Nussloch 1996

I really can't spend any more space on these structures, but I'd like to give you a peek at an absolutely sublime game. It is a masterful demonstration of the full range of IQP resources, but it's also one of the best games I've ever seen. I just can't play over it often enough.

1 d4 ♘f6 2 c4 e6 3 ♘c3 ♗b4 4 e3 0-0 5 ♗d3 d5 6 ♘f3 c5 7 0-0 cxd4 8 exd4 dxc4 9 ♗xc4

Note how a completely different opening results in the same structure. Serious students are encouraged to cross-reference here to find good examples of IQP play – the Nimzo Indian, Queen's Gambit Accepted and Queen's Gambit Declined are particularly fertile fields in this regard.

9 ... b6 10 ♖e1 ♗b7

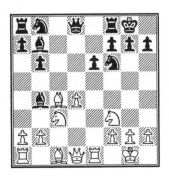

11 ♗d3!

A very interesting decision. Though the bishop was quite well placed on c4, Yusupov drags it back so that he can create a queen and bishop battery on the b1-h7 diagonal.

11 ... ♘c6

An aggressive deployment. The knight hits the pawn but weakens control over d5.

11 ... ♘bd7 is another way of handling the position, preparing ... ♘d5 and ... ♘7f6.

12 a3!

Perfect timing. Played a move earlier, this would've been met by ... ♗xc3, ... ♘bd7 and ... ♖c8 with reasonable play for Black, but now the c6-knight would feel awkward in this structure and so the bishop retreats.

12 ... ♗e7 13 ♗c2! ♖e8 14 ♕d3

This position has arisen a bundle of times in tournaments with *White* to play. In Barle-Grosar, Maribor 1988, White struck with the typical shot 15 d5!! exd5 16 ♗g5, when Black is defenceless, as the reader can verify for himself.

14 ... g6

Note how the queen and bishop battery forces a weakening of the kingside dark squares, allowing White to play ♗h6 for instance. It also makes the idea of h2-h4-h5 more effective, because now we have the g6-pawn to "latch on to".

15 h4!

An excellent move, increasing White's options on the kingside.

15 ... ♕d6 16 ♗g5 ♖ad8 17 ♖ad1 ♕b8 18 ♗b3!

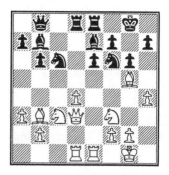

This is a great position for White. All of his pieces are perfectly placed. White's last move is typical: after ... g7-g6, White's light-squared bishop doesn't have much to do on the b1-h7 diagonal so it makes sense to shift it onto the a2-g8 diagonal where it prepares d4-d5 and eyes up e6 and f7.

18 ... a6?!

Black can't really afford this waste of time. The middlegame analysis from here is complicated and too far off the point – I'll just say that anyone who finds a flaw in the combination begun with Yusupov's next move is encouraged to send it in to Batsford. Answers on a postcard please.

19 d5! ♘a5 20 dxe6!! ♘xb3 21 exf7+ ♔xf7 22 ♕c4+ ♔g7 23 ♘e5+-♘g8 24 ♖xd8 ♕xd8 25 ♕f7+ ♔h8 26 ♕xb3 ♕d4 27 ♖e3 ♖f8 28 ♗xe7 1-0

Game Four
Pavasovic – Groetz
Mitropa Cup 2002

1 e4 c5 2 c3 d5 3 exd5 ♕xd5 4 d4 e6 5 ♘f3 ♘f6 6 ♗e3

This move almost invariably leads to IQP positions.

6 ... cxd4

Black has one main option to avoid the structure (I don't believe in 6 ... ♘c6?! 7 dxc5, when Black's compensation is almost invisible): 6 ... ♘bd7, when I would recommend 7 c4 ♕d6 8 ♘c3 cxd4 9 ♘xd4 a6 10 ♗e2 ♕c7 11 0-0 b6 12 ♗f3 ♗b7 13 ♖e1 ♘e5 (13 ... ♗e7 14 ♗f4! ♕xf4 15 ♗xb7 ♖a7 16 ♗f3 ♖c7 17 g3 ♕d6 18 ♘d5 ♘xd5 19 cxd5 ♘e5 20 ♗g2 0-0 21 dxe6 fxe6 22 ♘xe6 was winning for White in Sermek-Titz, Pula Open 2001) 14 ♗xb7 ♕xb7 15 ♗g5 ♘fd7 16 ♕h5 h6 17 ♘xe6!, winning as in Erenburg-Kacheishvili, Istanbul 2003.

7 cxd4 ♘c6 8 ♘c3 ♕d6

White continues the same way against 8 ... ♕d8 – the queen is just more passive here.

9 a3!

A very typical move, guarding against ... ♘b4 which can annoy a bishop on d3 while heading for the optimal d5-square.

9 ... ♗e7 10 ♗d3 b6 11 0-0 0-0 12 ♕e2

I like this move in IQP structures. There are several lines involving an early ♕c2, trying to put the brakes on ... b6 by Black by making threatening noises down the c-file, but ♕e2 is more thematic and aggressive. White plans to centralise his rooks and attack.

12 ... ♝b7 13 ♖ad1 ♖fd8

Black has a wide choice here, and it is unclear which option is best.

13 ... ♖ad8 14 ♝g5 ♖fe8 15 ♖fe1 g6 16 ♝b1 ♕b8 is the setup advocated by Rogozenko and looked pretty logical when it appeared in Pavasovic-Chan Peng Kong, Bled Olympiad 2002, but after the thematic 17 ♝a2! Black found himself under severe pressure. What he did wasn't convincing but it is difficult to suggest worthwhile alternatives. 17 ... ♘g4?! (17 ... ♘h5 18 d5! exd5 19 ♖xd5 ♝f8 20 ♘e4 ♖xd5 21 ♝xd5 ♘d4 22 ♝xf7+ ♔xf7 23 ♘xd4 ♕e5 [23 ... ♝xe4 gives rise to an enduring attack after 24 ♕c4+ ♔g7 25 ♘e6+ ♖xe6 26 ♕xe6 ♝f5 27 ♕c4!, for instance 27 ... ♕c8 28 ♕d4+ ♔g8 29 ♕d5+ ♔g7 30 ♝e7!] 24 ♘c3 ♕xe2 25 ♖xe2 ♖xe2 26 ♘dxe2 and White's technique was up to the task in Kobalia-Batsanin, Russian Team Championship 2004) 18 g3 ♝xg5 19 ♘xg5 ♘h6 20 ♘ce4 ♔g7 21 ♕f3 f5 (21 ... ♘f5 fails to 22 g4! ♘cxd4 23 ♖xd4 ♖xd4 24 gxf5 ♝xe4 25 f6+ ♔g8 26 ♘xe4 intending ♕e3, hitting the rook and threatening ♕h6) 22 ♘xe6+ ♖xe6 23 ♝xe6 fxe4 24 ♕c3 ♔f6 25 d5+ ♕e5 26 dxc6 ♕xc3 27 bxc3 ♖xd1 28 ♖xd1 ♝xc6 29 ♝d5 and Black, an exchange down for nothing, resigned.

13 ... ♖ac8 14 ♖fe1 ♖fd8 15 ♝g5 ♕b8 16 ♝b1 ♖d7 lost material after 17 d5! ♘xd5 18 ♘xd5 exd5 19 ♝f5 in Pavasovic-Podkriznik, Slovenian Championship 1999. 19 ... ♖cd8 20 ♝xd7 ♖xd7 21 ♝xe7 ♘xe7 22 ♘e5 and White was much better.

14 ♖fe1 h6

This is a useful precaution.

14 ... ♖ac8 15 ♝g5! threatens the d5-advance.

15 ♝b1 ♝f8 16 ♝c1!?

16 ... g6

16 ... ♘e7 17 ♘e5 ♘f5 was essayed in Pavasovic-Petrosian, Slovenian Team Championship 1999. This is an instructive example of how careful Black must be to keep any d5-break under control. He was routed after 18 d5!! ♘xd5 (18 ... ♗xd5 19 ♘xd5 ♘xd5 20 ♕h5 is just as good) 19 ♕h5 ♕e7 20 ♗xf5 ♘xc3 21 ♖xd8 ♖xd8 22 ♘xf7! ♖d5 23 ♘xh6+! gxh6 24 ♕g4+ ♗g7 25 ♗xe6+ ♔h8 26 ♗xh6 ♘e2+ 27 ♔h1 ♖d4 28 ♗xg7+ ♕xg7 29 ♕h5+ ♕h7 30 ♕xe2 ♖e4 31 ♕d2 ♖xe1+ 32 ♕xe1 ♕g7 33 f3.

17 ♗a2!

Again this typical idea – when ... g6 is played, switching to the a2-g8 diagonal to pressurise e6 and f7 can prove highly profitable.

17 ... ♘e7 18 ♘e5 ♘f5 19 ♗f4 ♕e7

Allowing a nice sacrifice, but alternatives don't inspire.

19 ... ♘h5 is Rogozenko's suggestion, with equality after 20 ♗e3 ♗g7, but 20 ♕g4! looks good, for instance 20 ... ♘xf4 21 ♕xf4 ♗g7 22 d5! with advantage.

19 ... ♘xd4 is risky: 20 ♕e3 ♘h5 21 ♖d2! (Rogozenko) is good for White.

20 ♘xf7! ♔xf7 21 ♗xe6+ ♔g7 22 d5

While there is nothing decisive here, White already has two pawns for his piece. Most importantly, all of his pieces are functioning at full capacity, while Black's can hardly move.

22 ... ♔h7 23 ♕f3 ♘g7 24 ♗g8+! ♘xg8 25 ♖xe7 ♗xe7 26 ♗e5

The game enters a new phase. There is rough material equality, but Black's best defensive piece has been exchanged off. The plan, as we saw before, is to push the passer, thereby disrupting Black's co-ordination.

26 ... ♖f8 27 ♕d3 ♗c5 28 ♘e4 ♖ad8 29 ♗xg7 ♔xg7 30 ♘xc5 bxc5 31 ♕c3+ ♘f6 32 ♕xc5 ♖xd5 33 ♖xd5 ♗xd5 34 ♕xa7+ ♖f7 35 ♕c5 ♗b7 36 b4

Black has exchanged the d-pawn, but lost material in the process. The position is now a technical win.

36 ... g5 37 a4 ℎd7 38 h3 g4 39 ♚h2 gxh3 40 ♚xh3 ℎd3+ 41 f3 ♚g6 42 a5 ℎd5 43 ♛c4 ℎd2 44 b5 ♛d5 45 ♛b4 ℎc2 46 ♛b1 ♛e6+ 47 g4 1-0

Chop, chop: The dxc5 Structure

Capturing on c5 is the core of my recommendation in the 2 ... d5 variation. This leads to rich, complex and fascinating positions which I'm hard-pressed to understand conceptually at the best of times, let alone explain with only a structural diagram for comfort. Immerse yourself in the annotated games and you'll learn how to handle this structure – here's the two-minute fortune-cookie version.

White just captured a pawn. This gives Black an automatic choice – to recapture or not to recapture.

If he recaptures, it must be with his queen from d5 (since this is the only piece immediately attacking the pawn, and White is threatening a quick b4 after which his gains begin to look permanent). This will leave his queen on c5, floating around in a relatively pawn-free centre. Black's structure is more useful since he has an extra centre pawn, and if both sides complete development he will be at least okay. Fortunately for White, he can gain some time on the black queen while developing and hopefully nail Black before move 20. The knight goes to a3, the dark-squared bishop can go to e3 or f4. The queen develops, often to b3, and castling queenside is often a good idea. Assuming that Black develops his bishop to g4, White can also consider a h3, g4, ♗g2 and ♘e5 plan which is very violent and hence gets a thumbs up. I don't want you to go crazy in these positions and start sacrificing pieces, but rather realise that playtime is the next 5-10 moves after which, if you haven't done something constructive, Black will be better.

If he doesn't recapture, then he exchanges queens on d1, when White must recapture with his king. In return for this inconvenience White gets to keep his extra pawn, which he must do with b4. In some lines Black actually goes a pawn up (when he plays ... e5, ... ♗g4 and ... e4, pinning the knight to the king and winning some material after h3 ♗h5, g4 ♘xg4, hxg4 ♗xg4 and ... exf3) – to visualise this just put Black's e-pawn on f3 and remove the white g- and h-pawns. Here Black boasts of both a passed h-pawn and a material advantage and thus demands very accurate play of White, but in most positions these defects are more than compensated for by the highly dangerous nature of White's queenside activity, which can advance with tempo and create a passed pawn close to promotion. The h-pawn, meanwhile, isn't queening in the foreseeable future – the nervous ones amongst you can always put a white bishop on f4 if you're getting queasy.

Game Five
Sveshnikov – Gashimov
Dubai Open 2003

1 e4 c5 2 c3 d5 3 exd5 ♕xd5 4 d4 ♘f6 5 ♘f3 ♗g4

This is one of Black's best defences to the c3-Sicilian. He plans ... e6, after which all of his pieces will be on good squares. The comfortable nature of the black development convinces me that exceptional measures are needed to fight for an advantage.

6 dxc5!?

White forces open the centre, leaving Black with a choice of evils – either he can exchange queens and face a strong queenside pawn roller, or he can capture the c5-pawn and allow his queen to be chased with tempo after ♗e3, ♘a3-b5 and so on.

6 ... ♕xc5

This is critical – I like White's chances after a trade on d1 (for which see the next game).

7 ♘a3! a6

It is generally accepted that this move is necessary (especially if Black intends to play ... ♕c7), since otherwise White's resource of ♘b5 is too valuable.

For instance, 7 ... ♘bd7 8 ♗e3 ♕c7 9 h3 ♗h5 transposes to Vlassov-Avrukh, Moscow 2002, which resulted in a rout after 10 ♘b5! ♕b8 11 g4! ♗g6 12 g5 ♘e4 13 ♘h4 a6 14 ♘xg6 hxg6 15 ♕d5! ♖h4 16 0-0-0 ♕c8 17 ♖d4 ♘dc5 18 f3 e6 19 ♕e5 f6 20 ♘c7+ ♔f7 21 ♕h2 e5 22 ♗c4+ ♔e7 23 gxf6+ gxf6 24 ♘d5+.

8 h3

I think this is the most precise.

Delaying h2-h3 gives Black extra options with his light-squared bishop, as illustrated by Motwani-Gormally, Edinburgh 2003 which continued 8 ♗e3 ♕c7 9 ♕a4+ ♘bd7 10 0-0-0 e5 11 h3 ♗e6! 12 ♘c2 h6 13 ♗e2 ♗e7 14 g4 0-0 15 g5 b5 16 ♕h4 ♘d5 17 ♖hg1 ♖fc8 with excellent play for Black.

8 ... ♗h5 9 ♗e3!

Again the most flexible. Rozentalis and Harley focus mainly on early ♕a4+ systems but I see no reason to rush with this move.

9 ... ♕c7

9 ... ♕c8 transposes to Erenburg-Livshits, Alushta 2002, in which after 10 g4 ♗g6 11 ♗g2 ♘bd7 12 g5 ♘e4 13 ♘h4 ♘d6 14 ♘xg6 hxg6 15 ♕a4 b5 16 ♕c2 ♖b8 17 0-0-0 ♕c7 18 ♖he1 ♘f5 19 ♕e4 e6 20 ♕c6 ♕xc6 21 ♗xc6 ♗d6 22 ♖xd6 ♘xd6 23 ♖d1 ♔e7 24 ♗xd7 White won material.

10 g4! ♗g6

11 ♗g2

There is something very appealing about this mode of development – without being pressured into 'doing something' with ♘c4-b6 or such, White simply brings fresh forces into the game and waits to see which development Black will adopt.

11 ♕a4+ ♘bd7 12 ♗f4 ♕c8 13 ♘e5 b5 14 ♕d4 ♗e4 illustrates the problem with neglecting to load the h1-a8 diagonal, though in Morgan-Wise, British Championship 2000, White eventually prevailed after the wild 15 ♖g1 e6 16 ♘xb5!?.

11 g5?! ♘fd7 12 ♘c4 b5 13 ♕d5 ♕c6 14 ♕xc6 ♘xc6 15 ♘cd2 e6 got nowhere in Cherniaev-Rowson, Hastings Premier 2004.

11 ... e6 12 ♕a4+ ♘bd7 13 ♗f4 ♕c8 14 ♘e5 ♗c5 15 0-0-0!?

The most active, though White was also better after the more conservative 15 0-0 0-0 16 ♘xg6 hxg6 17 ♕b3 ♖a7 18 ♘c2 b5 19 a4 bxa4 20 ♕xa4 ♘b6 21 ♕a2 ♘fd5 22 ♗h2 f5 23 ♖ae1 of Pavasovic-Ramirez, Cappelle la Grande 2003.

15 ... ♖a7!?

This is actually quite an enterprising defensive concept – Black prepares ... b5, when the rook will laterally defend the d7-knight. If this occurs and Black manages to castle, White can only beg for a draw, so Sveshnikov acts with required energy:

16 ♘xd7 ♘xd7 17 ♗d6! b5

17 ... ♗xd6 18 ♖xd6 b5 doesn't improve in view of 19 ♕d4!.

18 ♕f4 ♗xd6 19 ♕xd6 ♕c5 20 f4!

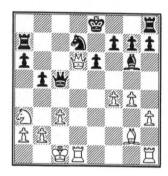

Putting his finger on the problem – due to the important defensive duties occupying the e6-pawn, the black bishop is in dire danger of being trapped.

20 ... b4 21 ♘c4 bxc3

This falls short, but the alternative 21 ... ♖c7 22 ♕xc5 ♖xc5 runs into 23 ♘d6+ ♔e7 24 ♖he1! with a tremendous position.

22 f5 cxb2+ 23 ♔b1 ♗xf5+ 24 gxf5 ♕xf5+ 25 ♖d3

Nominally White has an extra piece, but given the positions of the opposing pieces it would be more accurate to say that Black is down an entire army.

25 ... ♕c5 26 ♖hd1 ♕xd6 27 ♘xd6+ ♔e7 28 ♘xf7!

Simply winning. The rest is unnecessary – I've included the finish for completeness but there is nothing instructive in such positions so the reader should proceed to the next game!

28 ... ♖c8 29 ♔xb2 ♖c5 30 ♘d6 ♖ac7 31 ♖3d2 ♘e5 32 ♗f1 ♖5c6 33 ♗e2 g5 34 ♘e4 h6 35 ♖f1 ♖b6+ 36 ♔a1 ♖bc6 37 ♔b1 ♘g6 38 ♘f6 ♘f4 39 ♘g8+ ♔f8 40 ♘xh6 ♔g7 41 ♘g4 ♘xh3 42 ♘e5 ♖b6+ 43 ♖b2 ♖d6 44 ♘d3 ♖f7 45 ♖xf7+ ♔xf7 46 ♘c5 ♘f4 47 ♘e4 ♖d5 48 ♗xa6 ♔g6 49 ♗b7 ♖a5 50 ♘f2 ♔h5 51 ♗f3+ ♔h4 52 ♖b3 e5 53 ♖e3 ♖b5+ 54 ♔c2 ♖c5+ 55 ♔d2 ♖b5 56 ♔c3 ♖c5+ 57 ♔b2 ♖b5+ 58 ♔a1 ♖a5 59 a3 ♖c5 60 ♔b2 ♖b5+ 61 ♔a2 ♖c5 62 ♘g4 ♘g6 63 ♔b3 ♔g3 64 ♗e2+ ♔g2 65 ♔b4 ♖c7 66 a4 ♘f4 67 ♗f3+ ♔g3 68 a5 e4 69 ♗d1+ ♔g2 70 ♖xe4 ♘d5+ 71 ♔b3 ♖c3+ 72 ♔b2 ♖c5 73 a6 ♘c3 74 ♖d4 ♘xd1+ 75 ♖xd1 ♖b5+ 76 ♔c3 ♖a5 77 ♖d6 ♔f3 78 ♘f6 g4 79 ♘xg4 ♔xg4 80 ♔b4 ♖a1 81 ♔b5 ♔f5 82 ♔b6 ♔e5 83 ♔c7 ♖h1 84 ♖g6 ♔d5 85 a7 ♖h7+ 86 ♔b6 ♖h8 87 ♖g7 ♔d6 88 ♔b7 ♔d5 1-0

Game Six
Kosintseva – Paehtz
Istanbul 2003

1 e4 c5 2 c3 d5 3 exd5 ♕xd5 4 d4 ♘f6 5 ♘f3 ♗g4 6 dxc5 ♕xd1+

This is slightly less topical than 6 ... ♕xc5 these days, since White's queenside majority is very dangerous. That said, White must be well prepared here, since the main line leads to a position with huge mutual majorities and very unbalanced play.

7 ♔xd1 e5

7 ... ♘c6 has been met by 8 ♗e3 in some high level encounters, but after 8 ... ♘d5! Black has excellent chances of equalising. Instead Rozentalis and Harley's suggestion of 8 b4! is best, freeing the b2-square for the king. After 8 ... e5 9 ♔c2 a5 (9 ... 0-0-0 10 ♗b5 e4 11 ♗xc6 bxc6 12 ♘e5 ♗h5 13 ♘xc6 ♖d7 14 ♘d4 was winning in Lemmers-Aksluczyc, Valoz Cup 1999) 10 ♗b5 ♗xf3 11 gxf3 axb4 12 ♗xc6+ bxc6 13 cxb4 ♘d5 14 ♗d2 ♗e7 15 a3 0-0 16 ♘c3 White was a sound pawn up in Vajda-Moraru, Romanian Championship 2001.

8 b4! e4 9 h3 ♗h5 10 g4 ♘xg4 11 hxg4 ♗xg4 12 ♘bd2

12 ... exf3

Black can also try to prevent the bishop's development to d3 with 12 ... h5!? 13 ♗h3 ♗xh3 14 ♖xh3 exf3 15 ♘xf3 ♘c6 16 ♗e3 f6 and now Rogozenko gives 17 ♔c2 (instead of the unclear 17 ♘d4 ♘xd4 18 cxd4 0-0-0 19 ♔c2 ♗e7 20 ♖ah1 g6 21 ♔d3 ♖h7 22 ♔c4 ♖e8 of Asylguzhin-Loginov, Russian Championship 2002) 17 ... 0-0-0 18 b5!? as promising. This is the kind of position where most professionals, Rogozenko included, would *start* their analysis. In such an unclear situation it's pretty important to get some familiarity with the resulting positions before actually playing them. A good starting point is to try a couple of training games, preferably against a non-silicon opponent, and work from there. Take both sides, so as ·to familiarise yourself with Black's resources as well as White's, put about

15 minutes apiece on the clock and keep game scores, including notes of post mortem analysis. Of course, this kind of analysis is indicative of a rather professional approach to the game, but it's actually quite fun and really helps to illuminate both sides' resources. For instance, a recent training game I played against Fritz showed the strength of White's queenside majority: after 18 ... ♘e7 19 ♖ah1 g6 20 ♗d4 ♗g7 21 a4 ♖he8 22 ♔b3 ♗d7 23 ♘g5 ♘f5 24 ♘f7 ♖c8 25 ♘d6 ♘xd6 26 cxd6 ♗h8 27 ♗xa7 ♖e6 28 ♗d4 ♖xd6 29 a5 f5 30 ♗xh8 ♖xh8 31 c4 ♖a8 32 ♖a1 f4 33 c5! ♖d2 34 ♔c4! ♖xf2 35 ♖d3+ ♔e7 36 c6 bxc6 37 b6 ♖b2 38 ♖b3 ♖xb3 39 ♔xb3 ♖b8 40 ♔c4 ♔d7 41 a6 g5 42 a7 ♖a8 43 ♖b1 I pulled the plug.

13 ♗d3!

I like this move – several players have experimented with 13 ♗b5+ but e4 feels like the right spot for the bishop.

13 ... h5

Getting the kingside pawns rolling just can't be a bad idea.

13 ... ♘c6 14 ♖e1+ ♗e6 (14 ... ♗e7 15 ♔c2 a6 16 ♗e4 ♖c8 17 a4 h5 18 ♗a3 ♖h6 19 ♘xf3 ♖f6 20 ♖e3 ♖f4 21 ♗d5 ♖d8 22 ♗xc6+ bxc6 23 ♘d4 ♖xf2+ 24 ♔b3 ♗e6+ 25 ♘xe6 fxe6 26 ♖xe6 ♔f7 27 ♖xc6 h4 28 ♖c7 h3 29 b5 axb5 30 axb5 ♔f8 31 ♖e1 h2 32 ♖cxe7 h1=♕ 33 ♖xh1 ♔xe7 34 c6+ ♔f7 35 c7 ♖c8 36 b6 ♖f6 37 ♗c5 ♖c6 38 b7 was the thematic and winning continuation of Relange-Nunn, Hastings 1998) 15 ♘xf3 0-0-0 16 ♔c2 ♗e7 led to a clinical exploitation of the queenside majority in Emms-David, Escaldes 1998. White continued 17 ♗g5 h6 18 ♗xe7 ♘xe7 19 ♘d4 ♘d5 20 a3 ♘f4 21 ♗e4 ♗d7 22 a4 a6 23 ♘f5 ♗xf5 24 ♗xf5+ ♔b8 25 ♖e7 ♖hf8 26 c4 ♖de8 27 ♖ae1 ♘e6 28 ♖xe8+ ♖xe8 29 ♔c3 g6 30 ♗h3 ♖d8 31 ♗xe6 ♖e8 32 ♖h1 ♖xe6 33 ♖xh6 ♖f6 34 b5 ♔c7 35 ♖h8 axb5 36 axb5 b6 37 c6 ♖f3+ 38 ♔b4 ♖xf2 39 ♖a8 g5 40 ♖a7+ ♔c8 41 c5, when Black resigned.

13 ... ♘d7 14 ♖e1+ ♗e7 15 ♔c2 h5 16 ♘c4 ♗e6 17 ♘a5! b6 18 ♗e4! ♖c8 19 ♘c6 bxc5 20 ♘xa7 ♖c7 21 ♘b5 ♖c8 22 ♗b7 0-0 23 ♗xc8 ♖xc8 24 bxc5 was too good in Miljanic-Vuckovic, Petrovac 2004.

14 Ξe1+ Ձe7 15 Ձe4 ᗡc6 16 ⬧c2 ⬧f8 17 ᗡxf3 Ξe8 18 Ձf4 Ձf6 19 Ձd5!

This is much better for White. She's rounded up the f3-pawn, the h-pawn is innocuous while the queenside majority is as threatening as ever.

19 ... Ձf5+ 20 ⬧b3 Ձe6 21 Ձxe6 Ξxe6 22 Ξxe6 fxe6

The e-file exchanges have brought a fresh advantage in the shape of a weak e6-pawn. The big point, however, is still White's queenside majority – although it doesn't contain any passed pawns yet, it is clearly more dangerous than the black h-pawn.

23 Ξd1 ⬧e7 24 b5 ᗡb8 25 Ձd6+ ⬧f7 26 ⬧c4 Ξd8 27 a4 g5 28 Ξe1 ᗡd7 29 a5 Ξc8 30 ⬧b4 g4 31 ᗡd2 Ձd8 32 ᗡc4 Ձf6 33 Ξd1 ⬧g6

34 c6! bxc6 35 b6!

This is a typical break in this structure – see the note to Black's 12th move for another example.

35 ... axb6 36 axb6 ᗡxb6

A good practical attempt, but Black has no real drawing chances. Kosintseva wraps up smoothly.

37 ♘xb6 ♖d8 38 ♘c4 h4 39 ♖g1 ♔h5 40 ♖e1 ♖e8 41 ♘e5 h3 42 ♘d3 ♔g6 43 ♗g3 ♔f5 44 ♔c4 e5 45 ♘b4 ♖e6 46 ♘c2 e4 47 ♗h2 ♗h8 48 ♘e3+ ♔g5 49 ♖g1 ♔h5 50 ♖xg4 ♖f6 51 ♖g8 1-0

Game Seven
Jonkman – Christiansen
Canadian Open 2003

1 e4 c5 2 c3 d5 3 exd5 ♕xd5 4 d4 ♘c6 5 ♘f3 cxd4
After 5 ... ♘f6 I like 6 dxc5!?

6 ... ♕xc5 (I think 6 ... ♕xd1+ isn't a good idea here, since Black can't mobilise his ... ♗g4 and ... e5 idea quickly enough. Of the limited recent praxis in this line, Skytte-Jiretorn, Rilton Cup 2001 is a typical example and continued 7 ♔xd1 e5 8 b4 ♗f5 9 ♗e3 0-0-0+ [9 ... ♘d5 10 ♗b5 and again I don't think Black has enough for the material] 10 ♔c1 ♘d5 11 ♔b2 f6 12 ♗c4 ♗e7 13 ♘bd2 when White was a pawn up for not very much) 7 ♘a3 e5 (7 ... ♗g4 is only a temporary inconvenience. Jonkman-Muhren, Vlissingen Open 2001 continued 8 ♕e2 ♗f5 9 h3 ♘ge5 10 ♗e3 ♕a5 11 ♘xe5 ♕xe5 12 ♕b5! ♕xb5 13 ♘xb5 ♔d7 14 0-0-0+ ♔c8 15 ♗d3 g6 16 ♗c4 ♘e5 17 ♖d5! ♘c6 (17 ... ♘xc4 18 ♖c5+ ♔b8 19 ♖xc4 and Black is much too passive) 18 ♖d2 a6 19 ♘d4 ♘xd4 20 ♗xd4 f6 21 f4 ♗h6 22 g4 e5 23 ♗b6 ♗e4 24 ♖e1 ♗c6 and elegantly concluded 25 g5! fxg5 26 ♖ed1!) 8 ♗e3 ♕e7 9 ♗b5 ♘g4 10 ♕a4 ♕c7 11 ♘c4! ♘xe3 12 ♘xe3 ♗d7 13 0-0-0 f6 14 ♘d5 ♕d8 15 ♖he1 ♗d6 16 ♖d2 a6 17 ♗xc6 ♗xc6 18 ♕b3 ♗c5 19 ♘xe5! fxe5 20 ♖xe5+ ♔f8 21 ♖f5+ ♔e8 22 ♘f6+ and Black resigned in Sermek-Caposciutti, Montecatini Terme 1999.

After 5 ... ♗g4 it should be no surprise that I'm recommending 6 dxc5!? ♕xd1+ (6 ... ♕xc5 7 ♗e3 is untested: Rozentalis and Harley give 7 ... ♕a5 8 ♕b3 ♕c7 9 ♘a3 ♗xf3 10 gxf3 with a huge initiative for White) 7 ♔xd1 e5 (7 ... ♖d8+ 8 ♘bd2 e5 9 b4 e4 10 h3 ♗h5 11 g4 ♗xg4 12 hxg4 exf3 13

♔c2 ♘f6 14 g5 ♘g4 15 ♘xf3 ♗e7 16 ♖g1 ♘xf2 17 ♗e3 ♘e4 18 ♗d3 f5 19 gxf6 ♘xf6 20 ♖xg7 and White had more pawns than Black in Sveshnikov-Breder, Bled Open 2001) 8 b4 a5 9 ♗b5 ♘ge7 10 a3 0-0-0+ 11 ♘bd2 e4 12 h3 ♗h5 13 g4 with clearly the better chances.

6 cxd4 e5 7 ♘c3 ♗b4 8 ♗d2 ♗xc3 9 ♗xc3

This position is identical to one often enocuntered in the Chigorin Defence, with the crucial difference that in that position white and black pawns are on e2 and c7 respectively. This omission enables White to rapidly develop his light squared bishop with tempo on the black queen.

9 ... e4 10 ♘d2 ♘f6 11 ♗c4 ♕g5 12 d5 ♘e5 13 ♗b5+

13 ... ♔f8!?

An important resource for Black in this line – as far as I know, this game was its first outing.

13 ... ♗d7 is much better explored, with the position after 14 ♗xd7+ ♘exd7 15 0-0 0-0 16 d6! scoring well for White – the d-pawn is pivotal. A couple of masterclasses from c3-Sicilian experts: 16 ... ♖fe8 17 ♘c4 ♖e6 (17 ... ♖ad8 18 ♕d4 ♘c5 19 ♘e3 ♘d3?! traded the d-pawn at too high a cost in Pavasovic-Forster, Montecatini Terme 1997. After 20 ♕xa7 ♖xd6

21 ♕xb7 ♘h5 22 ♕c7 ♖ed8 23 ♕a5! Black was struggling, even before the unfortunate 23 ... ♕g6?! 24 ♘f5 ♖e8?? 25 ♘e7+) 18 ♗xf6 ♖xf6 19 ♕d4 ♖c8 20 ♕xe4 b5 21 ♕b7 ♖d8 22 ♕c7 ♖g6 23 ♘e3 ♘b6 24 ♖ad1 and White consolidated his extra pawn in Emms-Hall, Harplinge 1998.

14 ♕b3 e3 15 ♗b4+?

I'm not a fan of this one.

My recommendation is 15 ♘e4!

...when 15 ... ♕xg2 (15 ... ♘xe4 16 ♕b4+ ♔g8 17 ♕xe4 exf2+ 18 ♔xf2 ♘g4+ 19 ♔g1 ♗f5 20 ♕f3 ♕e3+ 21 ♕xe3 ♘xe3 22 d6 is a better endgame for White) 16 ♕b4+ ♔g8 17 ♘xf6+ gxf6 18 0-0-0 exf2 19 ♕f4 ♕g6 20 ♕xf2 is clearly better for White.

15 ... ♔g8

White's position now goes rapidly downhill.

16 fxe3 ♕xg2 17 0-0-0 ♗g4 18 ♖dg1 ♕xd5 19 ♗c3 ♖c8 20 ♔b1 ♖xc3 21 bxc3 h5 22 ♔c1 a6 23 ♗f1 ♕c5 24 e4 ♕e3 25 ♗c4 ♘xe4 26 ♖g2 ♗f3 27 ♖hg1 ♗xg2 28 ♖xg2 b5 29 ♖e2 ♕g1+ 30 ♔c2 ♘xc4 31 ♘xc4 ♕g4 32 ♖e3 ♕g2+ 0-1

A shame. I think White missed a good chance on move 15.

Game Eight
Pavasovic – Movsesian
Croatian Team Championship 2003

1 e4 c5 2 c3 d5 3 exd5 ♕xd5 4 d4 g6

This is increasingly popular these days, for much the same reason as the line seen in the Sermek-Fercec game – Black keeps lots of tension in the position and White can't easily simplify for a quick draw. As this was never our intention anyway, 5 ... g6 needn't worry us too much.

5 ♘f3

White has some other attractive options with ♘a3-b5 at this point, but nothing is clear cut there and in any event Black can force a ♘f3 system through the move order 4 ... ♘f6 5 ♘f3 g6.

5 ... ♗g7 6 ♘a3!

Preparing ♗c4.

6 ... ♘f6

6 ... cxd4!? is a tricky move. I think that 7 ♗c4 ♕e4+ (7 ... ♕d8 8 ♘b5 a6 9 ♘bxd4 ♘f6 10 ♕a4+ ♘c6 11 ♘xc6 bxc6 12 ♘e5 0-0 13 ♕xc6 left White a solid pawn up in Pavasovic-Pikula, Serbia 2004) 8 ♗e3! is best, as in Pinski-Markowski, MK Cafe Cup Open A 1999, when after 8 ... ♘h6 (8 ... dxe3 9 ♗xf7+ ♔f8 10 ♕d8+ ♔xf7 11 ♘g5+) 9 ♘b5 0-0 10 ♗d3 ♕d5 11 cxd4 ♘f5 12 0-0 ♘xe3 13 fxe3 ♕d8 14 ♕e2 ♘c6 15 ♖ad1 I prefer White – his central control is excellent and Black's bishops are somewhat devoid of purpose.

7 ♗c4 ♕e4+ 8 ♗e3 0-0 9 0-0 cxd4 10 ♘xd4!

This is best – alternative recaptures have led to nothing.

10 ... ♘c6

10 ... ♕e5 isn't an improvement: 11 ♕f3 ♘bd7 12 ♖fe1 ♕b8 13 ♗f4! e5 14 ♗g3 a6 15 ♖ad1 ♕a7 16 ♘b3 ♘h5 17 ♗h4 ♘df6 18 h3 b5 19 ♗f1 ♗b7 20 ♕e3 ♕xe3 21 ♖xe3 ♘d5 22 ♖ee1 ♘b6 23 ♘a5 ♗d5 24 c4 bxc4 25 ♘3xc4 ♘xc4 26 ♘xc4 ♗xc4 27 ♗xc4 ♖fc8 28 b3 and White had a classically better endgame in Sermek-Feletar, Pula 2001.

11 ♖e1 ♕h4 12 ♘xc6 bxc6 13 ♕f3!

White now has an enduring structural advantage. Movsesian tries whipping up some kingside counterplay but it never looked like hitting the mark.

This is Pavasovic's improvement over his game with Zarnicki from the Pinamar Masters 2002, when 13 ♕a4 allowed 13 ... ♗e6! with no problems.

13 ... ♘g4 14 ♗f4 ♕f6 15 ♖ad1 h5

16 ♗c7! ♗f5

16 ... ♕xf3 17 gxf3 wins the e7-pawn.

17 h3 ♘h6 18 ♕e3 ♖fe8 19 ♗f4! g5

Otherwise ♗g5, but now Black is clearly busted.

20 ♗xg5 ♕g6 21 ♕g3 e5 22 ♗h4 ♔h7 23 ♗b3 a5 24 ♗a4 ♕e6 25 ♗b3 ♕g6 26 ♕xg6+ ♗xg6 27 ♗a4 ♖e6 28 ♘c4 ♘f5 29 ♗d8 e4 30 ♗g5 ♗f8 31 ♖d8 ♖xd8 32 ♗xd8 e3!?

The last roll of the dice.

33 ♘xe3 ♗c5 34 ♗g5 f6 35 ♗b3 ♖e5 36 ♗c2 ♖e8 37 ♗xf6 a4 38 ♗xf5 ♗xf5 39 ♗d4 ♗d6 40 c4 ♔g6 41 ♗c3 ♗e6 42 g4 hxg4 43 hxg4 ♗f7 44 ♔g2 ♗f4 45 ♔f3 ♗g5 46 a3 ♖e7 47 ♘f5 ♖xe1 48 ♗xe1 ♗xc4 49 ♔g3 ♗d3 50 f4 ♗d8 51 ♘h4+ ♔h6 52 ♗d2 ♗c7 53 ♗c3 ♗c2 54 ♘f5+ ♔h7 55 ♘d4 ♗e4 1-0

Game Nine
Mamedyarov – Mamedov
World Junior Championship 2003

1 e4 c5 2 c3 d6

2 ... e5 is another interesting try. This used to be my favourite when I was little, in part because I was angling for a good Ruy Lopez with Black but mainly because I was too lazy to learn a proper defence to the c3-Sicilian. The main defect of the move is obviously that it weakens the d5-square, and it is this aspect that I'll be focussing on in my recommendations (White has some sharper stuff, but none of it is overly convincing). 3 ♘f3 ♘c6 4 ♗c4 ♕c7!? is the move which somewhat rehabilitated this line for Black – while the move is useful in general, it prepares to laterally defend the f7-pawn against any quick stuff with ♕b3 and ♘g5 (4 ... ♗e7 is also possible: after 5 d4 cxd4 6 cxd4 exd4 7 ♘xd4 ♘f6 8 ♘c3 0-0 9 ♘c2! a6 10 0-0 b5 11 ♗d5 ♗b7 12 ♘e3 ♘xd5 13 ♘cxd5 ♘e5 14 b3 ♖e8 15 ♗b2 ♗f8 16 ♘f5 White had a bind in Cherniaev-Webb, Portsmouth Open 2003). 5 d3 ♘f6 6 ♗g5 is the start of Schmittdiel's plan, which simply aims to win full control of d5. After 6 ... ♗e7 7 ♘a3 a6 8 ♘c2 b5 9 ♗b3 ♘a5 10 ♗xf6 ♗xf6 11 ♗d5 ♘c6 12 ♘e3 ♖b8 13 h4! h6 14 ♕b3 d6 15 g4! ♘a5 16 ♕c2 ♗e6 17 ♔e2! Black's position had little to recommend it in Schmittdiel-Burr, Bundesliga 2002.

2 ... b6 is a favourite of Israeli GM Artur Kogan who has a massive score with the move, and I've played it myself with Black whenever looking for an offbeat position against the c3-Sicilian, but objectively White has a choice of ways to maintain an advantage. I think the simplest is 3 d4 ♗b7 4 f3, after which 4 ... e6 5 ♗e3 ♘f6 6 ♘d2 ♘c6 7 a3 ♗e7 8 ♗d3 a5 9 ♘e2 ♗a6 10 ♗xa6 (Rozentalis and Harley recommend 10 ♗c2 but I don't really see the point – it's true that pieces should generally be kept on the board when one is pushing a space advantage but this rule doesn't apply when keeping a miserable bishop and conceding a bunch of light squares) 10 ... ♖xa6 11 0-0 0-0 12 ♘f4 cxd4 13 cxd4 a4 14 ♕e2 ♖a8 15 ♖ac1 ♕b8 16 d5! was good for White in Rozentalis-Tyomkin, Montreal 2000.

2 ... ♕a5 is another move which, while playable, consents to an inferior position. To be honest I'm somewhat loathe to recommend a line here, since there are a plethora of ways to an edge against such a move and the reader will probably be served better by five minutes quiet thought at the board than by anything I can provide here. However, while the main approach seems to be ♘f3, ♗c4 and castling, I quite like the 3 g3!? of Pavasovic-Teofilovic, Croatian Championship 2002. After 3 ... ♘c6 4 ♗g2 g6 (4 ... ♘f6 5 ♘e2 h5!? 6 h3 h4 7 g4 ♘e5 8 d4 cxd4 9 f4 d3 10 ♘d4! [Gallagher] is good for White) 5 ♘e2 ♗g7 6 0-0 d6 7 h3 e5 8 ♘a3 ♘ge7 9

♘c4 ♕c7 10 a4 0-0 11 d3 ♗e6 12 ♘e3 ♔h8 13 ♘d5 ♕d7 14 ♔h2 ♖ae8 15 a5 White was doing well.

2 ... g6 suffers the same defect as all of these offbeat lines, namely insufficient struggle for the centre. After 3 d4 cxd4 4 cxd4 d5 White has several promising options, but as I write this in my pokey Bulgarian hotel room (good old European Team Championships), my Round One bulletin gives the interesting tussle Sermek-Weiss, which saw 5 ♘c3!? dxe4 6 ♗c4 ♘f6 7 ♕b3 e6 8 d5 exd5 9 ♘xd5 ♘xd5 10 ♗xd5 ♕c7 (10 ... ♕e7 is a bit greedy, and I like 11 ♗d2!? when Erenburg-Bitansky, Tel Aviv 2002 continued [Rozentalis and Harley only consider 11 ♕c3 ♕b4 with equality] 11 ... ♘c6 12 ♗xc6+ bxc6 13 ♕c3 e3 14 ♗xe3 ♕b4 15 ♗d4 ♖g8 16 ♘f3 ♗e6 17 0-0 ♕xc3 18 ♗xc3 0-0-0 19 ♘g5 with an advantage for White) 11 ♘e2 ♗d6 12 ♘c3 ♗e5 13 ♘xe4 ♘c6 14 0-0 ♘d4 15 ♕d3 0-0 16 ♗e3 ♕c2 17 ♖ad1 ♘e2+ 18 ♔h1 ♕xd3 19 ♖xd3 ♘f4 20 ♗xf4 ♗xf4 21 ♖f3 ♗e5 22 ♘g5 ♔g7 23 ♘xf7 ♗xb2 24 ♖b3 ♗d4 25 ♘d6 ♗xf2 26 ♘e4 ♗b6 27 ♖xf8 ♔xf8 28 ♖f3+ ♔g7 29 ♖f7+ ♔h6 30 ♖f8 ♗c7 31 ♘f6 ♗e5 32 ♘g4+ when Black resigned as he drops an exchange.

2 ... e6 is met by 3 d4 d5 4 e5 and we're in the French chapter.

3 d4 ♘f6 4 ♗d3!

The best response.

4 ... cxd4

4 ... g6 runs into trouble after 5 dxc5! dxc5 6 e5!. After the provocative 6 ... ♘fd7 Pavasovic-Fauland, Austrian Championship 2002 continued 7 e6! fxe6 8 ♘f3 ♘c6 9 ♕e2 ♗g7 10 h4 ♘de5 11 ♗e4 ♕d6 12 ♘a3 ♘xf3+ 13 gxf3 ♗d7 14 ♗e3 b6 15 h5 gxh5 16 f4 ♖c8 17 ♘b5 ♕b8 18 0-0-0 ♘d4 19 cxd4 cxd4+ 20 ♔b1 dxe3 21 ♕xh5+ ♔f8 22 ♖xd7 ♕xf4 23 ♕f3 ♕xf3 24 ♗xf3 exf2 25 ♖f1 ♗h6 26 ♘c7 ♗e3 27 ♗b7 ♖b8 28 ♖d3 ♖xb7 29 ♘xe6+ ♔f7 30 ♖xe3 ♖d7 31 ♖xf2+ ♔e8 32 ♖c3 when Black resigned.

4 ... ♛c7 5 ♘f3 ♝g4 6 0-0 e6 was tried in Korneev-Cifuentes Parada, Dos Hermanas Open 2004, and now the simplest is 7 h3 ♝h5 8 ♖e1 with an edge.

5 cxd4 g6 6 h3! ♝g7 7 ♘c3 0-0 8 ♘f3 ♘c6 9 0-0 e5

While this closes the g7-bishop out of the game somewhat, the idea is known from numerous Pirc/Modern positions. Black simply must establish some central influence. The bishop wasn't doing much on the long diagonal in any event, and can re-emerge via f8 at some point in the future.

10 dxe5 dxe5 11 ♝e3

11 ... ♝e6

My game against Adam Hunt in the Hilton Premier 2003 continued 11 ... ♖e8 12 ♝b5 ♝d7 13 ♛b3 ♘a5 14 ♛a4 ♝xb5 15 ♛xb5 a6 16 ♛e2 ♖c8 17 ♖fd1 ♛c7, when the game's 18 ♝g5 was good enough for an edge but 18 ♖ac1! would have been even better.

12 ♝b5!

There's no other way to generate play.

12 ... ♛a5 13 ♛a4! ♛xa4 14 ♝xa4 ♘h5 15 ♖fd1 ♖fc8 16 ♖ac1

White is a little better here, no more. This position is definitely drawn with best play, and yet I'm recommending it. Why? On a pragmatic note, White can play for a win with virtually no risk, whereas Black finds it more difficult to generate play. However, I also feel it's vital to learn how to squeeze such positions to create maximum difficulties for one's opponent. Innumerable Eastern European GMs come to mind who have made a living from winning precisely these kinds of positions on a regular basis – symmetrical pawns, material equality but slightly more active pieces which can cause huge difficulties. While I have tried to avoid recommending sterile positions, such are largely inevitable in the context of any repertoire and the ability to handle them well is a vital element of every chess player's arsenal.

16 ... ♘f4 17 g3!

Putting the question to the knight. Taking on h3 leaves the steed cut off and retreating is a least a little silly, so Black is committed to violence...

17 ... ♘d4! 18 gxf4 ♘xf3+ 19 ♔g2 exf4 20 ♗xf4 ♘d4 21 ♖d3!

After a fairly forced sequence we arrive at a position where White holds the advantage, mainly due to the fact that he has some pawn control over a d-file outpost while Black can boast of no similar benefit. Mamedyarov's powerful exploitation of this edge is enormously instructive.

21 ... a6 22 ♗e3 b5 23 ♗d1 b4 24 ♘d5 ♖xc1 25 ♗xc1 a5 26 ♗e3 ♘c6 27 f4!!

The b2-pawn is irrelevant, while the e5-square is crucial.

27 ... ♗xb2 28 ♗a4! ♘d8 29 ♗b6!

The slicing bishops compel Black to grant a passed d-pawn, which soon proves fatal.

29 ... ♗xd5 30 exd5 ♗f6 31 d6 ♘e6 32 ♔f3 ♔f8 33 ♖d5 ♗d8 34 ♗xd8 ♖xd8 35 ♔e4 ♘g7 36 ♔d4 ♘e6+ 37 ♔e5 ♘g7 38 ♖xa5 ♘f5 39 ♖a6 h5 40 ♔d5 h4 41 ♔c5 f6 42 ♔d5 g5 43 fxg5 fxg5 44 ♔e5 ♘e3 45 d7 g4 46 ♖e6 1-0

CHAPTER TWO
The French Defence

"One of my most unsuccessful openings. Almost all the games in which I chose it ended in my defeat – fortunately, there weren't all that many of them... I felt these losses were not accidental. Black, in the French, must play with great accuracy, and this is a quality I never had a great measure of, neither now nor in my earlier days."

GM Mikhail Tal

1 e4 e6 2 d4 d5 3 e5

3 ♘c3 and 3 ♘d2 are also good moves, but they give Black more options. With 3 e5 (The Advance Variation) White secures an immediate central and kingside space advantage.

This line has always been something of a black sheep. It is less often seen today than White's two knight moves, but has been a very happy playground of its high-level adherents (most recently Movsesian and Grischuk) who have used it to deadly effect.

Black has numerous defensive tries and it can be quite easy to get confused amongst the variations. This chapter is split into several sections so that the material will be more manageable. After 3 ... c5 4 c3, we have:

I: Classical Systems. These arise after 4 ... ♘c6 5 ♘f3 ♗d7 6 ♗e2 ♘ge7 7 ♘a3 and are covered in the first four games. Obviously the game revolves around White's centre, since if White can simply complete development his central space will guarantee him a middlegame advantage. My recommendations centre around the move h4!, which is useful in many French positions and gives rise to interesting positions here.

II: An early ... ♕b6. Here the queen pressurises the b2- and d4-pawns, so my approach involves a3, intending b4. Black then has a choice: he can stop b4 by meeting a3 with ... c4, though this has the disadvantage of removing pressure from the white centre; or he can allow b4, when White's queenside play gives him fresh aggressive options. As these lines are so important and popular, I have devoted five games to them.

Finally I deal with some of the niggly offbeat ideas which don't threaten White's edge but with which you should be familiar.

Room Raiders: A Note on White Pawn Advances

The Advance Variation gives White an immediate central and kingside spatial advantage. White's task is to maintain this advantage and increase it. Obviously he can't generate central pawn play anymore, but both the kingside and the queenside are fertile fields for further forays.

On the kingside, the h4-advance is a cornerstone of the modern handling of this line. The positional justifications behind this are several. First, the move itself gains space – now Black will find it difficult to play ... g5, while the h1-rook is activated. It's worth pointing out that White frequently doesn't castle in these lines, instead preferring to leave his rook on h1 and play ♔f1. The move controls g5, which can sometimes be important, and h4, which is vital. Given that f5 is a natural square for a black knight, White frequently wants to kick it with g4 – if the pawn is not on h4, then frequently Black has a ... ♘h4 resource (supported by a bishop on e7) which can frustrate the further advance of the white pawns. Second, the possibilty of further expansion is introduced – a further h5 and (if allowed) h6, which will weaken Black's kingside dark squares. If Black checks the advance of the pawn with either ... h5 or ... h6, then his kingside is less flexible and thus more vulnerable to attack.

On the queenside, a setup with a3 and b4 is often seen. This is almost exclusively a response to an early ... ♕b6 by Black, which exerts unpleasant pressure on d4 and b2. Once the pawn gets to b4, then after an exchange on d4, White has the option of further expansion but Black can undermine the structure with ... a5 or even (with a white bishop on b2) ... ♘a5-c4, when the black queen pins the b-pawn to the bishop. I see this white queenside expansion as a primarily defensive measure, gaining time which can be invested on the kingside.

When Bishops Go Bad: Black's Problem Piece

Black's problem piece in this line is his light-squared bishop. After committing his central pawns to light squares on the first two moves, this piece is doomed to a substandard existence for quite a while. Black has two responses to this problem. The first (and most common) is to grin and bear it, instead taking comfort in his pressure against d4 and his ... c5 and ... f6 pawn breaks. The second and more radical approach is to try and exchange this bishop early, either with ... b6, ... ♕d7 and ... ♗a6 or with ... ♕b6, ... ♗d7 and ... ♗b5. From a positional point of view both of these latter plans are fully justified – the trade off is that they take some time to implement, during which White can solidify his centre and get rolling on a wing.

Game Ten
Movsesian – Borovikov
European Rapid Championship 2002

A word on rapid games as a source of opening ideas. While the quality of these encounters is variable, they still constitute a fertile ground for high-quality opening play. The Melody Amber tournaments come to mind, where the top ten have regularly used big novelties in rapid and blindfold matches. Still, some of these games must be taken with a grain of salt, not just because of blunders but also inaccurate recording, as I'm pretty sure was the case right at the end of this one.

1 e4 e6 2 d4 d5 3 e5 c5 4 c3 ♘c6 5 ♘f3 ♘ge7 6 ♘a3 cxd4 7 cxd4 ♘f5 8 ♘c2 ♗d7 9 ♗e2 ♕b6 10 h4!?

A somewhat rare choice, championed by Movsesian. The move is a typical example of the h4-push – White simply gains space and doesn't mind some slight inconvenience to his king. Indeed, most main routes from here result in endgames, where both a h4-pawn and a centralised king are useful.

10 ... ♘b4

In Sarajevo 2000, Mikhail Gurevich surprised Movsesian with 10 ... f6 11 g4 ♘fxd4!? 12 ♘cxd4 ♘xe5, a piece sacrifice which no-one has attempted since. Movsesian ended up losing this game, but his play can be improved in several places. In particular, after 13 g5 ♗c5 14 0-0 ♘xf3+ 15 ♘xf3 ♕b4 16 ♘e1 ♕xh4 17 ♘g2 ♕b4 18 ♗d3 0-0-0 19 a3 ♕b6 20 b4 ♗d4 21 ♗e3 ♔b8 22 ♕f3 ♗xe3 23 fxe3 ♖hf8, 24 ♗xh7!? (instead of Movsesian's 24 ♕g3+) is suggested by Psakhis, when 24 ... ♗b5 25 ♖f2 d4 26 ♖d1 leads to a clearly preferable position for White – the pawns will never prove dangerous enough here, while the white king is amply protected by pieces.

11 ♘xb4

11 ... ♗xb4+

11 ... ♕xb4+ was Ulibin's choice against Movsesian in Pula 1999. After 12 ♔f1 ♗b5 13 g4 ♗xe2+ 14 ♔xe2 ♕c4+ 15 ♕d3 ♘e7 16 h5 h6 17 ♗d2 ♖c8 18 a3 ♔d7 19 ♖ac1 ♕xd3+ 20 ♔xd3 ♖xc1 21 ♖xc1 ♘c6 22 ♘g1 g6 23 hxg6 fxg6 24 ♘e2 g5 25 ♖h1 White was obviously better due to the h6 weakness, eventually breaking with f4 and winning.

12 ♔f1

12 ... ♗b5

Shirov-Gurevich, Eurotel Trophy 2002 continued 12 ... h5 13 a4 ♖c8 14 g3 ♗e7 15 ♔g2 ♖c7 16 a5 ♕b4 17 b3 ♗b5, when 18 ♗a3!? ♗xe2 19 ♕xe2 ♕xb3 20 ♗xe7 ♘xe7 21 a6! b6 22 ♖hc1 ♖c3 23 ♖ab1 ♕c4 24 ♕d2! ♖xc1 25 ♖xc1 ♕xa6 26 ♖c7 ♕a3 27 ♕g5 (the downside of Black's 12th move) 27 ... ♔d8 28 ♖b7 gave White good compensation.

13 g4 ♗xe2+ 14 ♔xe2 ♕a6+ 15 ♕d3 ♕xd3+ 16 ♔xd3 ♘e7 17 h5 h6 18 a3 ♗a5

This is a typical French endgame. Black has managed to exchange his bad bishop, which is a weight off his mind. However, White maintains his central space advantage (relatively unimportant, since he can't play there) and his kingside one (very important, since a g5-break is a constant threat). Black has to show great patience in order to bring his position to safety.

19 ♘h4

Personally, I prefer this to 19 ♗e3 ♔d7 20 ♘h4, when 20 ... ♖ag8 21 ♖ag1 g5 22 ♘g2 ♘c6 23 f4 gxf4 24 ♘xf4 ♗d8 allowed Black to hold in Movsesian-Berelovich, Bundesliga 2003.

19 ... ♔d7 20 f4 ♖ac8 21 ♗e3 g6 22 ♘f3 ♖cg8 23 ♖ag1

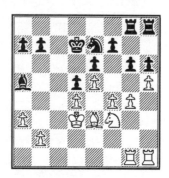

This is an ideal endgame for White. Black constantly has to be on the lookout for a kingside breakthrough.

23 ... ♗d8 24 ♖h2 ♖g7 25 hxg6! fxg6 26 ♖gh1 ♘g8 27 ♘g5!

The advantage has crystallised – the weak h6-pawn and huge difference in piece mobility don't bode well for Black.

27 ... ♗e7 28 ♗d2 ♗d8 29 a4 a6 30 ♗e3 ♗e7 31 b3 ♗f8 32 ♗d2 ♗e7 33 b4 ♗d8 34 b5 a5 35 b6!

35 ... ♘e7

35 ... ♗xb6? loses to 36 ♖b1.

36 ♖xh6 ♖xh6 37 ♖xh6 ♘c6 38 ♘h7 ♗xb6 39 ♗e3 ♔e7 40 ♘f6 ♗d8 41 ♗f2 ♔f7 42 ♗h4 ♗b6 43 ♖h8 ♗xd4 44 ♗g5 ♗xe5

A pretty desperate attempt.

44 ... ♗c5 45 ♗h6 is clearly better for White.

45 ♘e8??

Simply 45 fxe5 wins the game.

45 ... ♖g8 46 ♘d6+??

This just loses to a bishop capture on d6. The past couple of moves have illustrated my initial comments – whether the players went crazy at this stage or the game is recorded badly is irrelevant for our purposes, since we've already milked it for instructive material.

46 ... ♔g7 47 ♗f6+ ♔f8 48 ♖h7 1-0

Game Eleven
Movsesian – Lamprecht
Bundesliga 2002

1 e4 e6 2 d4 d5 3 e5 c5 4 c3 ♘c6 5 ♘f3 ♗d7 6 ♗e2 ♘ge7 7 ♘a3 cxd4 8 cxd4 ♘f5 9 ♘c2 ♘b4

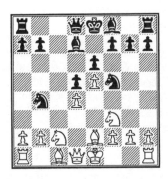

10 0-0

The endgame after 10 ♘xb4 ♗xb4+ 11 ♗d2 ♕a5 12 a3! ♗xd2+ 13 ♕xd2 ♕xd2+ 14 ♔xd2 is perhaps a little better for White, but remains a quiet technical position. Movsesian's choice is more aggressive.

10 ... ♘xc2 11 ♕xc2 ♖c8

Most lines here involve both ... ♕b6 and ... ♖c8. A twist was seen in Potkin-Berkes, World Junior Championship 2002 which continued 11 ... ♕b6 12 ♕d3 a6 13 a4 ♗b4 14 h4 a5 15 g3 h6 16 ♔g2 0-0-0, an approach which looks perfectly reasonable. After 17 ♗d2 ♔b8 18 ♖fc1 ♖c8 19 b3 ♖hd8 20 ♗f4 ♘e7 21 ♖xc8+ ♖xc8 22 ♖c1 White has an enduring edge due to his space advantage and slightly safer king, but Black is solid.

12 ♕d3 ♕b6 13 a4 ♗b4 14 h4

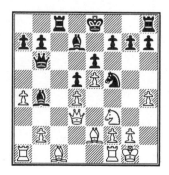

14 ... h6

14 ... a6 15 ♗g5 h6 16 ♗d2 transposes to Movsesian-Morozevich, Sarajevo 2000. After 16 ... ♕a5 17 ♗f4! ♖g8 18 g3, Morozevich decided to try and improve his king with a somewhat eccentric manoeuvre. 18 ... ♔d8!? 19 ♕d1 ♔c7 20 ♗d3 ♔b6 21 ♘e1 g5 22 hxg5 hxg5 23 ♗c1 ♔a7 24 ♘c2 ♔a8 25 ♔g2 ♖c4 26 b3 ♖xd4 27 ♘xd4 ♘xd4 28 ♗h7 ♖c8 29 ♗xg5 left White an exchange up for virtually nothing.

15 ♗d2!?

Threatening a5.

15 h5 is also very logical. Movsesian-Brumen, Nova Gorica 2000 continued 15 ... ♘e7 16 ♗f4 ♘c6 17 ♖fc1 ♘a5 18 ♖xc8+ ♗xc8 19 b3 ♗d7 20 ♔h2 ♗e7 21 ♗d2 ♗b4 22 ♗e3 ♗e7 23 ♗d1 ♘c6 24 g4 ♕a6 25 ♕c2 ♘b4 26 ♕d2 ♕d3 27 ♕b2 0-0 28 ♘e1 ♕h7 29 ♖c1 ♗c6 30 ♕d2 f6 31 exf6 ♗d6+ 32 f4 ♖xf6 33 ♔g3 g5 34 hxg6 ♕xg6 35 ♘f3 ♕d3 36 ♘e5 ♗xe5 37 dxe5 ♖f7 38 ♕xd3 ♘xd3 39 ♖c3 ♘b4 40 ♗xa7 d4 41 ♖c4 and Black resigned.

15 ... ♕a5

15 ... ♗xd2 16 ♕xd2 is quite comfortable for White, who entertains ideas of a5 and ♗d3.

16 ♗f4!

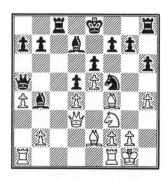

A nice idea Movsesian borrowed from his game against Morozevich.

16 ... ♕d8 17 g3 ♕e7 18 ♔g2 ♖c6 19 h5! ♕d8 20 ♕d1! ♗e7 21 ♗d3!

Movsesian's 19th and 21st moves were typical. The h5-pawn prevents ... h5 and discourages ... g5, thus deciding the battle of who owns the kingside. Meanwhile the bishop is optimally placed on the b1-h7 diagonal.

21 ... 0-0 22 ♗b1 ♕b6 23 g4!

A good time to start some trouble on the kingside, just when the other black monarch has gone walkies on the queenside.

23 ... ♘h4+ 24 ♘xh4 ♗xh4 25 ♕d3 f5 26 exf6 ♗xf6 27 ♗e3

27 ... ♔f7

27 ... ♕xb2 is very risky: 28 ♖a3! ♕b4 29 ♖b3 ♕xa4 30 ♖xb7 with a strong attack.

28 a5 ♕b4 29 ♖a3! ♔e7 30 ♖b3!

The rook lift wins control of critical squares on the queenside.

30 ... ♕xa5 31 ♗d2 ♕c7 32 ♗b4+

Decisive.

32 ... ♖d6 33 f4 ♕c4 34 ♖d1 ♗c6 35 ♕e3 ♔d7 36 ♗xd6 ♔xd6 37 ♖c3 ♕b5 38 ♖d2 ♔d7 39 ♗g6 ♕b4 40 g5 ♗e7 41 ♖e2 ♕d6 42 gxh6 gxh6 43 f5 exf5 44 ♕xh6 f4 45 ♖f3 ♕f6 46 ♖e5 ♕h4 47 ♗f5+ ♔d8 48 ♕e6 1-0

Game Twelve
Minasian – Gaprindashvili
IECC 2002

1 e4 e6 2 d4 d5 3 e5 c5 4 c3 ♘c6 5 ♘f3

5 ... ♗d7

5 ... ♘ge7 6 ♘a3 cxd4 7 cxd4 ♘f5 8 ♘c2 amounts to the same thing after 8 ... ♗d7 9 ♗e2. Alternatives fail to impress:

8 ... ♘h4 was Potkin's nihilistic approach against Motylev in Togliatti 2003. After 9 ♘xh4 ♕xh4 10 ♗e2 ♗d7 11 0-0 f5 12 b4! ♕d8 13 b5 ♘a5 14 ♘e3 ♗e7 15 ♗d2 0-0 16 ♕e1 b6 17 f4 ♖c8 18 ♖b1 White was much better.

8 ... ♘b4 9 ♗e2 ♘xc2+ 10 ♕xc2 ♕a5+ (10 ... ♗d7 11 0-0 transposes to main lines) 11 ♗d2 ♗b4 12 a3 ♗xd2+ 13 ♕xd2 ♕xd2+ 14 ♔xd2 left White a whole tempo up on a standard endgame in Grischuk-Pert in National I, Clemont-Ferrand 2003. I include the game in full since it is a lesson in how to conduct this typical endgame, albeit a very favourable verison: 14 ... ♗d7 15 b4 0-0 16 b5 f6 17 ♖hc1 ♖fc8 18 ♗d3 ♘e7 19 a4 ♖xc1 20 ♖xc1 ♖c8 21 ♖a1! (White wants to exchange one rook [so that Black can't double on the c-file] but not two – now he has potential pawn breaks on both sides of the board) 21 ... h6 22 h4 ♖f8 23 g4 ♔f7 (Obviously 23 ... fxe5 24 ♘xe5 ♖xf2+ 25 ♔e3 isn't smart) 24 g5! fxg5 25 hxg5 ♔e8 26 ♔e3 hxg5 27 ♘xg5 ♘f5+ 28 ♗xf5 ♖xf5 29 ♘h3 ♖h5 30 ♘f4 ♖h7 31 ♖g1 ♔e7 gave a typical good knight-bad bishop endgame. 32 ♘d3 b6 33 ♘f4 ♔e8 34 ♔f3 ♔e7 35 ♔g4 ♖h6 36 ♖c1 ♔d8 37 ♘h3 ♗e8 38 ♘g5 ♗h5+ 39 ♔g3 ♗e8 40 f4 ♖g6 41 ♖h1 ♔c7 42 ♖h8 ♗d7 43 ♔g4

♖h6 44 ♖a8 ♔b7 45 ♖g8 ♖g6 46 ♖f8 a5 47 ♖h8 ♖h6 48 ♖xh6 gxh6 49 ♘f7 ♔c7 50 ♘d6! The energy with which Grischuk handled this endgame, wiping out the former World U-18 Champion, is instructive.

6 ♗e2 ♘ge7 7 ♘a3 cxd4 8 cxd4 ♘f5 9 ♘c2

9 ... ♕a5+

9 ... ♗e7 10 0-0 h5 was Kaidanov's interesting choice against Grischuk in the New York Open 2000. After 11 ♖b1 ♕b6 12 b4 a5 13 a3 axb4 14 axb4 ♖a2 15 b5 ♘a7 16 ♗d3 ♕a5 17 ♘e3 ♘xe3 18 ♗xe3 ♗xb5?! (Black was worse anyway due to his misplaced knight) 19 ♗d2 ♕a6 20 ♖xb5 ♘xb5 21 ♕b1 0-0 22 ♗xb5 White had won material.

10 ♗d2 ♕b6 11 ♗c3 ♘b4

11 ... a5 12 g4! (the quiet 12 0-0 ♗e7 13 a4 0-0 14 ♗b5 left Black well placed after 14 ... f6! in Carlsen-Hansen, Copenhagen 2004) 12 ... ♘fe7 13 ♕d2 h5 14 g5 ♘f5 15 ♗d3 ♘b4 16 ♗xf5 exf5 17 ♗xb4 axb4 18 0-0 ♗e7 19 ♘e3 ♗e6 20 ♘g2 g6 21 ♘f4 0-0 22 ♖fc1 left White better in Jonkman-Romero Holmes, Groningen 2002.

12 ♘e3 ♘xe3 13 fxe3 ♗b5 14 0-0 ♗e7

15 ♗xb4!

Starting some favourable exchanges.

15 ... ♗xe2 16 ♕xe2 ♕xb4 17 ♖ac1 0-0 18 ♖c7 ♗d8 19 a3 ♕b3 20 ♖c3 ♕a4 21 ♖fc1 ♕d7 22 ♘e1 ♗a5 23 b4 ♗b6 24 ♘d3 ♖fc8 25 ♕c2

It's pretty remarkable that Minasian didn't convert from here. Black can't do anything.

25 ... ♖xc3 26 ♕xc3 h6 27 ♘c5!?

Very committal, but not bad if followed up correctly.

27 ... ♗xc5 28 bxc5?

I think this is a big mistake, squandering most of the winning chances.

28 **♕xc5!** is best, still dominating the c-file. White remains much better though Black has some drawing chances.

The rest isn't particularly interesting:

28 ... ♖c8 29 h3 ♕a4 30 ♕b4 ♕a6 31 a4 ♕d3 32 ♖c3 ♕d2 33 ♖b3 ♕d1+ 34 ♔h2 b6 35 ♖c3 ♕e1 36 cxb6 ♕xc3 37 b7 ♕xb4 38 bxc8=♕+ ♔h7 39 ♕c2+ ♔g8 40 ♕c8+ ♔h7 41 ♕d7 ♕a3 42 ♕xa7 ♕xe3 43 ♕a5 g6 44 ♕c5 h5 45 ♕b4 h4 46 a5 ♕f4+ 47 ♔g1 ♕e3+ 48 ♔h2 ♕f4+ 49 ♔g1 ♕e3+ ½-½

Game Thirteen
Grischuk – Graf
Bled Olympiad 2002

1 e4 e6 2 d4 d5 3 e5 c5 4 c3 ♘c6 5 ♘f3 ♗d7 6 ♗e2 ♘ge7 7 ♘a3 ♘g6

This is the other square for the knight. To be honest, I'm not sure what the piece does here – g4 is no longer a threat, sure, but there is far less pressure on d4 which unties White's hands a great deal.

8 h4

Why not?

8 ♘c2 is more conservative: 8 ... ♗e7 9 0-0 0-0 10 ♖e1 cxd4 11 cxd4 ♖c8 12 ♗d3 was a little better for White in Dvoirys-Tukmakov, Geneva Open 2001.

8 ... cxd4 9 cxd4

9 ... ♗xa3

Ehlvest-Minasian, 2nd IECC 2001 continued 9 ... ♗b4+ 10 ♔f1 h6 11 ♘c2 ♗e7 12 ♗d3! (possibly even better than Movsesian's 12 h5) 12 ... ♘f8 (12 ... 0-0 13 ♖h3! f5 14 ♖g3 left White well placed on the kingside in Shirov-Gurevich, French Team Championship 2004) 13 ♖h3 ♕b6 14 ♖g3 g6 15 ♔g1 ♖c8 16 b3 which looked nice for White. After 16 ... ♘b4 17 ♘xb4 ♗xb4 18 ♗e3 ♗b5 19 ♗xb5+ ♕xb5 20 ♖c1 ♖c6 21 h5 ♖xc1 22 ♗xc1 ♕a6 23 a4 ♕c6 24 ♗d2 ♗xd2 25 ♕xd2 gxh5 26 ♘h4 ♕c8 27 ♖c3 ♕d7 White had very promising pressure, though the game was later drawn.

10 bxa3 h6

10 ... ♕a5+ 11 ♔f1 and Grischuk comments that 'the queen is worse on a5 than d8'.

11 h5 ♘ge7 12 0-0

In this position it's tough to see the a-pawns as 'weaknesses'. Statically I guess they're a little repulsive but at the moment White has a half-open b-file to work on.

12 ... ♘a5 13 ♖b1 ♗c6?!

Grischuk criticises this, but his alternative 13 ... ♕c7 14 ♗d3 ♘c4 15 ♘d2 0-0-0 16 ♕f3! is also good for White.

14 ♗d3 ♘c4 15 ♘h4!

Another typical move, opening the queen's path to the kingside.

15 ... ♕a5 16 ♕g4

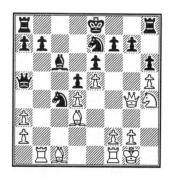

16 ... ♔d7

16 ... ♘d2 17 ♗xd2 ♕xd2 18 ♖bd1 ♕g5 19 ♕h3! (Grischuk) maintains the advantage.

17 ♖b4! ♖ag8 18 f4 f5 19 exf6 gxf6 20 ♕e2

White now has a fresh e-file weakness to work on, while the g6-square remains weak.

20 ... ♘d6 21 f5 exf5 22 ♘xf5 ♘exf5 23 ♗xf5+ ♘xf5 24 ♖xf5 ♕d8 25 ♖b3 ♖h7 26 ♕f3 ♖e8 27 ♖xf6 ♔c8

28 ♖xc6+!

The cleanest kill.

28 ... bxc6 29 ♕g4+ ♕d7 30 ♕g3 ♔d8 31 ♗xh6! ♖xh6 32 ♖b8+ ♔e7 33 ♕g7+ ♔d6 34 ♕xh6+ 1-0

Game Fourteen
Grischuk – Apicella
National I, Bordeaux 2003

1 e4 e6 2 d4 d5 3 e5 c5 4 c3 ♘c6 5 ♘f3 ♕b6 6 a3 c4 7 ♘bd2 ♘a5 8 g3 ♗d7 9 h4!

The closed nature of the position makes this move particularly apt in this context – almost all of the white chances lie on the kingside.

9 ... f5

9 ... ♘e7 10 ♗h3 h6 (the 10 ... f5 11 0-0 h6 12 ♖b1 ♖g8!? of Potkin-Vysochin, Cappelle la Grande 2004 should of course be met with 13 h5!, when Black can't play on the kingside without spoiling his structure. It seems counterintuitive to allow open files on the side where one's king sits, but a kingside attack [by White!] is quite common in this variation – if he needs, ♔h2 and ♖g1 can tidy up and prepare play on the g-file) 11 0-0 0-0-0 12 ♖e1 ♔b8 13 ♖b1 ♘c8 (13 ... ♔a8 14 ♕c2 ♘ec6 15 ♘h2 ♗e7 16 ♘hf1 is Torre-Mariano, Makati 2002, but I prefer 16 ♘df1!?, intending ♗e3, f4, h5 and ♘g4 as in the Vysochin game) 14 ♕c2 ♕c7 15 ♘f1 ♘b6 16 ♗e3 ♗a4 17 ♕e2 ♗e7 18 h5 ♕c6 19 ♘3h2 ♕e8 20 f4 and White's play was beginning to bear fruit in Vysochin-Hassan, Golden Cleopatra 2002.

9 ... h5?! is too weakening: Radulski-Oms Pallise, Andorra la Vella 2002 continued 10 ♗h3 ♗e7 11 0-0 ♘h6 12 ♖b1 0-0-0 13 ♖e1 ♔b8 14 ♘f1 ♘f5 15 ♗g5 ♖de8 16 ♗xf5 exf5 17 ♗xe7 ♖xe7 18 ♘e3 ♗e6 19 ♘g2 ♕b3 20 ♕e2 a6 21 ♘f4 g6 22 ♘g5 and White had a textbook clear advantage; 9 ... h6 was the more subtle treatment of Vysochin-Andreev, Lasker Memorial

Open 2002. After 10 ♗h3 ♕c6 11 ♕e2 ♕a4 12 ♘f1 ♘b3 13 ♖b1 ♘e7 14 ♗e3 0-0-0 15 ♘1h2 ♘f5 16 0-0 ♗e7 17 h5 ♖dg8 I like 18 ♔h1, intending g4 ♘h4 ♘xh4 ♗xh4 f4!; 9 ... 0-0-0 10 ♗h3 f5 was played by Pelletier against Reefat at the Bled Olympiad, but here of course White should play 11 exf6 when 11 ... gxf6 12 0-0 affords easy play against the e6-weakness.

10 exf6 ♘xf6 11 ♘e5 ♗d6 12 ♗h3 ♗xe5

Black elimintates the outpost, but at the cost of his vital bishop. Now the dark squares are permanently weak.

13 dxe5 ♘g8 14 ♕g4 g6 15 0-0 ♘e7 16 ♘f3 ♘b3 17 ♗e3 ♕c7 18 ♖ad1 h6 19 h5 g5 20 ♘d4 ♘xd4 21 cxd4

It's tough to find nice things to say about the black position, while a rapid march of the f-pawn is definitely on the cards.

21 ... 0-0-0 22 ♗d2 ♘c6 23 ♔h2 b5 24 f4! gxf4 25 ♖xf4

White's play on the kingside is now overwhelming. The fact that the kings have castled on opposite sides isn't really relevant here, as neither side can rustle up a big attack. Black needs to get going on the queenside, but always seems too slow.

25 ... ♕b6 26 ♖f6 b4 27 axb4 ♘xb4 28 ♗xh6 ♘d3 29 ♖d2 ♘xb2 30 ♗g7 ♖he8 31 h6 a5 32 h7 a4 33 ♕f3 ♕b4 34 ♖f2 c3 35 ♖f8!

Queening.

35 ... ♕b3 1-0

Game Fifteen
Vysochin – Polivanov
Chigorin Memorial 2002

1 e4 e6 2 d4 d5 3 e5 c5 4 c3 ♕b6 5 ♘f3 ♘c6 6 a3 ♘h6 7 b4 cxd4 8 cxd4 ♘f5 9 ♗b2 ♗e7 10 h4!

This is the most well tested move, and I think it is the best.

However, readers should also be aware of 10 &d3!?, which basically tries to get an improved version of the &xf5 and &c3 idea which you can see later. Black must be active, and 10 ... a5! is the only move worth considering. It is noteworthy that both Lastin and Motylev have played 10 &d3 recently, so obviously they have faith in its strength, and they certainly had no problems in their games: 11 ♕a4 0-0 (11 ... &d7 is superfluous: 12 b5 0-0 13 0-0 ♘a7 14 ♘c3 ♘h4 15 ♘xh4 &xh4 16 ♕d1 f5 17 ♘a4 ♕d8 18 ♕b3 b6 19 ♘c3 &e8 20 a4 and White had a dream Advance position: Motylev-Alavkin, Russian Team Championship 2004) 12 b5 f6 13 &xf5! (13 0-0 fxe5 14 dxe5 &d7 15 ♘c3 ♘cd4 16 ♘xd4 ♘xd4 17 ♖ad1 ♖f4 18 ♔h1 ♖af8 is what NOT to do: Molander-Korchnoi, Curacao 2002) 13 ... exf5 14 0-0 &e6 15 ♘c3 ♘a7 16 ♕b3 ♖fd8 17 ♖fe1 fxe5 18 ♘xe5 &f6 19 a4 ♕xd4 20 ♘e4 ♕xe4 21 ♖xe4 fxe4 22 f3 and the queen prevailed in Lastin-Ivanov, Aeroflot Open 2004.

10 ... h5 11 &d3

11 ... a5!

The most energetic and thus, in the opinion of most commentators, the best.

11 ... g6 is a little slower, and Black was treated to a nice demonstration of White's resources in Shabalov-Akobian, US Championship 2003. The tournament winner continued 12 &xf5! gxf5 13 ♘c3 ♖g8 14 g3 &d7 15 &c1!. Going for the standard plan. 15 ... ♖c8 16 ♘e2 a5 17 b5!. White chooses the queenside continuation which gives his opponent the most material but the least activity, highly indicative of the spirit with which these lines must be handled. 17 ... ♕xb5 18 &g5 a4 19 ♖b1!? ♕a5+ 20 ♔f1 &xa3 21 ♖a1 ♕b4 22 ♘f4 ♖h8 23 ♔g2 b5 24 &f6 ♖h6 25 ♖e1 ♕f8 26 ♕e2 &e7 27 &g5 ♖h8 28 ♖ec1 ♖b8 29 ♖ab1 &xg5 30 hxg5 ♕a3 31 g6! fxg6 32 ♘xe6! &xe6 33 ♖xc6 ♕e7 34 ♖xb5 ♔f7 35 ♘g5+. The infiltration is poetry. 35 ... ♕xg5 36 ♖c7+ ♕e7 37 ♖xe7+ ♔xe7 38 ♖c5 ♖hc8 39 ♕a6 ♖xc5 40 ♕a7+ ♔e8 41 dxc5 ♖c8 42 ♕xa4+ &d7 43 ♕d4 &e6 44 f4 and White's extra material proved quite decisive.

12 ♗xf5 exf5 13 ♘c3 ♗e6 14 b5

14 ... a4!

A vital move.

After the inattentitive 14 ... ♘a7? 15 a4! Black is worse everywhere. In Shirov-Taddei, Arthur Andersen Simul 2001, he didn't last long after 15 ... ♘c8 16 0-0 ♕d8 17 g3 ♘b6 18 ♗a3! ♖c8 19 ♘e2! ♘c4 20 ♗xe7 ♕xe7 21 ♘f4 g6 22 ♘g5 ♖g8? 23 ♘h7 ♕d8 24 ♘f6+.

15 ♕d3

Defending the c3-knight and thus creating a genuine threat of capture on c6, followed by ♖b1 and cxb7 with unpleasantness.

15 ... ♘a7 16 0-0 ♖c8 17 ♗c1 ♖c4 18 ♘e2!?

Oddly enough, I had this idea myself when studying the Grischuk-Lputian game, but Vysochin beat me to it. White foregoes negotiations regarding the severance package of the b5-pawn and moves his knight to the kingside, where ♗g5 and ♘f4 will soon follow.

Grischuk essayed 18 ♖d1?! against Lputian in the Bled Olympiad. After Black's excellent handling we can probably say that this move is too slow, but the game is instructive for two reasons. The first is its capacity to teach a salutory lesson about what happens to White when he acts with insufficient energy in these positions. The second is that Grischuk was obviously interested in forcing the black knight to recapture on b5, rather than allowing the capture with the queen. This is puzzling at first since the knight looks horrible on a7 and seems to be actively placed on b5, but once you start seeing that the pressure on d4 and a3 is likely to be of less significance than White's ♖b1 resource, it becomes clear that Black really wants his steed on c6. 18 ... ♘xb5 19 ♘e2 (19 ♘xb5!? ♛xb5 20 ♗g5 ♗xg5 21 ♘xg5 gives White a much more favourable version of the game. 21 ... ♛c6 22 ♖ab1 ♖c3 23 ♛d2 ♖xa3 24 ♖dc1 ♛d7 25 ♛a5 gives White excellent compensation for the pawns) 19 ... ♛c6 20 ♗g5 ♗xg5 21 ♘xg5 ♘c3! Things are clearly going awry for White already – Black's canny queenside regrouping has left Grischuk with no time to get his ♘f4 bind locked in, and forces a very unfavourable exchange. 22 ♘xc3 ♖xc3 23 ♛e2 g6 24 ♖d3 0-0 25 ♖ad1 ♖c8 26 ♖xc3 ♛xc3 27 ♛b5 ♛b3 28 ♖b1 ♖c1+ 29 ♔h2 ♛xb5 30 ♖xb5 ♖c4 31 ♖xb7 ♖xd4 32 ♘xe6 fxe6 33 ♖e7 ♖xh4+ 34 ♔g3 ♖e4 35 ♖xe6 ♔f7 36 ♖f6+ ♔e7 37 ♖xg6 ♖g4+ 38 ♖xg4 fxg4 and the pawn ending proved winning for Black.

18 ... ♛xb5

After 18 ... ♘xb5 I recommend that White ignores the pressure against the d4-pawn and continues 19 ♗g5! anyway. After the further 19 ... ♗xg5 20 hxg5 g6 the rooks are ready to roll on the b- and c-files while ♘f4, g3 and ♔g2 can be played automatically. White has excellent compensation.

19 ♗g5 ♛b3?!

Trying to put out the flames by consenting to a markedly inferior endgame. Still, I'm not sure what to recommend for Black here.

20 ♛xb3 axb3 21 ♗xe7 ♔xe7 22 ♖fb1 ♖hc8

22 ... ♖c2 23 ♖xb3! ♖xe2 24 ♖xb7+ is an important tactic.

23 ♖xb3 b5 24 ♘f4 g6 25 g3

This is the kind of endgame every 1 e4 player dreams of against the French, as it can arise from 3 e5, 3 ♘c3 or 3 ♘d2. White can gradually press with absolutely zero risk while Black must be attentive to every threat – one of those positions which, while probably drawn with best play, in practice greatly favours the attacker.

25 ... ♖c3 26 ♖ab1 ♖8c4 27 ♔g2 ♔e8 28 ♘g5 ♗d7 29 e6!

'The transformation of the advantage', as Dvoretsky says. White lets Black trade his miserable bishop in order to generate a weakness on g6.

29 ... ♗xe6 30 ♘gxe6 ♖xb3 31 ♖xb3 fxe6 32 ♘xe6 ♘c6?!

32 ... ♔f7 is probably more tenacious, but after 33 ♘g5+ ♔f6 34 ♘f3 White's advantages remain.

33 ♖xb5 ♘xd4 34 ♖b8+ ♔f7 35 ♘f4 ♖c7 36 ♖b6 ♖a7 37 ♘xg6 ♖xa3 38 ♘f4

The three black pawns allow a clear evaluation.

38 ... ♘c2 39 ♘xd5 ♘e1+ 40 ♔f1 ♖a1 41 ♖f6+ ♔g7 42 ♖xf5 ♔g6 43 ♖g5+ ♔h6 44 ♔e2 ♘c2 45 ♘f4 1-0

Game Sixteen
Grischuk – Radjabov
Wijk aan Zee 2003

1 e4 e6 2 d4 d5 3 e5 c5 4 c3 ♕b6 5 ♘f3 ♘c6 6 a3 ♘h6 7 b4 cxd4 8 cxd4 ♘f5 9 ♗b2 ♗d7

One of the most complicated lines in the Advance French. So pay attention!

10 g4

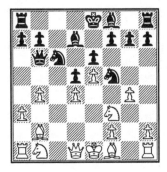

Critical, and necessary. The point is that Black can't play ... ♘h4 and so is going to lose some time.

As for the alternatives, White has scored horribly with 10 ♗e2, and his success with 10 h4 is solely attributable to Black players missing 10 ... h5! (thanks to FM Neil Berry for showing this move to me), after which White is simply worse.

10 ... ♘fe7

10 ... ♘h6 has been a favourite of Lputian, but leaves White with an easier time getting an advantage – the knight is horribly placed and will consume a lot of time getting to a respectable square. 11 ♖g1 f6 12 exf6 gxf6 13 ♘c3 ♘f7 14 ♘a4 ♕c7 (14 ... ♕d8 15 ♘c5 was long known to be better for White after 15 ... b6 16 ♘xd7 ♕xd7 17 ♖c1 and h4, but Vallejo Pons-Hillarp Persson, Hotel Bali Stars 2003 saw a different treatment with 15 ... ♗c8 16 ♖c1 ♘d6 17 ♗d3 ♕e7 18 g5 f5 19 ♘e5!? ♘xe5 20 dxe5 ♘e4 21 ♕h5+ ♔d8 22 ♘b3 ♖g8 23 h4 ♗d7 and now, instead of 24 ♗d4, 24 ♕d1! would leave the e4-knight in big trouble) 15 ♖c1 ♕f4 16 ♘c5 ♗xc5 17 dxc5 ♘ce5 18 ♘xe5 ♘xe5 19 ♖g3 a6 20 ♗e2 ♗b5 21 ♕d4 ♕xd4 22 ♗xd4 ♖f8 23 g5 ♗xe2 24 ♔xe2 with a better ending in Short-Lputian, European Team Championship 1999.

11 ♘c3 ♘a5!

This must be played, or else 12 ♘a4 and Black has too many pieces with too few squares.

12 ♘d2 ♖c8 13 ♖c1

This is the critical position for the 9 ... ♗d7 line. White has more space everywhere, and it's up to Black to demonstrate a weakness before he gets squashed.

13 ... ♘g6

13 ... h5 was essayed in Ivanchuk-Bareev, FIDE Grand Prix 2002, but it seems that White can take advantage of Black's omission of ... ♘g6 with 14

♗a1! when 14 ... ♘ac6 (14 ... ♘c4 15 ♗xc4! dxc4 16 ♘ce4 is the point, threatening both the c4-pawn and ♘d6+) 15 ♘a4 is nice for White.

Jonkman-Vysochin, Tanta Open 2002 continued 13 ... ♘c4 14 ♗xc4 dxc4 15 ♘ce4 ♘d5 16 ♘xc4 ♖xc4! 17 ♖xc4 ♗e7 18 0-0 0-0 19 ♖c5!? ♗xc5 20 dxc5 ♕d8 and now, while the game's 21 ♘d6 left White with some advantage, I'd prefer 21 ♕d2 ♕h4 22 f3 with a clear plus.

14 h4!

The most consistent. White has also tried 14 ♗b5, but without particular success.

14 ... ♗e7 15 g5

Grischuk tried 15 h5 in a previous game but got nothing.

15 ... h6

15 ... 0-0!? was Potkin-Hug, Istanbul 2003. This position looks like the definition of "castling into it", but in truth White has no clear route to an advantage. I'm including the whole game so readers can examine for themselves where White can improve, but I think that my 16th move suggestion looks good, though practical tests are needed to show how good. 16 ♖g1 ♘xh4 17 ♗d3 g6 18 ♕g4 ♘f5 19 ♗xf5 exf5 20 ♕h4 ♖fe8 21 ♘xd5 ♖xc1+ 22 ♗xc1 ♕c6 23 ♘xe7+ ♖xe7 24 ♗b2 ♕c2 25 ♖h1 f6 26 gxf6 ♖f7 27 d5 ♗a4 28 ♔f1 was agreed drawn, but the alternatives are fascinating:

a) Psakhis gives 16 ♕g4 ♗xb4! 17 axb4 ♕xb4 18 ♖b1 ♖xc3 19 ♗xc3 ♕xc3 20 h5 ♘e7 as 'unclear'. As Morozevich once commented, 'this is normally the assessment used by a lazy annotator, but this position really is unclear!'. After 21 ♖h3 ♕c7 22 h6 (22 g6 h6 is no clear improvement) 22 ... g6 I'd feel uncomfortable with both colours! I suppose the black king is weaker since it can be mated either on the back rank or on g7, but actually getting to these squares is another matter.

b) 16 ♗a1!?

...is a move I stumbled upon after a couple of hours of analysis (Psakhis doesn't mention it in his notes) – so far it looks good and I suppose I'd recommend it ahead of the alternatives. The idea can be seen after 16 ... ♘c4 (16 ... ♘c6 17 ♘a4 is, as always, good for White) 17 ♗xc4 dxc4 18 ♕g4, when the c-file has been closed and h5 is now a real threat. Of course this isn't the end of the story since Black can play on both the d-file and the a8-h1 diagonal, but after 18 ... ♗c6 19 ♖h3! (the best square, protecting the a3-pawn against and ... ♕a6 stuff, while also covering c3 – as will become apparent, the c3-advance is a vital resource for Black in several variations) 19 ... ♖fd8 20 ♘e2! (threatening the c4-pawn) 20 ... ♗d5 21 h5 ♘f8 22 ♘f4! I've yet to find a route to equality for Black. The f4-knight is awesome, both preparing g6 and retaining the option of taking on d5. Though it isn't a typical formation, I think the white pieces co-ordinate beautifully. 22 ... a5 23 g6 axb4 24 gxf7+ ♔xf7 25 axb4! ♕xb4 26 ♖g3 ♔e8 (the natural 26 ... b5 loses: 27 ♕xg7+ ♔e8 28 ♗c3! ♕a4 29 ♖a1 ♕c2 30 ♖a7 ♖d7 31 ♖xd7 ♘xd7 32 ♘xd5 exd5 33 e6 with too much: 33 ... ♘f8 34 ♕f7+ ♔d8 35 ♗a5+!) 27 ♕xg7 ♕b5 28 ♘xd5 exd5 (it's best to keep some pawn control over e4, as illustrated by the variation 28 ... ♕xd5 29 ♖f3 ♖c6 30 ♕f7+ ♔d7 31 ♗b2!! ♖e8 32 ♗a3 ♖cc8 33 ♖e3! followed by ♘e4 with an insufferable attack) 29 ♖f3 with a continuing attack. From my study of this position I've found a couple of themes – White plays ♗c3 and follows with ♖b1 or ♖a1, trying to bring another piece into play. Also, there is the motif ♕f7+ and ♖f6! to increase the pressure.

16 gxh6 ♖xh6 17 h5 ♘h4

Of course the knight is taboo for the moment, but it needs to reach the f5-square and must start its journey immediately.

For instance, 17 ... ♘c4 18 ♘xc4 dxc4 19 ♖g1 allows a breakthrough on g7.

18 ♕g4 ♘f5 19 ♗d3! ♗f8

19 ... ♘xd4 is more testing, however White retains an advantage after 20 ♕xg7 ♗f8 21 ♕g4 ♘ab3 22 ♘xb3 ♘xb3 23 ♖b1!, for instance 23 ... ♗c6 (23 ... a5 24 ♕d1! is good for White) 24 ♖h3 followed by ♘e2, taking control of d4.

20 ♘e2 ♘c4 21 ♘xc4 dxc4 22 ♗xf5 exf5 23 ♕g2

While the position remains complex, the assessment is clear – the white central pawn roller beats any trumps which Black might have. The black bishops can't move.

23 ... a5 24 ♗c3 axb4 25 axb4 ♖a8

25 ... g6 is another way to play: 26 hxg6 ♖xg6 27 ♕f3 ♗xb4 28 d5! with excellent compensation.

26 d5 ♖a2 27 ♔f1 ♕a6 28 ♖e1! ♔d8 29 ♖h3!

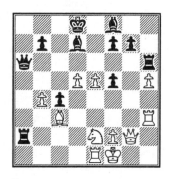

White has a clear advantage, in large part due to his much safer king.

29 ... f4

To show a thematic variation, 29 ... ♔c8 30 ♘d4 f4 31 ♖f3 ♖xh5? (31 ... ♖a3 is more tenacious) 32 e6! wins.

30 ♖h4 ♕a3 31 e6!

Here, the breakthrough gains only an exchange, but it proves more than enough.

31 ... ♖xe2

31 ... fxe6 32 dxe6 ♖xe6 33 ♖xf4 ♗xb4 34 ♕xb7! leaves the black monarch too exposed: note that 34 ... ♗xc3 35 ♕b8+ ♗c8 36 ♖xc4 is no problem for White.

32 ♖xe2 ♕xc3 33 ♖h3 ♕c1+ 34 ♖e1 ♕d2 35 exd7 ♗xb4 36 ♖a1! ♖a6

A very big concession – the side with an exchange less is always advised to keep the rooks on – but the alternative 36 ... ♗c3 37 ♖a8+ ♔xd7 38 ♕e4 costs a king.

37 ♕xg7 ♗c5 38 ♖f3 ♖xa1+ 39 ♕xa1 ♕xd5 40 ♕h8+ ♔xd7 41 ♖xf4 c3

Otherwise the h-pawn would be unstoppable.

42 ♕xc3 ♕h1+ 43 ♔e2 ♕xh5+ 44 ♖f3 b6 45 ♕f6 ♔e8 46 ♕c6+ ♔e7 47 ♕b7+ ♔e8 48 ♕e4+ ♔f8 49 ♔d3

White has a clear advantage, but an analysis of how to win this endgame would clearly take us too far off track. Suffice it to say that Grischuk's technique has always been remarkable, and his prosecution of the advantage here should be played over at least once.

49 ... ♗d6 50 ♔c2 ♕c5+ 51 ♔d1 ♕h5 52 ♕d3 ♔e7 53 ♕e2+ ♔f8 54 ♕d3 ♔e7 55 ♕e4+ ♔f8 56 ♕c6 ♗c5 57 ♔c2 ♕h7+ 58 ♔d2 ♕h5 59 ♕a8+ ♔e7 60 ♕b7+ ♔f8 61 ♕c8+ ♔e7 62 ♕c7+ ♔e8 63 ♕c6+ ♔f8 64 ♕a8+ ♔e7 65 ♖f4 ♕g6 66 ♖e4+ ♔d7 67 ♕b7+ ♔d6 68 ♖f4 ♔e6 69 ♕c6+ ♔e5 70 ♕c7+ ♔e6 71 f3! f5 72 ♕c6+ ♔f7 73 ♕d5+ ♔f6 74 ♔d3 ♕g5 75 ♕e4!! ♕g6 76 ♔c4 ♕f7+ 77 ♕d5 ♕xd5+ 78 ♔xd5 ♗e3 79 ♖c4 f4 80 ♖c6+ ♔f5 81 ♖c8 ♔f6 82 ♖f8+ ♔e7 83 ♖f5 ♗d2 84 ♖e5+ ♔d7 85 ♖h5 ♗e3 86 ♖h7+ ♔d8 87 ♔e6 ♗c5 88 ♖d7+ ♔c8 89 ♖f7 ♗e3 90 ♔d6 ♔b8 91 ♔c6 b5□ 92 ♔xb5 ♔c8 93 ♔c6 ♔d8 94 ♔d6 ♔e8 95 ♔e6 ♗d2 96 ♖c7 ♔f8 97 ♔f6 ♔e8 98 ♖e7+ ♔d8 99 ♖e4 1-0

Game Seventeen
Grischuk – Gurevich
National I, Bordeaux 2003

1 e4 e6 2 d4 d5 3 e5 c5 4 c3 ♗d7 5 ♘f3 ♕b6

This is a tricky little system. Black's idea is to play an early ... ♗b5 to get rid of his problem piece and leave his queen actively placed on the queenside. However, he retains the option of transposing into normal lines with ... ♘c6. Thus 6 ♗e2, for instance, which isn't a bad move at all (Movsesian crushed Volkov a couple of times here) is a non-starter for us since 6 ... ♘c6 brings us into territory where we'd rather have played a3. Speaking of which...

6 a3!?

...is a good move here too and constitutes my recommendation.

6 ... ♗b5

Logical and consistent.

6 ... ♘c6 7 b4 cxd4 8 cxd4 transposes to stuff we've looked at already, while 6 ... a5 is the next game.

7 b4!?

The main move here is probably the pawn sacrifice 7 c4!?, which is actually less fun than it looks – in several lines Black returns the pawn for a somewhat dull position. Grischuk's move is very consistent, plus it's played by Grischuk, which is always a ringing endorsement.

7 ... cxd4

7 ... cxb4?! has no independent significance: White can transpose to the text with 8 ♗xb5+ ♛xb5 9 cxb4. Anyone wishing to exploit this move-order error (if it proves to be an error) should take a peek at Shirov-Feygin, Bundesliga 2001, which continued 8 axb4 ♘d7 9 ♗d3 ♗xd3 10 ♛xd3 ♘e7 11 0-0 ♘c8 12 ♘g5 h6 13 ♘h3 when Shirov subsequently played on the queenside and drew after many adventures but I'd be sorely tempted to play for f4-f5 with good chances.

8 ♗xb5+ ♛xb5 9 cxd4 ♘d7

9 ... a5 10 ♘c3 ♛c6 doesn't look too promising after 11 ♗d2!. Now 11 ... axb4 12 axb4 ♖xa1 13 ♛xa1 ♛a6 14 ♛b1 (14 ♛a4+ ♛xa4 15 ♘xa4 ♘c6 16 b5 ♘a7 17 ♔e2 ♘e7 18 b6 ♘ac6 19 ♖c1 h6 20 ♘c5 ♘d8 21 h4 was also clearly better for White in Peng Xiaomin-Tovsanaa, 2nd World Cities Ch., Shenyang 1999) 14 ... b5 15 0-0 ♘e7 16 ♛d3 ♘ec6 17 ♘xb5 ♔d7 18 ♘g5 ♗e7 19 ♘xf7 ♖f8 20 ♘fd6 ♗xd6 21 exd6 was the winning continuation of Shirov-Ljubojevic, Amber Blindfold, Monaco 2002.

10 ♘c3 ♛c6 11 ♘a4!

This seems like the optimal setup.

11 ♗b2 ♘b6 12 ♘d2 ♘e7 13 0-0 ♘f5 14 ♖c1 ♕d7 15 ♘e2 was too passive in Alekseev-Rustemov, Russian Championship 2001.

11 ... ♘e7 12 ♗e3 ♘b6 13 ♘xb6 ♕xb6 14 0-0 ♘c6

From here on the simplicity of White's play is breathtaking, just one typical move after another until Black cracks.

14 ... ♘f5 15 ♖c1 ♕d8 was tried in Carlsen-Rustemov, Aeroflot Open 2004, and now I like 16 ♕e2 intending to double on the c-file.

15 ♘e1!

With three aims:

1   Re-routing the knight to c5

2   Allowing the white queen access to the kingside.

3   Creating the option of f2-f4.

15 ... ♗e7 16 ♕g4 g6 17 ♘d3 0-0

17 ... h5 doesn't bring any particular relief after 18 ♕d1!, when 18 ... ♘xd4?? loses to (amongst other things) 19 ♘f4.

18 ♘c5 ♕c7 19 ♖ac1 ♖fc8 20 h4!

99% of times this is played to soften up the black kingside structure (the luft for White's king is also welcome), but here Grischuk plays a slight twist:

20 ... b6 21 ♘d3 ♕d7 22 h5 ♗f8 23 ♘f4 ♗g7 24 h6!! ♗xh6 25 ♘h5 ♗g7 26 ♘xg7 ♔xg7 27 ♕h4

Childsplay for someone of Grischuk's ability. The dark-square weaknesses are terminal.

27 ... ♔g8 28 ♗g5 f5 29 exf6 ♘d8 30 ♕h6 ♖c4 31 ♖xc4 dxc4 32 d5 a5 33 ♖e1 ♖a7 34 f7+ 1-0

Game Eighteen
Svidler – Volkov
Russian Championship 2003

1 e4 e6 2 d4 d5 3 e5 c5 4 c3 ♕b6 5 ♘f3 ♗d7 6 a3 a5
Putting the brakes on b4.

7 b3!?

Putting the brakes on ... a4! Strangely enough, all of the recent high level games in this line have featured Volkov as Black.

7 ♗e2 is also played but Black had no problems after 7 ... a4 8 0-0 ♘c6 9 ♗d3 ♘a5 10 ♗c2 ♘c4 11 ♖a2 ♘e7 12 ♖e1 ♘c6 13 ♔h1 ♗e7 in Charbonneau-Shulman, American Continental 2003, though he later lost.

7 ... ♘a6

Against Zviaginsev in the Russian Team Championships 1999 Volkov chose 7 ... ♘e7, and after 8 ♗e2 cxd4 9 cxd4 ♗b5 10 ♗xb5+ ♕xb5 11 ♘c3 ♕a6 12 a4 ♘ec6 13 ♘b5 ♕b6 14 0-0 h6, instead of the game's 15 ♗a3 with equality I like 15 ♗e3!, intending ♘e1-d3-c5, a queen sortie to the kingside and shoving the f-pawn up the board. I prefer White.

7 ... ♘c6 8 ♗e3 ♘h6 (8 ... ♖c8 9 ♗d3 cxd4 10 cxd4 ♘a7 11 0-0 ♗b5 12 ♗xb5+ ♘xb5 was Volkov's choice against Najer at St Petersburg 2004, and now I think that 13 ♕d3 followed by a4 and ♘a3 is an edge) 9 ♗d3 ♘f5 10 ♗xf5 exf5 11 0-0 cxd4 12 cxd4 h6 13 ♘c3 ♗e6 14 ♘a4 ♕b5 15 ♘e1 ♗e7 16 ♘d3 ♖c8 17 ♘ac5 0-0 18 ♖c1 ♖fe8 19 ♖c3 ♘a7 20 a4 is very nice for White: Vorobiov-Volkov, Aeroflot Open 2004.

8 ♗e3 ♖c8 9 ♗d3 ♘e7

After 9 ... ♘h6 as in Sveshnikov-Volkov, Togliatti 2003, White can transpose to the text with 10 0-0 ♘f5, but Sveshnikov's continuation is also promising: 10 ♗xh6 gxh6 11 0-0 ♗g7 and now the game's 12 ♖a2 was interesting but I'd prefer 12 ♘bd2 followed by ♕e2 and doing something with the rooks on the queenside.

10 0-0 ♘f5 11 ♗xf5 exf5 12 ♖e1

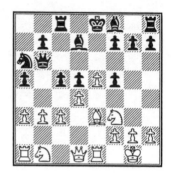

12 ... c4?!

With hindsight, possibly the losing move.

12 ... ♗e6 was also pretty grim, however, despite Svidler's typically pessimistic annotation that White 'doesn't have much of an edge'. White can preserve the advantage in several ways, possibly the most thematic of which is 13 dxc5 ♗xc5 14 b4! ♗xe3 15 ♖xe3 followed by ♘d4 with advantage.

13 bxc4 ♖xc4 14 e6! ♗xe6

14 ... fxe6 15 ♘e5 is no improvement, since White threatens both ♘xc4 (if he wants) and ♕h5+.

15 ♘e5 ♖c7 16 ♕a4+ ♔d8 17 c4 f6

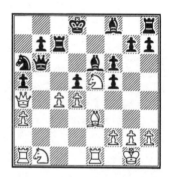

Now what?

18 c5!!

Svidler points out that 18 cxd5 ♗xd5 19 ♘c3 ♗b3 20 d5 ♘c5 is 'messy' (for him – 'utterly incomprehensible' for me).

18 ... ♕b2 19 ♘d3 ♕xa1 20 ♕xa5!!

It's no surprise that Svidler won the tournament – this concept is absolutely superb. White is a rook down but is going to get his material back with interest.

20 ... ♕a2

Even Fritz's suggested 20 ... f4 21 ♘xf4 ♗f7 is no good after 22 ♘d3!: 22 ... ♕a2 23 ♗f4 ♕c4 24 ♘b4 ♕xd4 25 ♘xa6 ♕xf4 26 g3 and White wins.

Svidler's notes suggest 20 ... ♗c8!, preparing to meet 21 ♘c3 with b6, as the only way to survive. The following analysis is his and, while pretty remote from our purposes, is worth playing over as an example of how a top player looks at a position: 21 ♘d2 ♕a2 22 ♕c3 ♗xc5 (22 ... f4 23 ♗xf4 ♗f5 24 ♗xc7+ ♔xc7 25 ♕a5+ ♔d7 26 ♘b4 ♘xb4 27 ♕xb4 wins) 23 dxc5 d4 24 ♕xd4+ ♖d7 25 ♕c3 ♕d5 26 ♘f4 ♕c6 27 ♘c4 ♖e8 28 ♘a5 ♕c7 29 c6 ♖d6 30 ♖b1 ♖xc6 31 ♘xc6+ ♕xc6 32 ♕b3 ♔e7 33 ♖c1 ♕d6 34 h4 ♔f8 35 h5 and White still holds the initiative.

21 ♗f4 ♕c4 22 ♘b4 ♔e8 23 ♗xc7 ♔f7 24 ♕b6 ♗c8

24 ... ♘xc7 25 ♕xc7+ ♗e7 26 ♕xb7 is even worse.

25 ♘xa6 ♕xa6 26 ♕xa6 bxa6 27 ♘c3 ♗e6 28 ♖b1 ♗e7 29 ♖b7 ♖e8 30 f3 g5 31 ♖a7 f4 32 ♗d6 ♔f8 33 ♖xa6 ♗xd6 34 ♖xd6 ♗f7 35 ♘xd5 ♖e1+ 36 ♔f2 ♖c1 37 ♔e2

Svidler suggests 37 ♘xf6 ♗c4 38 g4 as the simplest win.

37 ... ♖c2+ 38 ♔d1 ♖xg2 39 c6 ♗h5 40 c7 ♗xf3+ 41 ♔c1 ♖g1+ 42 ♔d2 ♖g2+ 43 ♔e1 ♖e2+ 44 ♔f1 ♖c2 45 ♖d8+ ♔f7 46 c8=♕ ♖xc8 47 ♖xc8 ♗xd5

The transformation hasn't helped Black at all – the two passers are too fast.

48 a4 ♔e6 49 a5 ♔d7 50 ♖c3 ♗b7 51 ♖b3 ♗a6+ 52 ♔f2 f5 53 ♖b6 ♗c8 54 d5 1-0

Game Nineteen
Grischuk – Bareev
European Club Cup 2001

This is the game where I try to take care of some odds and ends in the Advance. Because the position is so closed, at least to begin with, Black has a large degree of flexibility in choosing how to place his pieces (which isn't to say that any or all of these lines are as good as their better-established counterparts). What has been shown earlier in the chapter is the bread-and-butter and will undoubtedly inform the majority of your games – my aim here is to take the mystique out of a couple of move-orders and systems which, though rare, can be somewhat discomforting to play against.

1 e4 e6 2 d4 d5 3 e5 c5

3 ... b6 is another rare line, trying to get the light-squared bishop off ASAP. The drawback is that White can put the time expended to good use elsewhere, as Movsesian demonstrated against Tibensky in the Slovakian Championship 2002: 4 c3 ♕d7 (the impetuous 4 ... ♗a6 is unfortunate: 5 ♗xa6 ♘xa6 6 ♕a4+) 5 h4! ♗a6 6 ♗xa6 ♘xa6 7 h5!. This pawn, as so often happens, comes in very handy later. Movsesian makes the interesting comment that he preferred not to kick the a6-knight with ♕e2 or ♕d3, since it doesn't have any better prospects than dragging itself back into play via b8 and c6. While I guess White needs to be careful not to allow an effective knight sortie to b4 after ... c5, ... cxd4 cxd4, Movsesian's point is an excellent one. Indeed, the queen could well find a better home on d2 or g4. 7 ... c5 8 ♘e2 f6 (both Psakhis and Movsesian analyse 8 ... ♘e7 9 ♘d2 ♘c6 10 ♘f3 as being slightly better for White – it's tough to see the point of Black's position) 9 ♗f4 ♘e7 10 ♘d2 ♘c6 11 ♘f3 ♖c8 12 0-0 ♘ab8 13 ♖e1 ♗e7?. Inattentive, but White was much better in any event. Movsesian now finds a nice line to build on his gains: 14 exf6 gxf6 (14 ... ♗xf6 fails to the same idea, and leaves Black's pawn structure crippled) 15 ♗xb8 ♖xb8 16 ♘f4 ♘d8 17 ♕e2 ♔f7 18 c4 ♗d6 19 ♕d2 ♕c7 20 ♘h3 dxc4 21 ♖ad1 ♖f8 22 ♖e4. White has a substantial initiative which Movsesian exploits superbly. 22 ... ♔g8 23 dxc5 ♗xc5 24 ♖g4+ ♔f7 25 ♕c2 ♔e8 26 ♖xc4 ♕e7 27 b4 ♗d6 28 ♖cd4 ♘b7 29 ♘d2 ♘d8 30 ♕d3 ♘b7 31 ♘e4.

4 c3 ♘c6 5 ♘f3 ♘h6

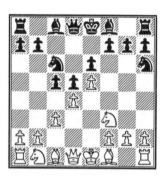

Why this way? The answer can be gleaned from examining the more standard 5 ... ♘ge7: 6 ♘a3 cxd4 7 cxd4 ♘f5 8 ♘c2 ♗d7 9 ♗e2 and we're back in a main line. By going via h6, Black tries to discourage this ♘a3-c2 manoeuvre by threatening ... cxd2 and ... ♗xa3, disrupting White's pawn structure. While this is double edged (he is giving up his good bishop, after all), I'm recommending a different treatment.

5 ... ♗d7 6 ♗e2 f6 is rare but interesting. Black is obviously hitting the pawn chain as hard as he can, both at its base and its head. The problem is

that he starts this fight from a position of relative weakness, in that White controls more space and can get his pieces to better squares in less time. When an early ... f6 is played, it's standard practice to allow Black to capture on e5, rather than take on f6 and assist his development (...♘xf6) or central control (...gxf6). After ... fxe5, should one recapture with the knight or the pawn? In general, the knight is preferable, since the knight on f3 blocks both an f4-advance and the queen's path to the kingside. In this particular position though, Black generally intends to castle queenside, so it can be a good idea to maintain the f3-knight for defensive purposes. Grischuk-Kolev, Istanbul Olympiad 2000 continued 7 0-0 ♕b6 8 ♘a3 fxe5 9 dxe5 ♘h6 10 c4! d4 11 ♗d3 ♘f7 12 ♖e1 ♗e7 13 h4 0-0-0 14 ♘c2 ♖dg8 and now Grischuk recommends 15 ♖b1 g5 16 hxg5 ♘xg5 17 ♗xg5 ♗xg5 18 b4 cxb4 19 a3, when I prefer White.

6 ♗d3 cxd4 7 ♗xh6!

A rare move – Khalifman and others played 7 cxd4 here.

7 ... gxh6 8 cxd4 ♗d7

After the alternative 8 ... ♗g7 9 ♘c3 0-0 10 ♗c2 f5 11 a3 ♗d7 12 ♘e2 ♘e7 13 ♕d2 ♖c8 14 ♗d3 ♔h8 15 h4 ♖g8 16 ♘f4 White was better in Morawietz-Tuerk, Cologne 1994.

9 ♘c3 ♕b6

Bareev appreciates how critical his position is. If he doesn't try this, White will simply castle and play on the queenside.

10 ♗b5! ♖g8

After 10 ... a6 11 ♗xc6 ♗xc6 12 ♕c2 the black bishops are impotent in the resulting closed structure while the white centre is utterly solid – I'd castle kingside and then arrange queenside play with b4.

11 0-0!

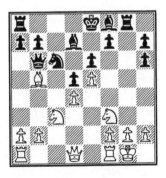

I'd love to know how many of the subsequent moves were stored on each player's laptop before the game. The only answer we can make with confidence is (in Bareev's case) "not enough."

11 ... ♘xe5

Winning a pawn, surely?

12 ♘xe5

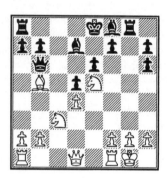

12 ... ♗xb5 13 ♕h5 ♖g7 14 ♖fe1

Threatening 14 ♘xd5.

14 ... ♖d8?

This is the last point at which Bareev could have saved the game.

14 ... ♗e7! was the only move, when 15 ♕xh6 ♔f8 16 ♖ac1 leaves White comfortably better but Black is still playing. Note that 14 ... ♗c6 loses to 15 ♘xf7!

15 ♘xb5 ♕xb5 16 ♘xf7!!

The point.

16 ... ♖xf7 17 ♖xe6+ 1-0

It's all over after 17 .... ♗e7 18 ♖xe7+! ♔xe7 19 ♖e1+ ♔f8 20 ♕xh6+ ♔g8 21 ♕g5+.

CHAPTER THREE
The Scotch Opening

"Previously I would blunder a pawn with 2 f4? exf4, but now I have grown up."

GM Alexander Morozevich

1 e4 e5 2 ♘f3 ♘c6 3 d4 exd4 4 ♘xd4

This is the Scotch. Part of the appeal of this opening is that its positional demands are so outrageous – White seeks to exchange a pivotal e5-pawn for a meaningless d2-one, and questions Black's right to any significant central influence. Here, unlike in many lines of the Ruy Lopez, Black can't hold his e5-strongpoint and must allow the liquidation, leaving a position where White will get a very easy edge unless Black does something aggressive. Take a peek:

Balinov – Hicker
Schwarzach Open 1999

1 e4 e5 2 ♘f3 ♘c6 3 d4 exd4 4 ♘xd4 d6?!

No-one does this, for the simple reason that it fails to pressurise White's centre and allows him a free hand in developing. After

5 c4 ♘f6 6 ♘c3 ♗e7 7 ♗e2 0-0 8 0-0 ♗d7 9 ♗e3 ♖e8 10 f3 ♘xd4 11 ♕xd4 ♗c6 12 b4!

White has a clear advantage – Black is trying to play a hedgehog formation but has absent mindedly left his half-open c-file at home.

Thus Black is obliged to create some play, and he can do so against either d4 (4 ... &c5, 4 ... ♕f6) or e4 (4 ... ♘f6, 4 ... ♕h4?!). In all these lines he risks compromising his structure to create play – White's job is to make it to move 20 without any nasty accidents occurring, and then convert his edge. If Black doesn't play precisely he can easily end up in a prospectless position – here we are mainly concerned with the lines where he generates some serious play.

The Scotch breaks down into two main lines. The first, 4 ... ♘f6 5 ♘xc6 bxc6 6 e5 ♕e7! 7 ♕e2 ♘d5 8 c4, is met by either 8 ... &a6 or 8 ... ♘b6, and these lines are covered in the first five games.

The second line, 4 ... &c5, gives rise to huge theory after 5 &e3, but I've opted for 5 ♘xc6 which has been the choice of many Scotch experts, notably Rublevsky. This is covered in the next two games.

Of the odds and ends, pay attention to 4 ... &b4+ which is one of Black's better options. 4 ... ♕h4 is just a bad move, no matter how many people write books about it, and gives rise to huge attacking chances.

To be honest, I find it very difficult to explain each Scotch variation in conceptual terms – grand summaries here are of virtually no value. I'll leave the reader to plunge into the games and find out whether he likes this stuff. One word of advice, however – in the Scotch, more than in any other line of my acquaintance, White is seeking a HUGE long-term advantage. In most lines he gains a clearly better structure right from the word 'go', and if he reaches move 20 without Black making a dent, the game can be a very pleasent experience. The trade-off is that Black gains a lot of activity very early on, so just be careful. Basically I'm trying to say that in this line more than any other, you should learn your theory and be alert for the early stage of the game. Of course this advice should be followed in all openings, but if you don't do it here you'll get creamed.

Game Twenty
Smeets – Timman
Lost Boys Open 2002

1 e4 e5 2 ♘f3 ♘c6 3 d4 exd4 4 ♘xd4 ♘f6 5 ♘xc6 bxc6 6 e5 ♛e7 7 ♛e2 ♘d5 8 c4 ♝a6 9 b3 g5!?

This is almost certainly Black's best. Unleashed by Anand against Gazza in their '95 World Championship match, the move has several benefits over its little sister 9 ... g6, not least the availability of a ... ♘f4-e6(g6) regrouping which takes care of one of Black's problem pieces. Another idea is that, in several endgames which are likely to arise from the main lines, Black effectively saves a tempo over lines where he looks to a kingside pawn storm for counterplay.

The move has been effective in practice – of White's two main replies, 10 ♝a3 seems to be fine for Black in the positions arising after 10 ... d6! 11 exd6 ♛xe2+ 12 ♝xe2 ♝g7! 13 cxd5 ♝xe2 14 ♔xe2 ♝xa1 15 ♜c1 0-0-0!, while 10 g3 has had mixed results in practice, even though Black players have failed to make use of Wells' recommendation (after 10 ... ♝g7 11 ♝b2 0-0-0 12 ♘d2 ♘b4 13 ♘f3), 13 ... c5! 14 ♝g2 ♝b7 with easy equality.

Thus I've plumped for a third option which seeks to exploit the downside of 9 ... g5. The move received nods of approval from Wells but is still relatively untested – of its most recent outings, however, it was used by Smeets to beat two much stronger players in the Lost Boys Open of 2002.

10 h4!? ♝g7 11 ♝b2

11 ... ♘f4

11 ... h6 12 ♕e4 (12 ♘d2 is also possible, when 12 ... 0-0-0 13 0-0-0 ♖de8 14 g3 ♘b6 15 f4 ♗b7 16 hxg5 hxg5 17 ♖xh8 ♗xh8 18 ♘f3 gxf4 19 gxf4 a5 20 ♕f2 a4 21 ♘d4 f6 22 ♘f5 gave White some kingside pressure in Dworakowska-Vijayalakshmi, Moscow 2001) 12 ... ♘b6 13 hxg5 hxg5 14 ♖xh8+ ♗xh8 15 ♘d2 d5 16 ♕e3 dxc4 17 ♘xc4 ♗xc4 18 ♗xc4 ♘xc4 19 bxc4 0-0-0 20 ♔f1! occurred in Smeets' encounter with Jonkman two rounds before the text. Black, effectively a pawn down, could find nothing better than 20 ... ♕b4 after which 21 ♕b3 ♕xb3 22 axb3 ♖e8 23 ♖xa7 ♔d7 24 ♖a5 ♖b8 25 ♖c5! was a much superior endgame which White converted nicely: 25 ... ♔e7 (not 25 ... ♖xb3?? 26 e6+ ♔d6 27 exf7 ♖b8 28 ♖xg5!, winning) 26 ♖xc6 ♖xb3 27 ♖xc7+ ♔e6 28 ♗d4 ♖d3 29 ♖c6+ ♔f5 30 ♖d6 ♖d2 31 c5 ♖c2 32 e6 ♗xd4 33 e7 ♗xc5 34 ♖d5+ ♔e6 35 ♖xc5!.

11 ... 0-0-0 was the continuation of the stem game Palac-Giorgadze, Pula 1997. 12 ♘d2 ♖de8 (12 ... ♘b4 13 0-0-0 ♘xa2+ 14 ♔b1 ♘b4 15 ♕e3 is Palac's analysis, with a white advantage) 13 hxg5 ♘f4 14 ♕g4 ♗xe5 15 0-0-0 f6 16 ♘f3 ♗xb2+ 17 ♔xb2 ♘e6 18 gxf6 ♕xf6+ 19 ♔b1 ♗b7 20 ♗d3 ♖eg8 21 ♕h4 ♕xh4 22 ♘xh4 c5 23 ♖h2 ♘f4 24 ♗f5 ♗c6 25 ♖d2 ♖e8 26 ♖h1 ♖e7 27 f3 gave White an enduring edge because of his passed f-pawn, though very accurate defence enabled Black to hold the draw. While Wells seems to think this is a pretty clear draw, I would certainly doubt my abilities to bring the position to safety with Black, who has two weaknesses (on d7 and h7) and a dead lost king and pawn ending awaiting him if too many pieces come off.

12 ♕e3 h6 13 ♘d2!

I prefer this to the messy 13 g3 ♘g6 14 f4 gxf4 15 gxf4 h5 16 ♗d3 ♗h6 17 e6 of Van der Wiel-Erwich, Amsterdam 2002.

13 ... ♘g6 14 ♘f3

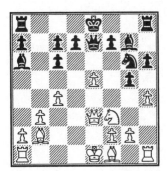

The pressure on Black's kingside forces an immediate concession.

14 ... gxh4

Wells analyses 14 ... g4 15 h5 gxf3 16 hxg6 fxg6 17 gxf3 g5 18 ♗d3 as in White's favour.

15 0-0-0 0-0 16 ♕d4! ♖ad8 17 ♕xa7 ♘xe5!? 18 ♕xc7!

The correct response to Timman's mixing attempts.

18 ♕xa6 ♖a8 19 ♕b7 ♖xa2 gives Black a decisive attack.

18 ... ♘xf3 19 ♗xg7 ♕g5+ 20 ♔c2 ♔xg7 21 gxf3 d5 22 ♖d4!

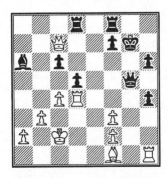

Either Smeets is underrated or in exceptional form. Here he latches on to the g- and f-file weaknesses, with a beautiful position.

22 ... ♗c8 23 ♖hxh4 ♗f5+ 24 ♔b2 ♗g6

Timman has covered up well, but now Smeets can switch to Plan B: a winning endgame.

25 ♕f4! dxc4 26 ♗xc4 c5 27 ♖xd8 ♖xd8 28 ♔c3! ♖d1 29 a4 ♖c1+ 30 ♔b2 ♖c2+ 31 ♔a3 ♖xf2 32 a5 ♖xf3 33 ♕xg5 hxg5 34 ♖g4 f5 35 ♖xg5 ♔f6 36 a6! 1-0

Very well played.

Scotch Endgame

There is a very interesting endgame in the Scotch, as shown in the diagram. Black has a rook and two pawns for two pieces, which is rough material equality, but the position is far from dead drawn. If Black can open files and mobilise his c- and d-pawns (all three of them!), White will be unable to deal with the onslaught. So the immediate white task is to stop Black's counterplay and prevent his rooks from gaining any meaningful employment, whereupon he can turn to exploiting his extra piece.

Typical ideas: The best route for the white knight is to a4 via c3, from where it threatens to hop into c5 and pressurise the black pawns. The white rook should aim for play on the a-file via the ♖c1-c3-a3 manoeuvre (after playing b4 to hold the black c-pawns) or ♖d1-d4-a4. Once these manoeuvres are completed, a role for the white king and bishop should become clearer – at the start, however, the move ♗f3 can come in handy, stopping a rook invasion on e2. For Black, the best plan is to double rooks on the e-file and transfer the king to d8.

Game Twenty-One
Rublevsky – Geller
Russian Championship 2004

1 e4 e5 2 ♘f3 ♘c6 3 d4 exd4 4 ♘xd4 ♘f6 5 ♘xc6 bxc6 6 e5 ♕e7 7 ♕e2 ♘d5 8 c4 ♗a6 9 b3 g6 10 g3

I think the double fianchetto is the best response to Black's setup.

When I started working on this book, 10 f4 was my recommendation. It is certainly a critical move, and was the scene of a brilliant Kasparov victory over Karpov. However, Kasparov himself recently demonstrated the antidote, against Radjabov in Linares 2004: 10 ... f6 11 exf6 ♕xe2+ 12 ♗xe2 ♗b4+ 13 ♗d2 ♗xd2+ 14 ♘xd2 ♘xf4 15 ♖f1 ♘xe2! (previously only 15 ... ♘xg2+ was played, with huge compensation for White) 16 ♔xe2 ♔f7 17 ♔d3 ♖ae8 when White had less than nothing, since 18 ♘e4 ♖e5! would have led to a slight advantage for Black.

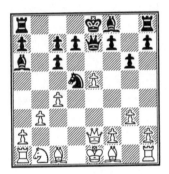

10 ... ♗g7 11 ♗b2 0-0

11 ... 0-0-0 12 ♗g2 ♖he8 13 0-0 ♗xe5 14 ♗xe5 ♕xe5 15 ♕xe5 ♖xe5 16 cxd5 ♗xf1 17 ♔xf1 cxd5 is another version of the endgame we reach in the text. After 18 ♘c3 c6 19 ♖c1 ♔b8 20 ♘a4 ♖e7 21 ♗f3 ♖de8 22 h4 ♖g8 23 b4 ♖c8 24 ♘b2 ♖c7 25 ♘d3 ♔c8 26 ♖c3 ♔d8 27 ♖a3 ♖e8 28 ♘c5 White was better since the black rooks were ineffective in Macieja-Grabarczyk, Polish Championship 2000.

12 ♗g2 ♖ae8

12 ... ♖fe8 is marked as dubious by Kasparov in his annotations to a game against Ivan Sokolov. 13 0-0 ♗xe5 (the aforementioned Kasparov-Sokolov, Yerevan Olympiad 1996 continued 13 ... ♘b6 14 ♖e1 d5 [If 14 ... f6 Kasparov suggests 15 e6!] 15 ♕c2 ♖ad8 16 ♘d2 ♕c5 17 ♖ac1, when Sokolov's 17 ... d4 left him struggling after 18 ♘f3, but Wells analyses 17 ... dxc4 18 ♘e4 ♕b4 19 ♗c3 ♕b5 20 ♘f6+ ♗xf6 21 exf6 with a huge attack) 14 ♕xe5 ♕xe5 15 ♗xe5 ♖xe5 16 cxd5 ♗xf1 17 ♔xf1 cxd5, and now White can proceed thematically with 18 ♘c3 and play as illustrated in the diagram at the start of the section, but 18 f4!? is critical: 18 ... ♖e3 19 ♗xd5 ♖ae8 20 ♘d2 ♖e2 21 ♖d1 ♖xh2 22 ♗g2 ♖e7 (22 ... d6 23 ♔f2 ♖h5 24 ♖c1 ♖e7 25 a4 ♖c5?! 26 ♖xc5! dxc5 27 a5 ♔g7 28 a6 ♖e6 29 ♗b7 ♔f6 30 ♘c4 ♔e7 31 ♘e5 and Black could resign in Zezulkin-Biolek, Czech Team Championship 2002) 23 a4 ♖h5 24 b4 ♖f5 25 ♘e4 ♔g7 and Motylev-Moiseenko, Geller Memorial 1999 was agreed drawn after 26 ♔f2, but I would play on with White here – ♘c5 and ♗h3 is on the cards, or a c-file buildup with b5 and ♖c1.

13 0-0

13 ... ♗xe5

13 ... ♘b6 is Black's attempt to avoid the endgame. After 14 ♖e1 f6 (14 ... ♗b7 was well handled in Zezulkin-Kolosowski, Rubinstein Open 2001: 15 a4! d6 16 f4 ♘d7 17 ♘d2 f6 [capturing on e5 would lose material after 18 ♗a3] 18 e6! ♘c5 19 f5! gxf5 20 ♕h5 ♘xe6 21 ♕xf5 ♕f7 22 b4!. Now Black tried to avoid the impending kingside attack with 22 ... ♕g6, but after 23 ♕xg6 hxg6 24 ♘b3! ♘d8 25 ♘a5! ♗a6 26 b5 cxb5 27 axb5 ♗c8 28 ♘c6 ♘xc6 29 ♗xc6 ♖xe1+ 30 ♖xe1 a6 31 ♖e7 axb5 32 cxb5 ♗h6 33 ♗d4 ♗d2 34 ♗d5+ ♔h8 35 ♖xc7 ♗b4 36 b6 White was winning) 15 e6!? (a suggestion of Kasparov's from a similar position) 15 ... d5 16 ♗a3 c5 17 ♘c3 f5?! 18 ♘xd5 ♘xd5 19 ♗xd5 ♗xa1 20 ♖xa1 f4 21 ♗b2 h6 22 ♖e1 White's pressure on the a1-h8 diagonal was overwhelming in Zelcic-Borisek, HIT Open 2000.

14 ♕xe5 ♕xe5 15 ♗xe5 ♖xe5 16 cxd5 ♗xf1 17 ♔xf1 cxd5

18 ♘c3!

This is the right square for the knight, pressurising d5 and preparing ♘a4 (and maybe to c5).

However, in positions such as this it is more important to know general plans than merely to remember one's chosen variation, so the game Paragua-Antonio, Makati 2002 is instructive. Note especially White's set up of ♖c6, ♘d2 and ♗f3 which so effectively restrains the black pawns: 18 ♘d2 ♖fe8 19 ♗f3 ♖b8 (19 ... a5! is better, when the game was soon drawn in Movsesian-Bacrot, European Club Cup 2002) 20 ♖c1 c6 21 ♖c5 ♖e7 22 a3 ♖be8 23 ♖a5 d6 24 b4 ♖b8 25 ♘b3 c5!? 26 b5 d4. Now Black's central pawn roller looks very dangerous, but the white pieces manage to restrain it. Black would almost prefer his d6-pawn to be off the board so he could support his advanced d-pawn with a rook. 27 ♘d2 ♖d8 28 ♖a6 d3 (28 ... d5 loses material to 29 ♘b3) 29 ♖c6! (note how none of the pawns can move) 29 ... a6 (a good complicating attempt, but Paragua reacts excellently) 30 ♖xa6 d5 31 ♖c6 c4 32 a4! (again the pawns can't move!) 32 ... ♖ee8 33 ♖c5 ♖c8 34 ♖xd5 c3 35 ♘b3 ♖ed8 36 ♖xd8+ ♖xd8 37 ♔e1 ♖c8 38 b6 ♖c4 39 b7 ♖b4 40 ♗d5 ♔f8 41 a5.

18 ... c6

18 ... d4 hasn't been tried as far as I know, since after 19 ♘d5 (threatening both ♘xc7 and ♘f6+) Black loses material.

19 ♖d1

19 ♖e1? ♖e6 20 ♗h3 f5 21 ♖xe6?? as in Kalaitzoglou-Fontaine, Ikaros Open 2003 is completely the wrong idea: White exchanges rooks and fixes the black pawn structure. After 21 ... dxe6 22 f4 ♔f7 23 ♘e2 ♔e7 24 ♘d4 c5 25 ♘c6+ ♔d6 26 ♘e5 a5! 27 ♔e1 a4 28 ♘d3 axb3 29 axb3 ♖b8 30 ♘c1 c4! he could have resigned.

19 ... ♖fe8 20 ♗f3 ♔f8 21 ♘e2 ♔e7

22 ♖d4!

Again we see the rook lift.

22 ... ♖b8 23 ♖a4 ♖b7 24 b4 ♔d6 25 a3 ♖e8 26 ♘d4 h5 27 ♘b3! ♖e7 28 ♘c5 ♖c7 29 h4

Rublevsky has handled this endgame superbly – the black rooks are utterly impotent.

29 ... ♖e5 30 ♖a6 ♖e8 31 ♗e2 ♔e5 32 ♔e1 d6 33 ♘d3+ ♔e6

33 ... ♔d4? 34 ♔d2 leaves the black king facing threats of ♖a4 and b5.

34 a4 ♖b8 35 b5?!

This impatient move gives Black a chance – I'd prefer to play 35 ♔d2 with b5 later.

35 ... ♖b6?

35 ... c5! equalises: 36 ♗f3 d4 37 ♘f4+ ♔e5 38 ♘d5 ♖d7 39 b6 axb6 40 ♘xb6 ♖dd8 41 ♔d2 d5! 42 ♗g2 c4 43 ♘d7+!? ♖xd7 44 f4+ ♔f5 45 ♗h3+ ♔e4 and now taking the rook is too dangerous so White should repeat with 46 ♗g2+.

36 ♖a5 cxb5 37 axb5 ♖bb7 38 ♗f3 ♖c3 39 ♔d2 ♖b3 40 ♗xd5+ ♔xd5 41 b6+ ♔c4 42 ♖a4+ 1-0

Game Twenty-Two
Pavasovic – Jenni
Mitropa Cup 2002

1 e4 e5 2 ♘f3 ♘c6 3 d4 exd4 4 ♘xd4 ♘f6 5 ♘xc6 bxc6 6 e5 ♕e7 7 ♕e2 ♘d5 8 c4 ♗a6 9 b3 0-0-0

This is a very natural attempt for Black, in many ways his most logical. Its problems are twofold:

1 The black king is uncomfortable on the queenside, especially if White pulls off a ♕d2-a5 manoeuvre.

2 White's development is not interfered with.

10 g3 f6

This appears to be the modern trend. The guy to watch with Black here is GM Florian Jenni, who is one of the few to have a good score with the 9 ... 0-0-0 variation.

10 ... ♖e8 11 ♗b2 f6 is another way to win a pawn. The downside for White is that his bishop has been forced to b2, so some of the more aggressive plans with ♗a3 are ruled out. On the other hand, Black has significantly weakened his d7-pawn, quite a big deal if White castles queenside and gets in ♗h3. Rublevsky-Mikhalevski, Vilnius 1995 is the model game here, continuing 12 ♗g2 fxe5 13 ♘d2! h5!? (13 ... g6 14 0-0-0 ♗h6 15 ♔b1 ♖hf8 16 ♘e4 ♔b8 17 ♕e1 ♘f6 18 ♘xf6 ♖xf6 19 f4 ♖f7 20 ♕a5 ♗b7 21 ♗xe5 and White dominated in Thorhallsson-Sigfusson, Icelandic Championship 1991) 14 0-0-0 ♕b4 15 ♘e4 ♕a5 16 ♔b1 ♗a3 17 ♕d2 ♕xd2 18 ♖xd2 ♗xb2 19 ♔xb2 ♘b6 20 ♖c1 ♔b8 21 a4 d6 22 c5! ♘c8 23 cxd6 cxd6 24 ♘xd6 ♖d8 25 ♖cd1 ♖xd6 26 ♖xd6 ♘xd6 27 ♖xd6 and White has excellent chances.

10 ... g6 11 ♗b2 ♗g7 12 ♘d2 ♖he8 (12 ... ♖de8?! is the wrong rook: Magem Badals-Montolio Benedicto, Anibal Open, 2002 continued 13 0-0-0 ♘b6 14 f4 ♔b8 15 ♕f2 f5? 16 c5 ♗xf1 17 cxb6 ♗a6 18 bxc7+ ♔xc7 19 ♕xa7+ ♗b7 20 ♗a3 ♕e6 21 ♗d6+) 13 0-0-0 ♘b6 14 f4 d5 15 ♕f2 ♔b8 16 ♔b1 ♗b7 17 ♖c1 is better for White: Vysochin-Grabarczyk, Bank Pocztowy Open 2000.

10 ... g5 11 ♗g2 ♗g7 12 ♗b2 h5 (Makropoulou-Potapov, Nikea 2001 saw a typical endgame after 12 ... ♖de8 13 0-0 ♗xe5 14 ♗xe5 ♕xe5 15 ♕xe5 ♖xe5 16 cxd5 ♗xf1 17 ♔xf1 cxd5 .... Material is roughly level, so basically White's task is to fully co-ordinate before Black gets his rooks and central pawns rolling. General guidelines are tough to come by here, though I'd remind you of the typical rule that you shouldn't exchange rooks here – the two black rooks to a large extent duplicate each other's functions, and if things go wrong then exchange-down endgames are much easier to hold with an extra pair of rooks. The game is a good example of how to handle

this: 18 ♘d2 g4 19 f4 gxf3 20 ♘xf3 ♖e3 21 ♖d1 c6 22 ♔f2 ♖he8 23 ♗f1 ♖c3 24 ♗d3 h6 25 ♘d4 ♖c5 26 g4 ♔c7 27 h4 and I prefer White) 13 0-0 ♔b8 14 ♘d2 ♘b6 15 ♖fe1 d5 16 ♘f3 c5 17 ♕e3 ♗h6 18 ♕c3 d4 19 ♕a5 ♗b7 20 ♗a3 ♗f8 21 ♖ad1 and White is better: Voltsekhovsky-Lobzhanidze, Geller Memorial 1999

11 ♗g2! fxe5 12 0-0

Black is a pawn up, but his piece co-ordination and king safety are poor. On my database Black has scored awfully from this position, generally going down in under 25 moves.

12 ... e4

This is nearly universal.

12 ... ♖e8 was very well handled in Dworakowska-Dabrowska, Polish Women's Championship 2000. White first got her queen to a5 with tempo: 13 ♕d2! ♘b6 14 ♕a5 ♔b7, then weakened the c5-square: 15 ♗a3! ♕f6 16 ♗xf8 ♖hxf8, and finally threatened to occupy it: 17 ♘c3 d6 (ugly, but what else?) 18 ♗xc6+! ♔xc6 19 ♕xa6 e4 20 ♘d5 ♕e5 21 ♖ad1 ♖f7 22 a4 ♔d7 23 ♘xc7! e3 24 ♘xe8 and Black resigned.

13 ♕d2!

13 ♕xe4 ♕xe4 14 ♗xe4 has also been tried, with a 100% score over several games and a nice endgame for White, but the text is much more fun.

13 ... ♘f6

13 ... e3? looks like a blunder, especially after a vicious display from Alexander Motylev against Naes at Ubeda 2000: 14 ♕a5 ♔b7 15 cxd5 ♗xf1 16 ♗xe3! ♗a6 17 ♗f1! c5 18 ♗xa6+ ♔a8 19 ♘c3 ♕f6 20 ♗g5!! ♕xg5 21 ♕xc7 and Black stopped the clocks in view of 21 ... ♖b8 22 ♘b5 ♖xb5 23 ♕c8+ and 24 ♗b7 mate.

14 ♕a5 ♔b7

14 ... ♗b7 15 ♗f4 ♘e8 (15 ... d5 16 ♕xa7! is good for White: for instance 16 ... ♕c5 17 ♗h3+ ♘d7 18 ♕xc5 ♗xc5 19 ♘c3 ♔b8 20 cxd5 cxd5 21 ♘b5), as in Szieberth-Abdel Aziem, Tanta City Open 2001 should have been met by 16 ♘c3! with an excellent position for White.

15 ♗f4 d5 16 ♘c3

16 ... ♖d7

16 ... ♘h5! was Jenni's improvement against me in the European Team Championship 2003. Indeed, White needs to be careful over the next few moves: 17 cxd5 cxd5 (17 ... ♗xf1?? 18 dxc6+ ♔a8 19 ♗e3 ♕a3 20 ♘a4 wins) 18 ♘xd5 ♕c5 19 ♕xc5 ♗xc5 20 ♖fc1! ♗d4!. This is an improvement on Postny's analysis. (20 ... ♖xd5 21 ♗xe4 ♘xf4 22 gxf4 ♔c6 23 ♖d1 wins; 20 ... c6 21 ♖xc5 is good for White, as Postny analyses) 21 ♘xc7 (21 ♖xc7+ ♔b8 22 ♘b4 ♗b7 23 ♖c8+ ♔xc8 24 ♗h3+ ♖d7) 21 ... ♗d3 22 ♘e6 ♘xf4 23 gxf4 ♔b6 24 ♘xd4 ♖xd4 and now instead of 25 ♖c3, after which the game was eventually drawn, I think I should've tried 25 ♖d1 threatening ♗xe4. After a natural sequence like 25 ... ♖hd8 26 ♖d2 a5 27 ♖ad1 ♔c5 28 h3 g6 29 ♔h2 Black is well placed but White still has his extra pawn.

17 ♗h3 ♕b4 18 ♕xb4+ ♗xb4 19 ♗xd7 ♗xc3 20 ♖ac1 d4 21 ♗f5 c5 22 ♖xc3!?

The more materialistic 22 ♗e5 ♖e8 23 ♗xf6 gxf6 24 ♗xh7 is interesting. Fritz assesses this position as winning for White, for instance 24 ... ♔c6 25 ♗g6 ♖e7 26 h4 ♗c8 27 h5 ♗h3 28 ♖fe1 ♗xe1 29 ♖xe1 d3 30 h6 ♗g4 31 h7 ♖xh7 32 ♗xh7 d2 33 ♗xe4+ ♔d6 34 ♖f1 d1=♕ 35 ♖xd1+ ♗xd1 36 f4 with a clear extra pawn.

22 ... dxc3 23 ♗e5 ♔b6 24 ♗xc3 ♗c8 25 ♗xc8 ♖xc8 26 ♖d1 ♖e8 27 ♗xf6!?

Another enterprising transformation. Black will struggle in the rook endgame.

27 ... gxf6 28 ♖d7 h5 29 ♔f1 e3 30 ♖f7 exf2 31 ♖xf6+ ♔a5 32 ♔xf2 ♖e5 33 ♖c6 a6 34 h4 ♖f5+ 35 ♔e3 ♖e5+ 36 ♔f4 ♖e2 37 ♖xc5+ ♔b4 38 ♖xc7 ♖xa2 39 ♖b7+ ♔c3 40 c5 ♖f2+ 41 ♔g5 1-0

Game Twenty-Three
Nataf – McMahon
Zonal 2000

1 e4 e5 2 ♘f3 ♘c6 3 d4 exd4 4 ♘xd4 ♘f6 5 ♘xc6 bxc6 6 e5 ♕e7 7 ♕e2 ♘d5 8 c4 ♗a6 9 b3 ♕h4

This is a somewhat tricky move, but if White knows what he's doing then he should have no problem coming out of the opening with an advantage.

10 a3!

This is clearly best – Black's system depends to a large degree on the availability of ... ♗b4+, so control of this square is vital.

10 ... ♗c5

10 ... ♘f4 was essayed in Delchev-Galdunts, Bad Wildbad Open 2002, and now 11 ♕e4! looks like the simplest, when 11 ... ♘g6 12 ♕xh4 ♘xh4 is a promising endgame for White.

11 g3!

Giving up some material but putting the black queen into solitary confinement. Black must go for the exchange, since otherwise his piece placement makes no sense.

11 ... ♗xf2+ 12 ♕xf2

Not 12 ♔xf2? ♕d4+.

12 ... ♕e4+ 13 ♔d1 ♕xh1 14 ♘d2

14 ... 0-0

14 ... f5!? demands accurate handling on White's part – Black intends simply ... f4 and ... fxg3, trying to extract his queen from the box. In Macieja-Kaminski, Polish Championship 2000, White opted for 15 cxd5!?, and after 15 ... ♗xf1 16 ♕xf1 ♕xd5 17 ♗b2 0-0 18 ♔c2 the two pieces were preferable to the rook and pawns. Following 18 ... d6 19 ♖e1 ♖ae8 20 ♕f4 ♕c5+ 21 ♔b1 dxe5 22 ♖xe5 ♖xe5 23 ♗xe5 ♕xa3 24 ♕c4+ ♔h8 25 ♕xc6 ♕a5 26 ♘c4 I prefer White.

14 ... ♘c3+ 15 ♔c2 ♘e4 16 ♘xe4 ♕xe4+ 17 ♗d3! and Black still has trouble with his queen. In Kotsur-Frolov, Tomsk 1997, he was routed after 17 ... ♕g4 18 ♗f5 ♕h5 19 h4! f6 20 exf6 0-0 21 g4 ♕e8 22 ♗b2 gxf6 23 ♖g1! h6 24 g5 fxg5 25 ♕d4 ♕e7 26 ♕h8+.

15 ♔c2 f6

Wells analyses 15 ... f5 16 ♗b2! f4 17 cxd5! fxg3 18 ♗xa6 ♕xa1 19 ♕xg3 ♕h1 20 e6 g6 21 ♕e5, winning for White.

16 e6!

Keeping Black's rooks passive.

16 ... dxe6 17 ♗h3 ♖fe8

Mikhalevski anlayses 17 ... ♗c8 18 ♘f3! e5 19 ♗b2 ♕xa1 20 ♗xa1 ♗xh3 21 cxd5 cxd5 22 ♕c5 with a clear advantage.

18 ♘f3 e5 19 ♗b2 ♕xa1 20 ♗xa1 ♘b6 21 ♘d2 ♖ad8 22 ♘e4 ♗c8 23 ♗xc8 ♘xc8 24 g4 ♖e6 25 ♗c3 ♘d6

This is definitely inadequate, but otherwise Black would remain in a fatal bind – White just pushes his pawns on both sides.

26 ♘xd6 cxd6 27 ♕xa7 d5 28 ♕b6 ♖de8 29 a4 d4 30 ♗b4 g6 31 a5 f5 32 a6 f4 33 a7 f3 34 ♕b8 d3+ 35 ♔c3 1-0

Game Twenty-Four
Kasparov – Timman
Wijk aan Zee 2000

1 e4 e5 2 ♘f3 ♘c6 3 d4 exd4 4 ♘xd4 ♘f6 5 ♘xc6 bxc6 6 e5 ♕e7 7 ♕e2 ♘d5 8 c4 ♘b6 9 ♘c3!

The most active. Kasparov won three beautiful games in this line (twice against Adams in addition to the text) after which it was catapulted to the forefront of theory. The previous big line, 9 ♘d2, in my opinion gives Black reasonable play based on the rapid advance of his a-pawn.

9 ... ♕e6 10 ♕e4 ♗b4

10 ... ♗a6 11 b3 0-0-0 12 ♗b2 ♗b7 13 0-0-0

13 ... ♖e8 (13 ... ♗b4 14 f4 ♗xc3 15 ♗xc3 d5 doesn't fully solve Black's problems: 16 cxd5 cxd5 17 ♕d4 ♔b8 18 ♗b4 ♘c8 19 ♗c5 a6 20 ♔b2 f6 21 ♗d3 fxe5 22 fxe5 ♘e7 23 ♗xe7 ♕xe7 24 ♖c1 ♖hf8 25 ♖he1 ♕g5 26 ♖e2 was better for White in Stepovaia Dianchenko - Ubiennykh, Russian Women's Championship 2003) 14 f4 d5 (14 ... g6 15 ♗d3 ♗h6 was seen in Willemze-Mikhalevski, Vlissingen Open 2002, and now I like 16 ♕f3!?, preparing ♘e4 and with the tactical point that 16 ... ♕xe5 17 ♘e2 ♕c5 18 ♗xh8 ♖xh8 19 ♔b1 ♗g7 20 ♖he1 ♕a3 21 ♖d2 ♖e8 22 ♕f2! leaves Black with insufficient compensation for the exchange) 15 cxd5 cxd5 16 ♕c2 ♔b8 17 ♔b1 g6 18 ♗e2 c5 19 ♗f3 ♗e7 20 g4 d4 21 ♗xb7 ♔xb7 22 ♘e4 ♖c8 23 ♕g2 ♔b8 24 ♖he1 was much better for White in in Kasparov-Adams, KasparovChess Grand Prix 2000.

11 ♗d2 ♗a6 12 b3 ♗xc3 13 ♗xc3 d5

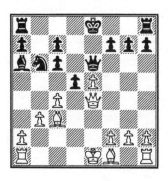

14 ♕h4!

This was Gazza's invigorating novelty – Black had previously been doing fine after both 14 cxd5 and 14 ♕f3.

14 ... dxc4 15 ♗e2! ♘d5

15 ... 0-0 16 0-0 ♘d5 17 ♗xc4 ♗xc4 18 ♕xc4 and the black pawn structure promises him the inferior game.

16 ♗xc4

In his first game against Adams, Kasparov tried 16 ♗d4 and got a good position after 16 ... c5?!, but later the improvement 16 ... ♕f5! was found, with good play for Black.

16 ... g5!? 17 ♕d4 ♗xc4 18 ♕xc4 ♘f4

18 ... 0-0-0 was played in Pavasovic-Mastrovasilis, Karadjordje 2004, and now the simplest is 19 0-0 when I prefer White.

19 ♕xe6+ ♘xe6

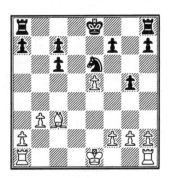

This was Michalevski's recommendation for Black, but the endgame is very pleasant for White. His bishop could soon come into its own and Black's pawns suck.

20 0-0-0 ♔e7 21 ♖he1 ♖hd8 22 ♖xd8 ♖xd8 23 ♖e4!

Preparing to swing to a4 (or possibly c4) and taking control of some vital squares on the fourth rank.

23 ... ♖d5

23 ... c5 24 ♖a4 ♖a8 was the much more passive continuation of Motylev-Sofronie, Ciocaltea Memorial 2000. The natural plan is to take advantage of the passivity of Black's rook to utilise the kingside majority, as Motylev stylishly demonstrated: 25 g3 ♔d7 26 ♔d2 ♔c6 27 ♔e3 ♔d5 28 f4 h6 29 f5! ♘d8 30 ♖e4 ♘c6 31 e6 fxe6 32 ♖xe6 ♘d4 33 ♖f6 a5 34 ♔d3 a4 35 ♖xh6 axb3 36 axb3 ♖a2 37 ♖h8 ♘xb3 38 ♖d8+ ♔c6 39 f6 g4 40 ♔e3 ♘d4 and Black resigned since 41 f7 is crushing.

24 ♔c2 c5

Timman tries his luck in a rook endgame. It's hard to see what else to suggest here.

25 ♖a4 ♘d4+ 26 ♗xd4 cxd4 27 ♖xa7 ♔d7 28 ♔d3 ♖xe5 29 ♖a4 c5 30 b4 ♔e6

Mikhalevski thinks 30 ... c4+ is the last chance, but analyses 31 ♔xc4 ♖e2 32 ♖a5 ♖xf2 33 ♖xg5 ♖xa2 34 ♔xd4 with excellent winning chances.

31 ♖a6+ ♔f5 32 b5 ♖d5 33 ♖c6 c4+ 34 ♔xc4 d3 35 ♔xd5 d2 36 g4+! 1-0

37 ♖c4+ and 38 ♖d4 follow.

Game Twenty-Five
Sutovsky – Van den Doel
European Team Championship 2003

1 e4 e5 2 ♘f3 ♘c6 3 d4 exd4 4 ♘xd4 ♘f6 5 ♘xc6 bxc6 6 e5 ♕e7 7 ♕e2 ♘d5 8 c4 ♘b6 9 ♘c3 ♕e6

9 ... g6 should also be mentioned: I like the 10 ♘e4 ♕e6 11 ♗g5! of Maiorov-Malaniuk, Kuban 1999, when after 11 ... ♗b4+ 12 ♔d1! ♗e7 13 ♗xe7 ♕xe7 14 ♕e3 ♗b7 15 ♘f6+ ♔d8 16 ♔c2 ♔c8 17 ♗e2 c5 18 ♖hg1 ♗c6 19 ♖ad1 ♔b7 20 ♗f3! ♘xc4 21 ♕b3+ ♘b6 22 ♘xd7! White was much better.

9 ... a5!? is a relatively novel treatment. The idea is to wait for 10 ♕e4 before playing 10 ... g6!, when White can't exploit the dark-squares with ♘e4 and ♗g5 anymore. Lautier-Hebden, Clichy 2001 continued 10 f4!? a4 11 ♕e4 g6 (11 ... ♗b7 12 ♗e3 ♕b4 13 ♖b1 ♗e7 14 ♗d2 d5 15 exd6 ♕xd6 [Postny] is slightly better for White) 12 ♗d3 ♗g7 13 0-0 0-0 14 ♗e3 f5 15 ♕f3 ♕b4 and now Postny analyses 16 ♕f2! (intending ♗c5) 16 ... ♖a5 17 a3 ♕b3 18 ♗b1 ♘a8 19 ♗a2 ♕b8 20 c5+ as 'strategically winning' for White.

10 ♕e4 d5

This is less combative than the lines examined in the last game. Black consents to a solid, slightly inferior endgame.

11 exd6 cxd6 12 ♗d3

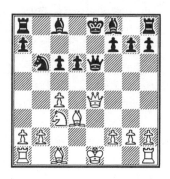

12 ... ♗a6

12 ... ♕xe4+ is the main alternative. Movsesian-Kharlov, ECC 2002 continued 13 ♗xe4 ♗b7 (13 ... ♗d7 14 b3 0-0-0 15 0-0 ♗e7 16 ♗e3 ♖he8 17 ♖ac1 ♔c7 18 ♖fd1 ♗f6 19 ♗f3 ♗f5 20 a4 and White was a little better in Rublevsky-Kunte, Bled Olympiad 2002) 14 b3 d5 (14 ... g6 15 ♗b2 ♗g7 16 0-0-0 0-0-0 17 ♗f3 c5 18 ♘b5 ♗xb2+ 19 ♔xb2 ♗xf3 20 gxf3 d5 21 cxd5 ♘xd5 22 ♖d2 a6 23 ♖hd1 axb5 24 ♖xd5 ♖xd5 25 ♖xd5 ♔c7 26 ♖xc5+ and White was clearly better in Pavasovic-Carlsen, Wijk aan Zee 2004) 15 cxd5 cxd5 16 ♗f3. Of course the d-pawn is passed, but for the moment it is more of a weakness than a strength. 16 ... ♗e7 (16 ... ♗b4 17 ♗d2 ♗a6 was Ivan Sokolov's choice against Rublevsky in the European Club Cup 2002. Now I like 18 a3 ♗xc3 19 ♗xc3 0-0 20 ♗d4 when the king can nestle on d2 and the d5-pawn looks weak) 17 ♗e3 ♗f6 18 ♖c1 ♖c8 19 ♔d2 0-0 20 ♘b5! d4. This is necessary, since otherwise ♘d4 would have resulted in a bind. Now Black loses a pawn but retains reasonable drawing chances in view of the opposite-coloured bishops. 21 ♗xb7 dxe3+ 22 fxe3 ♖ce8 23 ♔e2 ♖e7 24 ♖c7 ♖xc7 25 ♘xc7 ♗e5 26 ♘b5 ♖b8 27 ♗e4 ♘d5 28 ♘xa7 ♘c3+ 29 ♔f3 ♖b6 30 ♘c6 ♗f6 31 ♖c1 ♘xa2 32 ♖c4. After some tactical blows we arrive at a position where White has good winning chances. The opposite-coloured bishops remain but, with a rook and knight for each side, Movsesian can hope to push his passed pawn eventually.

12 ... f5 looks pretty ugly: after 13 ♕xe6+ ♗xe6 14 b3 d5 15 cxd5 ♗b4 16 ♗d2 ♘xd5 17 ♘xd5 ♗xd2+ 18 ♔xd2 ♗xd5 Black still had an inferior structure in Parligras-Rama, Istanbul 2002. For instance, 19 ♖he1+ ♔f7 20 g3 ♔f6 21 f4 ♖he8 22 ♔c3 is better for White.

13 ♗e3 ♕xe4 14 ♗xe4 ♖c8 15 c5!

Typically dynamic stuff from Sutovsky. This pawn sacrifice ruins Black's structure and kills both the c8-rook and f8-bishop.

15 ... dxc5 16 0-0-0 ♗e7 17 ♗f5 ♖d8 18 ♖xd8+ ♔xd8 19 ♖d1+ ♔c7 20 ♗f4+ ♔b7 21 ♖e1

21 ... ♗d8

21 ... ♗f6 is more active, and White needs to respond accurately. 22 ♘e4! (22 ♗d6 ♖d8 23 ♗xc5 is okay, but White really wants a knight on c5, not a bishop) 22 ... ♗d4 23 ♗e3!, when 23 ... g6 24 ♗xd4 (24 ♘d6+ ♔b8 25 ♘xf7 ♗xe3+ 26 ♖xe3 ♖f8) 24 ... cxd4 25 ♘c5+ ♔a8 26 ♗e4! leads to a bind after either 26 ... ♗b7 27 ♗f3 ♘c8 28 ♔d2 or 26 ... ♗b5 27 ♗f3 a5 28 ♖e7.

22 ♘e4 ♗c4 23 ♘xc5+ ♔a8 24 a4 g6 25 ♗e4! ♗d5 26 ♗d3! a5

26 ... ♗c4?? runs into trouble after 27 a5!, since 27 ... ♗xd3? 28 axb6 wins.

26 ... ♗xg2?? 27 ♗a6! is also comical.

27 f3 h5 28 ♗d2 g5 29 ♗xa5 ♘xa4 30 ♗b4 ♘xc5 31 ♗xc5 g4 32 ♗e4 ♗g5+ 33 ♔c2 ♖e8 34 ♔d3 ♗xe4+ 35 ♖xe4 ♖xe4 36 fxe4!

A really classy move. White intends to leave all the black kingside pawns as weaknesses.

36 ... ♔b7 37 e5 ♔c7 38 ♔e4 ♔d7 39 ♔f5 ♗c1 40 ♗d4 c5!

A good attempt, exchanging the queenside, but still insufficient.

41 ♗xc5 ♗xb2 42 ♔f6 ♔e8 43 ♗e3 h4 44 ♔f5 g3 45 h3 ♔d7 46 ♗g5 ♗c3 47 ♗xh4 ♗e1 48 ♗g5 ♗f2 49 h4 ♔e8 50 ♗h6 ♔e7 51 h5 1-0

Game Twenty-Six
Pavasovic – Korneev
HIT Open 2002

1 e4 e5 2 ♘f3 ♘c6 3 d4 exd4 4 ♘xd4 ♗c5 5 ♘xc6 ♕f6 6 ♕d2 dxc6 7 ♘c3 ♗e6 8 ♘a4!?

This move is Kasparov's novelty, unleashed on Short in their 1993 World Championship match. Black must choose between moving his bishop to a sub-optimal diagonal or playing ... ♖d8, an active move but one which foregoes queenside castling. While there has been substantial practice in this line, recent results have strongly favoured White and most Black players these days favour the lines presented in the next game.

8 ... ♗d6

8 ... ♖d8 9 ♗d3 ♗d4 is a major alternative. White can castle here, but I prefer 10 c3!?. For quite a while this move was frowned upon because of 10 ... ♗xf2+! 11 ♕xf2 ♖xd3 12 ♕xf6 ♘xf6 13 ♘c5 ♖d8 14 ♘xb7 ♖b8 15 ♘c5 ♖b5 16 b4 ♘xe4 17 a4 ♖xc5 18 bxc5 ♗c4, when Black has an excellent position in the event of 19 ♗e3, but Nataf-Lautier, Clichy 2001 continued with the much more purposeful 19 ♗f4! 0-0 20 ♗xc7 ♖e8 21 0-0-0 ♘f2 22 ♖d4 ♘xh1 23 ♖xc4 ♘f2 24 ♗b6!! a6 25 ♖d4 ♔f8 26 ♔c2 ♖e3 27 ♔b3 ♘d3 28 ♔c4 ♘e1 29 ♖d6, when Lautier managed to hold the draw but I'd severely doubt my ability to do likewise! The queenside activity is exceptionally dangerous.

9 ♕e3!?

Eyeing the a7-pawn and so discouraging queenside castling.

Pavasovic was previously successful with 9 f4 ♘h6 10 h3 ♕e7 11 ♗d3 f6 12 ♕f2 ♘f7 13 ♗e3 b6 14 0-0 with an edge in Pavasovic-Mikac, Slovenian Team Championship 1999, but I prefer the subtle queen move.

9 ... ♘h6 10 h3!

Leaving the h6-knight out on, well, h6. This game is a vivid illustration of the weakness of this piece.

10 ... ♕g6

10 ... ♕e7 is also possible: 11 ♗d3 f6 12 ♗d2 ♘f7 13 f4 with an edge in Tseshkovsky-Krasenkow, AIG Life rapid 2002.

11 g4!

Clamping down on f5 and so continuing to play against the black steed.

11 ... 0-0 12 ♗d2 b5 13 ♘c3 b4 14 ♘e2 ♖ae8 15 0-0-0! ♗xa2 16 f3!

Now the a2-bishop really is in trouble, but the time spent extracting it allows White to reach perfect co-ordination.

16 ... ♗c4 17 ♘f4 ♗xf4 18 ♕xf4 ♗xf1 19 ♖hxf1 c5

The last gasp.

19 ... f6 20 ♗xb4 ♖f7 21 h4! is hopeless.

20 g5 ♕a6 21 ♔b1 ♕a5 22 gxh6 ♖e6 23 ♕g5 ♖xh6 24 ♖g1 ♖g6 25 ♕e5 ♕b5 26 ♗e3 ♕e2 27 ♗xc5 ♖g2 28 ♖xg2 1-0

Game Twenty-Seven
Kovalevskaya – Stefanova
North Ural Cup 2003

1 e4 e5 2 ♘f3 ♘c6 3 d4 exd4 4 ♘xd4 ♗c5 5 ♘xc6 ♕f6 6 ♕d2

6 ... dxc6

After 6 ... ♕xc6 7 ♗d3 ♘f6 (7 ... ♘e7 8 0-0 0-0 9 b4! ♗d4 10 c3 ♗f6 11 ♕e2 ♕e6 12 f4 d6 13 ♕c2 ♘c6 14 a3 is good for White: Grischuk-Graf, Yerevan 2001) 8 ♘c3 0-0 9 0-0 ♖e8!? (9 ... ♗d4 10 ♕f4 d6 11 ♘e2 ♗b6 12 ♕h4 ♖e8 13 ♘c3 ♕c5 14 ♗g5 ♕e5 15 ♗xf6 ♕xf6 16 ♕xf6 gxf6 17

♘d5 ♔g7 18 a4 was good for White in Chandler-Lodhi, London 1994) 10 ♕e2 b6 11 ♘d5 ♘xd5 was rather wet in Rublevsky-Grischuk, Russian Championship 2003, but I prefer 10 ♕f4!?, keeping an eye on the c7-pawn and preparing to swing to h4.

6 ... bxc6 is no joke, having been essayed by both Ivan Sokolov and Lautier. That said, in avoiding a classically lost king-and-pawn endgame, Black makes the development of his queenside much more of a chore, and this should be enough to give White an edge. 7 ♘c3 (this is a more ambitious plan than the 7 ♗d3 ♘e7 8 0-0 0-0 9 ♘c3 d5 of Rublevsky-Sokolov, 1st European Blitz Ch, Neum 2000) 7 ... ♘e7 8 ♘a4 ♗b6 9 ♗d3 0-0 10 0-0 d6 11 ♔h1!? (Rublevsky's improvement over 11 ♖b1 ♘g6 12 ♔h1 ♘e5 13 ♗e2 ♕h4 14 ♕f4 ♕xf4 15 ♗xf4 ♖e8 16 f3 f5! when Black was well placed in Rublevsky-Lautier, Corsica Masters Rapid, Bastia 2001) 11 ... ♕g6 12 ♕e2 ♖e8 13 ♗d2 f5 14 e5 ♕g4 15 exd6 cxd6 16 ♘xb6 ♕xe2 17 ♗xe2 axb6 occurred in Rublevsky-Beliavsky, FIDE World Cup QF 2002. Now, instead of Rublevsky's 18 c4, I like 18 ♖fe1!?, when lines like 18 ... ♗e6 19 ♗d3 ♘d5 20 a4 look nice for White with his better structure and two bishops.

7 ♘c3

7 ... ♗d4

7 ... ♘e7 8 ♕f4 ♕e6 is a somewhat dubious gambit (Jeric-Korneev, HIT Open 2004 proceeded 8 ... ♗e6 9 ♕xf6 gxf6 10 ♗d2 0-0-0, and now instead of 11 f3?! ♗f2+!, simply 11 ♗d3 is good for White). The key is not to try to sit on the extra pawn, but instead play with additional vigour. An instructive game in this regard is Rublevsky-Beliavsky, Moscow 2002, which continued 9 ♕xc7 ♗d6 (9 ... ♗b4!? was Romanishin's choice against Manca in the Aosta Open 2004. As well as threatening the e-pawn, he also works ... ♘d5 ideas into the position. After 10 ♗d2 ♗xc3 11 ♗xc3 ♕xe4+, instead of the game's 12 ♔d2 ♕d5+ 13 ♔c1 [which is certainly playable], I suggest 12 ♗e2!, for instance 12 ... 0-0 [12 ... ♕xg2 13 0-0-0! ♘d5 14 ♕e5+ ♗e6 when White can immediately regain the pawn with a

slight endgame advantage or go for more with 15 ♗d4!?] 13 f3! [to prepare
a square on f2 for the king] 13 ... ♕e6 14 ♕e5 ♕xe5 15 ♗xe5 and White
has the two bishops in an open endgame) 10 ♕a5 b5 11 ♗e3 0-0 12 0-0-0!
♘g6 13 ♘e2! ♕e7 14 ♘d4 ♕xe4 15 ♗d3 ♕xg2 16 ♖hg1 ♕d5 17 ♗f1!!
♗f4 18 ♗g2 ♗xe3+ 19 fxe3 ♕c5 20 ♗xc6 ♖b8 21 h4 ♘e5 22 ♗e4 ♗g4
23 ♖df1 f5 24 ♗xf5 ♖be8 25 ♗xg4 ♖xf1+ 26 ♖xf1 ♘xg4 27 ♕xb5 ♕xb5
28 ♘xb5 a5 29 ♖e1 h5 30 e4 with a simple win for White.

7 ... ♕e7 8 ♕g5 f6 9 ♕g3 ♗e6 10 ♗e3 ♗d6 11 f4 ♘h6 12 ♗e2 0-0-0 13
0-0 ♗c5 14 ♘a4 ♗xe3+ 15 ♕xe3 ♔b8 16 ♖ad1 is slightly better for White,
though he later lost in Macieja-Mastrovasilis, Antalya 2004.

8 ♗d3 ♘e7 9 0-0 ♘g6 10 ♘e2!

Getting the bishop out of White's face as quickly as possible.

I really don't believe in White's position after 10 ♕e1 ♘e5 11 ♗e2. For
instance, Stefanova's game against Kosintseva from round 7 of the same
tournament proceeded 11 ... h5! 12 ♔h1 ♗e6 13 f4 ♘g4 14 e5 ♕g6 15
♗d3 ♗f5 16 ♗xf5 ♕xf5 17 ♕e4 ♕d7 18 ♘d1 0-0-0 19 ♗e3 ♘xe3 20
♘xe3 ♗xb2 and White didn't have enough for the pawn.

**10 ... ♗b6 11 ♘f4 ♘e5 12 ♗e2 ♘g4 13 ♘d3 ♕h4 14 ♕f4 g5 15 ♕g3
♕xg3 16 hxg3 ♖g8 17 ♗xg4 ♗xg4 18 ♖e1**

It would be easy to assume that, with White having doubled his pawns and Black holding the two bishops, this position is at least equal for Black. In fact White has an enduring edge. To begin with, the point was never that Black had doubled pawns, but rather that Black's structure is incapable of yielding a passed pawn by force. This is still the case, while White's majority is still healthy – she just pushes the f- and e-pawns to create a passer. As regards the two bishops, it is clear that the one on b6 is destined for exchange. The position is quite closed, which will probably leave White's knight at least equal to Black's remaining bishop.

18 ... c5 19 ♗e3 c4 20 ♘c5 0-0-0 21 f3 ♗h5?!

21 ... ♗e6 is no bed of roses but has to be tried – on g6 the bishop is a non-entity.

22 g4! ♗g6 23 ♔f2 ♖de8

23 ... ♗xc5 24 ♗xc5 ♖d2+ 25 ♗e2 ♖gd8 simply drops a pawn to 26 ♗e7 – Black can't use the d-file.

24 ♘a4 ♗a5 25 ♖eb1 a6 26 ♘c3!?

26 ... c6

26 ... ♗xc3 27 bxc3 leaves the c4-pawn too vulnerable after a4 and ♖b4.

27 ♘e2 ♗c7 28 ♖h1 f6 29 ♖ad1 ♖g7 30 ♘d4 ♗e5 31 c3 ♖d7 32 ♔e2 ♔c7 33 ♘f5 ♖xd1 34 ♔xd1 ♗xf5 35 gxf5 ♖e7 36 ♔c2 ♖d7 37 ♖h6 b5 38 a3 ♖g7

Ceding the d-file to threaten counterplay with ... g4.

38 ... a5 wouldn't make much of a difference: 39 ♗d4 ♔d6 40 ♔d2 and the king gets across anyway.

39 ♗d4 ♔d6 40 g3! ♖f7 41 ♔d2 c5 42 ♗xe5+ ♔xe5 43 ♔e3 a5 44 ♖h1 ♔d6 45 f4 gxf4+ 46 ♔xf4! b4 47 ♖h6 bxc3 48 bxc3 ♔e7 49 e5! ♔e8 50 ♖xf6 ♖b7 51 ♖a6 ♖b3 52 f6 ♔f7 53 ♔f5 1-0

An excellent display.

Game Twenty-Eight
Kasparov – Unzicker
Zurich 2001

1 e4 e5 2 ♘f3 ♘c6 3 d4 exd4 4 ♘xd4 ♗b4+!?

One of the most popular lines at top level, largely because of the late Tony Miles' impressive record with this move. White has been scoring very badly here, but it certainly has nothing to do with the objective merits of 4 ... ♗b4+. Kasparov managed a rather handy 2/2 against it, for instance.

5 c3 ♗c5 6 ♗e3 ♗b6 7 ♕g4!

Taking advantage of the two main effects of Black's bishop manoeuvre (the stabilisation of the White centre and the weakening of g7) to get a little aggressive.

7 ... ♕f6

7 ... g6?! is uninspiring: after 8 ♘d2 d6 9 ♕g3 ♘f6 10 ♗e2 ♕e7 11 0-0 ♗d7 12 ♘b5 0-0-0 13 ♗xb6 axb6 14 ♖fe1 ♘xe4 15 ♘xe4 ♕xe4 16 ♕xd6 cxd6 17 ♘xd6+ ♔c7 18 ♘xe4 White had a much better endgame in Rosito-Garcia Palermo, Argentinian Championship 2002 (though, to keep up White's record in this line, he somehow failed to win).

8 ♕g3 ♘xd4

After 8 ... ♕g6 9 ♘d2 (9 ♘f5 d6 10 ♗xb6 axb6 11 ♘e3 ♘f6 wasn't convincing in Nakamura-Goldin, American Continental 2003) 9 ... ♘ge7, I like the untested 10 0-0-0!? (I prefer simple development to the 10 ♘xc6 bxc6 11 ♗f4 of Mashinskaya-Zaiatz, Elista 2003, though there White had a small edge after 11 ... ♕xg3 12 ♗xg3 d5 13 a4 a5 14 0-0-0 0-0) 10 ... ♘xd4 11 ♗xd4 0-0 12 ♗d3 and White's central control and good development give him an edge.

Postny recommends 8 ... ♕e5 9 ♘d2 ♕xg3 10 hxg3, but Black is worse in the endgame. Perhaps he needs to bail out like this though, since the game is a rout.

9 cxd4

9 ... ♗xd4

After 9 ... ♘e7 10 ♘c3 ♕g6, White has an edge after 11 ♕xg6 (instead of the unclear 11 ♕h4 ♗a5 12 ♗d3 ♘d5! of Trent-Erwich, Smith & Williamson Young Masters 2002) 11 ... hxg6 12 ♗c4.

Postny analyses 9 ... d5 10 exd5 ♘e7 11 ♘c3 0-0 12 ♕e5 with a clear advantage.

10 ♗xd4 ♕xd4 11 ♘c3 ♘e7

After the more aggressive 11 ... ♘f6 12 ♖d1 ♕b6 13 e5 ♘h5 14 ♕g4 ♕xb2 (14 ... ♕g6 15 ♕f3! [even better than Postny's 15 ♕c4] 15 ... ♕g5 16 ♘d5 ♖b8 17 ♗e2! c6 18 ♕xh5 ♕xh5 19 ♗xh5 cxd5 20 ♖xd5 is nice for White), 15 ♘d5! ♕xe5+ 16 ♕e2! ♕xe2+ 17 ♗xe2 is the kind of elegant line which abounds in Kasparov preparation. After 17 ... ♔d8 18 ♗xh5 the pieces are stronger than the pawns.

12 ♕xc7 0-0 13 ♖d1 ♕b4 14 ♖d2 ♘g6 15 ♗e2 f5 16 ♗c4+ ♔h8 17 ♘d5 ♕a4 18 exf5 ♖xf5 19 0-0!

Black is busted.

19 ... ♕c6 20 ♗b3 ♕xc7 21 ♘xc7 ♖b8 22 ♖e1 b6 23 ♘b5 ♗b7 24 ♘d6 ♖ff8 25 ♘f7+ ♔g8 26 ♖xd7 1-0

Game Twenty-Nine
Van der Wiel – Pliester
Dutch Championship Playoff 2003

1 e4 e5 2 ♘f3 ♘c6 3 d4 exd4 4 ♘xd4

4 ... ♕h4?!

This line is risky to the point of stupidity. GM Pete Wells wrote in his seminal work *The Scotch Game* back in 1998 that "4 ... ♕h4?! seems to be rushing full steam ahead towards the status of 'unplayable'." Six years on, it has arrived. Though still essayed by some strong players, Black's score in this line is so abysmal as to make me pray for this queen sortie every time I play the Scotch. The temptation was overwhelming to give a really violent attacking game here – the number of IMs who have been steamrollered here without reaching move 20 is stunning. But things never seem to work out quite so well in my own games. Thus I've opted for a solid, bread-and-butter win by Van der Wiel, demonstrating the nature of White's compensation when Black doesn't drop his king. Bloodthirsty readers should check the notes for extra violence.

4 ... g6 is another offbeat try. White has several systems here but I like the rapid queenside castling of Ni Hua-Wu Wenjin, HeiBei 2001: 5 ♘c3 ♗g7 6 ♗e3 ♘ge7 7 ♕d2 0-0 8 0-0-0 d6 9 h4! when White's attack was much bigger after 9 ... h5 10 f3 ♘e5 11 ♗h6 a6 12 ♗e2 b5 13 g4 c5 14 ♘f5!.

4 ... ♘ge7 is okay but a little wet: Vallejo Pons-Campora, Spanish Championship 2000 continued 5 ♘c3 ♘xd4 6 ♕xd4 ♘c6 7 ♕e3 ♗b4 8 ♗d2 0-0 9 a3 ♗xc3 10 ♗xc3 d6 11 0-0-0 ♕e7 12 g4! f6 13 ♖g1 ♘e5 14 ♗e2 ♘f7 15 h4 ♖e8 16 f3 with an excellent position.

5 ♘c3!

The normal choice of strong players here. 5 ♘b5 is also a very dangerous move, and was formerly the main line, but nowadays players seem too tempted by the prospect of developing yet another piece.

5 ... ♗b4

It has to be done.

5 ... ♗c5?! 6 ♗e3 leaves the queen looking pointless on h4, even if 6 ... ♘ge7? 7 ♘f3 ♕h5 8 g4! was a somewhat harsh punishment in Kulaots-Geller, Aeroflot Open 2002.

6 ♗e2

6 ... ♛xe4

Karjakin-Malinin, Sudak 2002 is a comical game between two strong players. Black continued 6 ... ♘f6 7 0-0 ♗xc3 8 ♘f5! ♛xe4 9 ♗d3 ♛g4 10 f3 ♛a4 11 bxc3 0-0? 12 ♘xg7! ♔xg7 13 ♗h6+!. Amazingly, all this had already occurred in Vukovic-Mozetic, Banja Vrucica 1991! Not the toughest day's work for the young Ukranian supertalent. 13 ... ♔xh6 (13 ... ♔g8 14 ♛d2! collects material: [Pete Wells' suggested 14 ♛e1?! isn't clear after 14 ... ♘h5] 14 ... ♛h4 [14 ... ♛a5 15 ♗xf8 ♔xf8 16 ♛h6+ ♔e7 17 ♖ae1+] 15 ♗g5) 14 ♛d2+ ♔h5 (14 ... ♔g7 15 ♛g5+ ♔h8 16 ♛xf6+ ♔g8 17 ♛g5+ ♔h8 18 ♛h6) 15 g4+ ♘xg4 16 fxg4+ ♛xg4+ 17 ♔h1 d6 18 ♖f6 ♛g5 19 ♗e2+ ♗g4 20 ♗xg4+ and Black resigned – either capture on g4 drops a monarch, while 20 ... ♔h4 gets mated after 21 ♛f2+.

6 ... ♘ge7 7 0-0 0-0 8 ♘db5 ♗a5 was tried in Reinaldo Castineira-Golod, Anibal Open 2001, and the game is worth including in full for its instructive value. Note again that, if Black doesn't capture on e4, his system is entirely pointless. 9 ♘d5! ♘xd5 10 exd5 ♘e5 11 f4 ♗b6+ 12 ♔h1 ♘g6 13 f5 ♘e5 14 d6! c6 15 ♖f4! ♛d8 16 ♘c3 and White had a total bind at absolutely no cost. The finishing attack was sweet: 16 ... ♖e8 17 ♘e4 a5 18 ♛e1 f6 19 ♛g3 a4 20 ♖h4 ♖a5 21 ♗h6 g6 22 fxg6 hxg6 23 ♗c4+ ♖e6 24 ♗f4 ♔g7 25 ♛h3 ♛g8 26 ♗h6+ ♔f7 27 ♘xf6! ♘xc4 28 ♘xg8 ♖ae5 29 ♖f1+ and Black resigned.

After 6 ... ♗xc3+ 7 bxc3 ♛xe4, White can try to exploit Black's move order with 8 0-0 ♘xd4 9 cxd4 ♘e7 10 ♖e1 ♛h4 11 ♗d3 as in Reefat-Vladimirov, Goodricke Open 2000, or simply transpose to the game with 8 ♘b5.

7 ♘db5 ♗xc3+ 8 bxc3 ♔d8 9 0-0

9 ... ♞f6

In Oral-Kantorik, Slovakian Championship 2000, after 9 ... a6 10 ♗f3 (anyone who can't improve on my move 12 analysis can try 10 ♞d4 here, with typical and good compensation for the pawn) 10 ... ♕c4 Thomas Oral made my job a whole lot more difficult by punting 11 ♞d6!? cxd6 12 ♕xd6. This led to a beautiful victory after 12 ... ♞f6 (12 ... ♞ge7! is more tenacious, when I can only find a draw after 13 ♖e1 ♕xc3 14 ♗f4 ♕a5 15 ♗xc6 ♞xc6 16 ♗d2 ♕f5 17 ♗f4 ♕a5) 13 ♗e3 ♞e7 (13 ... ♕b5 14 ♖ab1 ♞e8 15 ♕a3 ♕e5 16 ♖fe1 ♞c7 17 ♗b6 ♕f6 18 ♗xc6 wins) 14 ♖fe1 ♞fd5 15 ♗xd5 ♞xd5 16 ♕xd5!!. 12 ... ♞ge7! looks like a good chance to half out, however, and so maybe 10 ♞d4 is the way to go.

10 ♖b1!

This remains flexible with the deployment of the dark-squared bishop and hence gets my vote, though 10 ♗e3 ♖e8 11 ♖e1 ♕d5 12 ♕c1 ♕f5 13 ♕a3 d6 14 ♖ad1 ♖e7 15 c4 ♗e6 16 ♗f3 ♖d7 17 ♗xc6 bxc6 18 ♞d4 ♕h5 19 ♗g5!! c5 20 ♗xf6+ gxf6 21 ♞c6+ ♚e8 22 ♕b2 ♕h4 23 ♕b7 ♖ad8 24 ♖d3 was a beautiful victory in Azmaiparashvili-Hector, San Sebastian 1991.

10 ... a6 11 ♞d4 ♞xd4 12 cxd4 ♖e8 13 ♗f3 ♕g6 14 ♗f4 d6 15 ♕c1!?

Already we can see the congenital defects in Black's position thrown into sharp relief. Black still has his extra pawn and no visible structural weaknesses, and yet stands worse. Why? I don't think it's a king safety issue (though of course d8 is far from an optimal square for this piece), rather it's a question of piece activity and more specifically piece co-ordination. The white pieces harmonise beautifully – both of the bishops and the b1-rook pressurise the queenside – while Black's pieces have no clear function. Note also that Van der Wiel could have captured on b7 but chose instead to improve his queen (it's headed for a3) – perhaps the most important quality to have when playing these positions is patience, an ability not to cash in too quickly.

15 ... ♗f5! 16 ♖xb7 ♗e4!

An excellent attempt at slapping some purpose on the position, albeit at the cost of a pawn.

17 ♖b3 ♔d7 18 ♕a3 ♗xf3 19 ♖xf3 ♕e4 20 ♗h6 ♕g6 21 ♗f4 ♕e4 22 ♗g5!

A good idea. The major piece position is unpleasant for Black.

22 ... ♕xd4

Forced, otherwise Black will have nothing to compensate for his structural weaknesses.

23 c3 ♕e5 24 ♗xf6 gxf6 25 ♕a4+ c6 26 g3!

Black doesn't so much have a structure as a collection of weaknesses. The only positive pawn play available to him, the advance of the c- and d-pawns, is obviously out of the question as it would expose the king too much.

26 ... a5 27 ♕b3 ♖ab8 28 ♕xf7+ ♖e7 29 ♕xf6 ♕xf6 30 ♖xf6 ♖b2 31 a4 ♖c2 32 ♖d1 ♖e6 33 ♖f3 d5 34 ♖b1 ♖a2 35 ♖b7+ ♔d6 36 ♖xh7 ♖xa4 37 h4 ♖a1+ 38 ♔g2 a4 39 ♖a7 a3 40 ♖f4!

40 ... a2 41 h5 c5 42 ♖fa4 ♖c1 43 ♖xa2 ♖xc3 44 h6 ♖b3 45 h7 ♖e8 46 ♖2a6+ ♔e5 47 ♖e7+ 1-0

CHAPTER FOUR
The Petroff Defence

"Many people think that the Petroff is a solid but unambitious opening which Black only plays to get his half point. I used to think so too before winning my last three games with it."

GM Alexander Motylev

1 e4 e5 2 ♘f3 ♘f6

This line has evolved from a dull, easy edge for White to one of the biggest pains in a 1 e4-player's life. Black is rock-solid, but also wins an unbelievable number of games, even at the very highest level. The main stuff here begins after 3 ♘xe5 (3 d4 is also big theory) 3 ... d6 4 ♘f3 ♘xe4 5 d4 d5 6 ♗d3, when anyone looking for an edge against either 6 ... ♗d6 or ... ♘c6 and ... ♗e7 is advised to find a novelty around move 20-25. I don't like the idea of rejecting lines merely because they're theoretical, but to learn and keep on top of the theory in this line really is a huge amount of work. In addition, the line isn't all that popular at lower levels, so boning up on this to the exclusion of all else could prove a waste of time.

Many GMs have thus been looking for early deviations to avoid some of this mess. 4 ♘xf7!!/?? was extensively tested a few years ago, and isn't played anymore for some reason. The significantly less interesting 5 ♕e2 ♕e7 6 d3 ♘f6 7 ♗g5 is an attempt at putting Black into a coma while grabbing a couple of tempi – the vast majority of games in this line end in draws.

The line I'm recommending, 5 ♘c3!?, was originally a Nimzowitsch recommendation. It lay unused for ages, until Alexei Shirov dusted it off to win excellent games against both Morozevich and Motylev in the Russia vs. The World match in 2002. The idea is pretty straightforward – after 5 ... ♘xc3 6 dxc3, White plans ♗f4, ♕d2 and long castling. There has been an explosion of interest here following Shirov's efforts – at present White seems to be doing pretty well.

Game Thirty
Fressinet – Koch
French Team Championship 2004

1 e4 e5 2 ♘f3 ♘f6 3 ♘xe5 d6 4 ♘f3 ♘xe4 5 ♘c3 ♘xc3 6 dxc3 ♗e7 7 ♗f4

7 ♗e3 poses fewer problems due to its inferior central control. Bosch believes Black equalises instantly with 7 ... ♘d7! 8 ♕d2 ♘e5 – indeed, he seems pretty comfortably placed.

7 ... 0-0 8 ♕d2 ♘d7

8 ... d5 9 0-0-0 ♗e6 10 h4 ♘d7 11 ♘g5 c5 12 g3 h6 13 ♘xe6 fxe6 14 ♗h3 ♖f6 15 ♖he1 ♕b6 16 ♖e2 ♖e8 17 ♖de1 was too much pressure in Fedorchuk-Lecocq, St Lo Open 2004.

9 0-0-0!

The only way to generate anything – castling kingside is an instant draw.

9 ... ♖e8

9 ... ♘c5 leads to an important tabiya after 10 ♗e3 (with 10 ♔b1 ♖e8! 11 ♗e3 ♗g4! 12 ♗e2 ♘e4 13 ♕e1 ♗f6 I was in trouble with White in a European Team Championship game) 10 ... ♗e6 (10 ... ♖e8 11 ♗c4 ♗e6 12 ♗xe6 ♘xe6 13 h4! gives White an aggressive position:

13 ... ♗f8 14 h5 h6 15 g4 ♗e7 16 ♖dg1 ♗g5 17 ♘xg5 ♘xg5 18 ♗xg5 hxg5 19 h6 ♕f6 20 hxg7 ♔xg7 21 ♖h5 ♖e5 22 ♖gh1 ♖ae8 23 ♖h7+ ♔g8

24 b3 ♖e1+ 25 ♖xe1 ♖xe1+ 26 ♕xe1 ♕f4+ 27 ♔b2 ♔xh7 28 ♕h1+ ♔g7 29 ♕xb7 ♕xf2 30 ♕xc7 ♕f4 31 ♕xa7 ♕xg4 32 a4! and, in Kayumov-Hilwani, Asian Championship 2003, White won by a tempo: 32 ... ♕d1 33 a5 g4 34 a6 g3 35 ♕e3 ♕g4 36 a7 g2 37 a8=♕ g1=♕ 38 ♕e7!;

13 ... c6 14 ♘g5 ♕a5 15 ♔b1 ♘f8 16 ♕d3 ♖ad8 17 f4 d5 18 g4 ♗d6 19 h5 ♕c7 20 ♖df1 f6 21 ♘h3 b6 22 g5 and White's pawn storm was bearing fruit while Black's was yet to start in Marechal-Laurent, Belgian Championship 2003;

13 ... ♕d7 14 ♔b1 ♕a4 15 ♘g5 ♘f8 16 ♖h3 c6 17 ♖g3 ♕xh4 18 ♖h3 ♕g4 19 f3 ♕f5 20 g4 ♕d5 21 ♕xd5 cxd5 22 ♘xh7 ♘xh7 23 ♖dh1 f5 24 ♖xh7 fxg4 25 fxg4 ♗f8 26 ♖h8+ ♔f7 27 ♗d4 ♔g6 28 a4 ♗e7 29 ♖8h5! left White perfectly placed in Apicella-Laurent, Touraine Open 2003)

11 ♔b1 and now:

11 ... a6 12 ♘d4 ♗d7 13 f3 ♖e8 14 h4 ♘a4 15 ♗g5 b5 16 ♗d3 ♘b6 17 ♕f4 c5 18 ♘f5 ♗xf5 19 ♗xf5 d5 20 ♖he1 g6 21 ♗h3 ♗xg5 22 hxg5 ♖e7 23 ♗g4 ♕e8 24 ♖h1 ♕f8 25 ♕f6 ♘d7 26 ♗xd7 ♖xd7 27 ♖xh7 was the seminal Shirov-Motylev, Russia vs. Rest of the World 2002;

11 ... ♕c8 was Karpov's choice against Shirov in Benidorm 2002. After 12 ♘d4 ♗d7 13 h4 ♖e8 14 f3 ♗f8 15 g4 ♘e6 16 h5 ♘xd4 17 cxd4 ♗c6 18 ♖h3 ♗d5 19 c4 ♗c6 20 d5 ♗d7 21 ♗d3 c5 22 ♗f4 b5 23 cxb5 ♕b7 24 ♕c2 h6 25 ♖g3 ♗xb5 26 g5 ♗xd3 27 ♕xd3 ♖ab8 28 ♖g2! White again had the bigger attack.;

11 ... ♗f6 12 ♘d4 ♕d7 13 f3 ♕a4 14 ♘xe6 ♘xe6 15 ♕d5 ♕c6 16 ♕f5 ♘c5 17 ♗c4 left White well placed in Nepomniachtchi-Lintchevski, World Youth Stars 2003.

10 h4!

This looks like the most flexible.

10 ♘d4 ♗f6 11 f3 ♘e5 12 ♔b1 ♗d7 13 ♗g3 a6 14 f4 ♘g4 15 ♗d3 c5 16 ♘f3 c4! 17 ♗xc4 ♘e3 18 ♗b3 ♘xd1 19 ♖xd1 ♗c6 and White had lost the thread, though he later won in Sveshnikov-Petrosian, Petrosian Memorial 2004.

10 ♗c4 ♘b6 11 ♗d3 ♗e6 12 h4 ♕d7 13 ♘g5 ♗f5 14 g4 ♕a4 15 ♔b1 ♗xd3 16 cxd3 ♗xg5 17 ♗xg5 ♖e6 18 h5 ♖ae8 19 ♗e3 ♘d5 and White's play fails to convince: Cheparinov-Pashikian, Antalya 2004.

10 ... ♘c5 11 ♘g5 ♗f6 12 ♗c4! ♗e6 13 ♘xe6 ♘xe6 14 ♗e3

The two bishops are a big asset in such a position, and make potential endgames considerably less palatable for Black. Koch obviously wanted to have something to suffer for, but his next move opens the kingside rather too much.

14 ... ♗xh4? 15 g4 h6 16 f4 ♕e7

17 ♖h3!

The pawn play can bring no further fruit, but doubling on the h-file draws attention to the h4-bishop.

17 ... g5 18 ♕h2 ♖ad8 19 ♔b1 d5 20 ♗d3 c5 21 ♗b5 ♖f8 22 f5!

The h4-bishop isn't the only black minor piece in trouble.

22 ... d4 23 ♗c1 ♘c7 24 f6 ♕xf6 25 ♕xc7

It's all over now.

25 ... dxc3 26 ♖f1 ♕e6 27 ♖xc3 ♖d4 28 ♕xc5 ♕xg4 29 ♖cf3 a6 30 ♗d3 ♕d7 31 b3 ♖d5 32 ♕c3 g4 33 ♖f5 ♗g5 34 ♗b2 1-0

Game Thirty-One
Sandipan – Singh
Indian Championship, 2003

Here I deal with early Petroff deviations and some ... ♗g4 systems.

1 e4 e5 2 ♘f3 ♘f6 3 ♘xe5 d6

3 ... ♘xe4?! is a mistake, but not an absolutely fatal one. After 4 ♕e2 ♕e7 (obviously the knight can't move) 5 ♕xe4 d6 6 d4 dxe5 7 dxe5 ♘c6, most recent high-level games have continued 8 ♗b5, where Black gets reasonable compensation for the pawn. I prefer 8 ♘c3! ♕xe5 9 ♕xe5+ ♘xe5 10 ♗f4, as in Vasiukov-Chekhov, Kischniev 1975, when after 10 ... ♗d6 11 ♗g3 ♗d7 12 0-0-0 0-0-0 13 ♘e4 ♗c6 14 ♘xd6+ cxd6 15 f3 ♖he8 16 ♖d4! White had the two bishops and a structural advantage.

4 ♘f3 ♘xe4 5 ♘c3

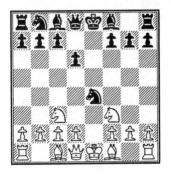

5 ... ♘xc3

This is clearly best.

My game against Gwaze in the British Championship 2003 continued 5 ... ♘f6 6 d4 ♗e7 7 ♗d3 0-0 8 h3 a6 9 0-0 b5 10 a4 b4 11 ♘e4 ♗b7 12 ♘g3 ♖e8 13 ♖e1 when White was aggressively placed.

5 ... ♗f5 6 ♕e2 1-0 is the infamous Zapata-Anand (!), Biel 1988. 6 ... ♕e7 7 ♘d5 would be decisive.

6 dxc3 ♘c6

Khalifman-Atalik, Kallithea 2002 continued 6 ... ♗e7 7 ♗f4 ♘d7 8 ♕d2 ♘c5 9 0-0-0 ♗g4 10 ♗e2 0-0 11 h3 ♗h5 12 g4 ♗g6, and now I like 13 ♘d4 (the game actually continued 13 h4 ♖e8 14 h5 ♗e4 15 ♖hg1 ♘e6 16 ♗e3 c5 17 g5 d5 18 g6 hxg6 19 hxg6 fxg6 20 ♘e5 ♗f6 21 ♘g4 d4 22 ♗c4, when Khalifman gives 22 ... b5! 23 ♘xf6+ ♕xf6 24 ♗g5 dxc3! as good for Black) 13 ... ♘e6 14 ♗g3 for White.

7 ♗f4 ♗e7 8 ♕d2 ♗g4 9 ♗e2 ♕d7

9 ... h6 10 0-0-0 ♕d7 11 ♖he1 0-0-0 12 h3 ♗e6 13 ♗b5 a6 14 ♗a4 b5 15 ♗b3 ♗xb3 16 axb3 ♗f6 17 ♕d5 ♖he8 18 c4 bxc4 19 bxc4 ♖xe1 20 ♘xe1

♘b8 21 ♘d3 ♕e6 22 ♖e1 ♕xd5 23 cxd5 was slightly better for White in Jakovenko-Lastin, Russian Championship 2003.

10 h3

The immediate 10 0-0-0 is similar: 10 ... a6 (in Efimenko-Motylev, ECC 2002, Black tried doing without this move: 10 ... 0-0-0!? 11 h3 ♗e6, when the simplest is 12 ♔b1 intending ♖he1 followed by ♗b5 or ♘g5 though the edge here is miniscule) 11 h3 ♗e6 12 ♔b1 0-0-0 13 ♖he1 ♖he8 14 ♘g5 ♗xg5 15 ♗xg5 f6 16 ♗e3 ♘e7 17 f3 ♕c6 18 b3 ♘f5 19 ♗f2 d5 20 ♗f1 ♗f7 21 ♔b2 ♖xe1 22 ♖xe1 ♖e8 23 ♖xe8+ ♕xe8 24 ♕d3 and White had an edge because of his two bishops: Lobron-Navarro, Merida 2002.

10 ... ♗f5 11 0-0-0 a6 12 g4! ♗e6

12 ... ♗g6 13 ♖he1 0-0-0 14 ♕d5!? ♗f6? (14 ... ♖he8 just looks equal) 15 g5 ♗e7 16 ♘d4 ♘xd4 17 ♖xd4 c6 18 ♕a5 c5 19 ♗g4! ♗f5 20 ♗xf5 ♕xf5 21 ♖xe7 was Velimirovic-Nikcevic, Yugoslav Team Championship 2001.

13 ♘g5

The impending exchange of one of the black bishops makes White a slight favourite.

13 ... ♗xg5?!

This commits Black to weakening the kingside in order to castle long.

14 ♗xg5 h6 15 ♗h4 g5 16 ♗g3 0-0-0 17 f4! gxf4 18 ♗xf4 h5?! 19 gxh5 f6 20 h4 ♗g4 21 h6 ♘e5 22 ♖df1 ♗xe2 23 ♕xe2 ♕e6 24 ♔b1 ♖d7 25 ♖hg1 ♖hh7 26 ♗c1 c5 27 ♕f2 ♘g4 28 ♕f5!

A nice tactic to finish.

28 ... ♕xf5 29 ♖xf5 ♘xh6 30 ♖h5 1-0

CHAPTER FIVE
The Philidor Defence

"The Philidor was a slightly unpleasant surprise, and by no means a bad decision. The fact was that the last game began at 10 am rather than the usual 2 pm, and the cushion of a dozen or so moves of theory can be quite pleasant before the brain has switched on."

GM Luke McShane

1 e4 e5 2 ♘f3 d6

This line is the slightly less attractive sister of the Petroff. Black sets up a solid defence of the e5-pawn, at the cost of a slightly passive stance. Thereafter, he has two basic approaches, involving either holding the e5-pawn or playing ... exd4. Both are reasonably popular today, but White seems to be establishing a pretty comfortable edge here.

Tensing Up: The Exchangeless Structure

This is the Philidor structure when Black doesn't exchange on d4. The central situation is in White's favour, but there is more tension than in the previous diagram. If Black doesn't exchange on d4 when White must recapture with a piece, there are four probable structural changes:

1   White plays dxe5. In a pure sense, this is a concession, since the d4-pawn is better than the d6-pawn. Thus when White plays it he must have a concrete follow-up in mind. The move is often played when White has such an advantage in mobility that his pieces greatly benefit from the freshly-opened d-file.

2   White plays d5. This gains more space but closes the position to a large degree – often this move has the added benefit of blocking a bishop on b7.

3   White plays c3, Black exchanges on d4 and White recaptures with a pawn. Classically, this is a very favourable central situation for White, who has an extra central pawn and can advance with e5 at a suitable moment. Black's hopes rely on counterplay against the e-pawn and the prospect of a quick ...d5.

4   Black plays d5 immediately. This creates overwhelming central tension, and pure calculation will determine who emerges on top. White must be very attentive to the possibility of this break, which can often equalise at a stroke.

Game Thirty-Two
Shirov – Damljanovic
Bosnia 2003

1 e4 d6 2 d4 ♘f6 3 ♘c3 e5

This is a smart move-order from Black, angling for a Philidor while denying White the chance for a King's Gambit, Vienna etc. White can try to exploit this move order with 4 dxe5 dxe5 5 ♕xd8+ ♔xd8 6 ♗c4, but after 6 ... ♗e6!? 7 ♗xe6 fxe6 the endgame is far from clear. By all means give it a go if you're in the mood for a quiet game, but I prefer Shirov's treatment.

4 ♘f3 ♘bd7 5 ♗c4 ♗e7 6 0-0 0-0 7 ♖e1 c6 8 a4!

It would be a mistake to allow Black an active stance on the queenside.

8 ... b6 9 b3

The best way to develop the bishop. White needs to be prepared for a ... d5 break by Black, so bringing more pressure to bear on e5 is logical.

9 ... a6 10 ♗b2

10 ... ♖b8

Black has tried several moves here, but they all conform to the same paradigm. White, for his part, just puts the bishop on d3 (so ... b5 won't gain a tempo) and swings the c3-knight to g3.

10 ... ♕c7 11 h3 ♗b7 12 ♗d3 ♖fe8 13 ♘e2 ♗f8 14 ♘g3 g6 15 c3 ♗g7 16 ♕b1!? (I have to admit that White's last two moves are somewhat baffling to me, but Glek is just playing around with his space advantage and freeing up the e1-rook for some d- or e-file action. Black decides to break, but White still has residual activity which prevents full equalisation) 16 ... d5 17 dxe5 ♘xe4 18 ♘xe4 dxe4 19 ♗xe4 ♘xe5 20 ♘xe5 ♗xe5 21 c4 ♖e6 22 ♗f3 ♖ae8 23 ♖xe5 ♖xe5 24 ♗xe5 ♖xe5 25 ♕b2 ♖e7 26 ♖d1 ♖d7 27 ♖xd7 ♕xd7 28 ♕e5 a5 29 ♕b8+! ♔g7 30 ♕a7! (not the most conventional square for the queen, but it does the job. White plans c5 and chopping on

a5, and there is very little Black can do about it) 30 ... ♕c7 31 ♗e2 ♔f6 32 c5! ♕e7 33 ♗f1 bxc5 34 ♕xa5 ♔e6 35 ♕d2 ♕d6 36 ♗c4+ ♔e7 37 ♕xd6+ ♔xd6 38 ♗xf7 1-0 was the abrupt finish of Glek-Galdunts, Griesheim 2002.

10 ... ♗b7 11 ♗d3 ♕c7 12 ♘e2 ♖fe8 13 ♘g3 ♗f8 14 ♕d2 (This has the benefit of covering the b4-square, as compared to 14 h3 which I played against Vladimir Georgiev in the fifth round of the European Team Championship 2003. The game proceeded 14 ... ♖ad8 15 ♕c1 g6 16 a5!? b5 17 c4 b4 18 ♕d2 exd4 19 ♘xd4 ♗g7 20 ♘df5 [the only move, otherwise ... ♘c5 is strong] 20 ... gxf5 21 ♘xf5 ♖e5 22 ♖e3 ♖xf5 23 exf5 h6 24 ♖g3 d5 25 cxd5 ♕d6 26 ♖e1 cxd5 27 ♗d4 ♔f8 28 ♕b2 ♖c8 when I should have played 29 ♗b1 [stopping a ... ♖c3 sacrifice] when my opponent felt chances were equal but personally I like Black) 14 ... g6 and, in contrast to Glek's sly manoeuvring above, in Kindermann-Gulbas, European Club Cup 2002 White proceeded more actively on the queenside with 15 a5!? b5 16 c4, winning the a2-g8 diagonal for his bishop after 16 ... bxc4 17 ♗xc4. Following 17 ... h6 18 ♖ac1 exd4 19 ♘xd4 c5 20 ♘f3 ♖ad8 21 ♕f4 ♗g7 22 ♗c3 ♘e5 23 ♘xe5 dxe5 24 ♕f3 ♘h7 25 h4!, White had a substantial kingside initiative and stood better.

11 ♕d2 b5 12 ♗d3 ♖e8 13 ♘e2 ♗f8 14 ♘g3 g6

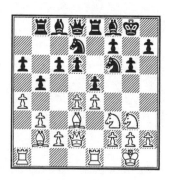

Now White has several options, but Shirov decides to improve his d3-bishop.

15 axb5!? axb5 16 c4 bxc4 17 ♗xc4

A very similar plan to the Kindermann game above. Now Damljanovic feels obliged to break in the centre, but as in Glek above, White's pieces are better prepared for the opening of the position.

17 ... d5 18 dxe5 dxc4 19 exf6 ♖xb3 20 ♗c3 ♘c5 21 ♘d4 ♖b7 22 ♖ad1 ♘d3?

This looks like a definite error.

Fritz recommends 22 ... ♕d7, guarding the c6-pawn. I think Shirov's intention might have been 23 e5 ♘d3 24 e6!? fxe6 25 ♘f3!, for instance 25 ... ♘xe1 (25 ... ♕d5 26 ♘e4 ♘xe1 27 ♕xe1 ♕f5 28 ♘e5 is similar) 26 ♕xe1 ♕c7 27 ♘e5 ♕b8 28 ♘e4 with a bind.

23 ♘xc6 ♕c7 24 ♘e7+ ♗xe7 25 fxe7 ♕xe7 26 ♖f1

Now Black has major difficulties on the dark-squares.

26 ... f6 27 f3 ♗e6 28 ♘e2 ♗f7 29 ♕e3 ♖d8 30 ♖a1 ♖bd7 31 h3 g5 32 ♘d4 ♕e5 33 ♖a5 ♕f4 34 ♘f5 ♕xe3+ 35 ♘xe3 ♖d6 36 ♘g4 ♘e5 37 ♘h6+!

Grabbing an exchange and ending the game.

37 ... ♔f8 38 ♗b4 ♔e8 39 ♗xd6 ♖xd6 40 ♖a8+ ♔d7 41 ♖a7+ ♔e8 42 ♘xf7 ♘xf7 43 ♖b1 1-0

Clearing the Ranks: The Exchange Structure

This is a very common structure, occurring in all the Philidor lines where Black plays an early ... exd4. White has a central space advantage through his e4-pawn, but of course this is slightly exposed to attack by ... ♘f6 and ...

♖e8. The fresh opening of the a1-h8 diagonal makes it more attractive for one or both sides to dump a bishop there, so mutual fianchettoes often occur. The main benefit of this structure for White is the weakened d5-square – if he posts a knight there, often Black won't be able to drive it away with ... c6 since that would leave his d6-pawn backward.

Game Thirty-Three
Potkin – Kobalia
Dos Hermanas Internet Final 2003

1 e4 e5 2 ♘f3 d6 3 d4

3 ... exd4

3 ... ♘d7 is an inaccurate move order. White can just transpose to normal stuff with 4 ♘c3 ♘f6 5 ♗c4 ♗e7, as has happened in several grandmaster games, but I think he should exploit Black's mistake with 4 ♗c4! c6 (4 ... ♗e7 5 dxe5 ♘xe5 6 ♘xe5 dxe5 7 ♕h5 wins a pawn) 5 0-0 ♗e7 6 dxe5 dxe5 7 ♘g5 ♗xg5 (7 ... ♘h6 8 ♘e6 fxe6 9 ♗xh6 ♘b6 10 ♕h5+ ♔f8 11 f4! gives White a winning attack) 8 ♕h5 ♕e7 9 ♕xg5 ♕xg5 10 ♗xg5 ♘gf6 11 f3 the two bishops gave White an enduring edge in the endgame of Tiviakov-Murshed, Dhaka 2003.

3 ... f5?! is very dodgy after 4 ♘c3!: Motwani analyses 4 ... fxe4 5 ♘xe4 d5 6 ♘eg5! h6 7 ♘f7!! ♔xf7 8 ♘xe5+, winning for White.

4 ♘xd4 ♘f6

4 ... g6 leads to a kind of Dragon position with a closed c-file. This is definitely good news for White, who can stop worrying about exchange sacs on c3 for instance. In Emms-Cox, 4NCL 2003, White had a very easy attack after 5 ♘c3 ♗g7 6 ♗e3 ♘f6 7 ♕d2 0-0 8 0-0-0 ♘c6 9 f3 ♘xd4 10 ♗xd4 ♗e6 11 ♗e3 a6 12 ♗h6 ♗xh6 13 ♕xh6 ♕e7 14 h4 b5 15 h5!.

5 ♘c3 ♗e7 6 ♗f4 0-0 7 ♕d2

7 ... ♘c6

Svidler-Ivanov, St Petersburg Blitz 1999 continued 7 ... c6 8 0-0-0 b5 9 f3 b4 10 ♘ce2 d5 11 ♘g3 dxe4 12 fxe4 c5, but Black was much worse after 13 ♘df5 ♗xf5 14 ♘xf5 ♕xd2+ 15 ♖xd2 ♗d8 16 ♗c4 ♘c6 17 e5 ♘h5 18 g3. The conclusion was short and sweet: 18 ... ♘xf4 19 gxf4 ♘d4 20 ♘xd4 cxd4 21 ♖xd4 ♗b6 22 ♖e4 ♖ad8 23 ♖d1 g6 24 ♗d5 a5 25 e6 fxe6 26 ♖xe6 ♔g7 27 ♖xb6.

After 7 ... d5 there have been several games with 8 ♘db5 but I prefer the simple 8 exd5! ♘xd5 9 ♘xd5 ♕xd5 10 ♘b5! of Van den Doel-Kovacevic, European Team Championship 2001, when White exerts unpleasant pressure. After 10 ... ♕e4+ 11 ♗e2 ♘a6 12 0-0 c6 13 ♘d6 ♗xd6 14 ♕xd6 ♕xc2 15 ♗d3 ♕c5 16 ♗xa6 ♕xd6 17 ♗xd6 ♖d8 18 ♗c7 ♖d7 19 ♖fe1 g6 20 ♖e8+ ♔g7, instead of the game's 21 ♗f1?, 21 ♗e5+! is pretty decisive: 21 ... f6 22 ♗c4 fxe5 23 ♗e6 ♖c7 24 ♖d1 and White should win.

7 ... a6 8 0-0-0 b5 (8 ... d5 9 exd5 ♘xd5 10 ♘xd5 ♕xd5 11 ♘b3 ♕c6 12 ♗d3 ♕a4 13 ♕e3 ♗h4 14 ♗xc7 ♖e8 15 ♕f4 ♕xf4+ 16 ♗xf4 ♗xf2 17 ♖hf1 ♗a7 18 ♖fe1 ♗e6 19 ♘a5! is better for White: Degraeve-Antoniewski, Belgian Team Championship 2004) 9 f3 c5!? 10 ♘f5 ♗xf5 11 exf5 ♘c6 is an interesting attempt, but so far has scored badly for Black. German GM Thomas Luther gave a model demonstration with White (after losing on the Black side!): 12 g4 b4 13 ♘d5 ♘xd5 14 ♕xd5 ♗g5 15 ♗xg5 ♕xg5+ 16 ♕d2 ♕xd2+ 17 ♖xd2 ♘d4 18 c3! bxc3 19 bxc3 ♘b5 20 ♗xb5 axb5 21 ♔b1 ♖fd8 22 ♖hd1 ♖a6 23 ♖d5 ♖c6 24 g5!. Now there comes a nice finish, but with Black so passive White is much better anyway: 24 ... f6?! 25 g6 ♔f8? 26 ♖xd6! ♖cxd6 27 ♖xd6 ♖a8 28 ♖a6! ♖d8 29 gxh7 and Black soon resigned in Luther-Sedlak, Reykjavik Open 2004.

8 0-0-0 ♘xd4 9 ♕xd4 ♗e6

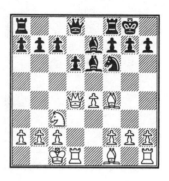

10 ♕d2

This is one of several good moves here. Basically White just wants to get busy on the kingside, and there are a few ways of setting this up. ♕d2 is largely prophylactic, anticipating ... ♘d7 and ... ♗f6 from Black. ♕d2 would be my choice, but some of the other moves are instructive too:

Ivanisevic-Jacimovic, European Team Championship 2001 continued 10 ♔b1 ♘g4 (10 ... ♘d7!, as in Brkic-Nevednichy, HIT Open 2004, looks like a better attempt) 11 ♕d2 ♗f6 12 ♗g3 ♗e5 13 f4 ♗xc3 14 ♕xc3 f5 15 ♗d3 ♕c8 16 ♖he1 fxe4 17 ♗xe4 ♘f6 18 ♗f3 d5, when 19 f5! ♗xf5 20 ♖xd5!! ♗g4 (20 ... ♘xd5 21 ♗xd5+ ♔h8 22 ♖e7 ♖f6 23 ♗e5 is horrible) 21 ♖de5 ♗xf3 22 ♕xf3 left White perfectly placed.

10 f3 ♘d7 (10 ... a6 11 g4 b5 12 ♘d5 ♘xd5 13 exd5 ♗d7 14 h4 c5 15 dxc6 ♗xc6 16 ♕f2 ♕c7 17 g5 f6 18 g6! hxg6 19 ♗d3 f5 20 ♕g3 ♖f6 21 h5 g5 22 ♗xg5 ♖f7 23 ♗f4 and White soon won in Nevednichy-Olarasu, HIT Open 2004) 11 ♕e3 ♗f6 12 g4 a6 13 g5 ♗e5 14 h4 ♕e7 15 ♗h2 ♗xh2 16 ♖xh2 ♘e5 17 ♗e2 f5 18 f4 ♘c6 19 h5 fxe4 20 h6 g6 21 ♘xe4 d5 22 ♘c5 ♖ae8 23 ♗f3 ♗f7 24 ♕xe7 ♖xe7 25 ♘xb7 ♖b8 26 ♘c5 and Black didn't have enough for the pawn in Lautier-Dorfman, French Championship 2002.

10 ... a6 11 f3 b5 12 g4 ♖e8 13 h4 ♘d7 14 g5 ♘e5 15 ♗e2 ♗f8 16 h5 ♕b8 17 ♔b1 b4 18 ♘d5 a5 19 h6!

White's attack is quicker. I'd draw the reader's attention to his choice of break – in these lines White seems to be playing for h6 rather than g6. Broadly speaking, g6 opens more lines and thus is more appropriate in most pawn storm scenarios. Here, however, the race isn't as violent as a Sicilian Dragon – rather the attacks are being primarily played for positional gains. The benefit of h6 is that it creates permanent mating threats on g7 and the back rank, and thus ties up the f8-bishop and one of Black's rooks.

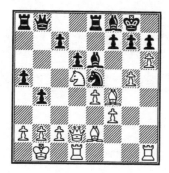

19 ... ♗xd5 20 ♕xd5 g6 21 ♗e3 c6 22 ♕d4 d5!?

Chucking a pawn for some activity, but White plays for the attack.

23 ♗f4 ♗d6

23 ... dxe4 24 fxe4 and White's bishop will win the game from c4.

24 ♗h2 ♗f8 25 f4 ♘c4 26 f5 ♕b7 27 fxg6 ♘a3+

27 ... fxg6 28 ♗xc4 dxc4 29 ♕xc4+ is winning.

28 bxa3 bxa3+ 29 ♔a1

An illustration of the comment at move 19. Here the piece chuck just leads to a loss.

29 ... fxg6 30 ♖b1 ♕e7 31 ♖hf1 ♕xg5 32 ♖xf8+ 1-0

CHAPTER SIX
The Caro-Kann Defence

"Just as any other 1 e4 player in the world, I've looked at enough CK in the last few years to grow completely sick of it."

GM Peter Svidler

1 e4 c6 2 d4 d5 3 exd5 cxd5 4 c4

The Caro-Kann has been one of the main veins of opening theory over the past several years. Theory has developed exponentially after both 3 ♘c3 and 3 e5, in particular the latter. To be honest, I don't really see the appeal of the Caro-Kann for non-professionals – although its main aim is to have a quiet life, White has the choice of several razor sharp lines all of which demand superb preparation. In lower-level tournaments where neither a draw with Black nor hours of preparation are always desired, the Caro-Kann just looks like a silly choice. At least that's what my opponents seem to think – a quick glance at my games shows that I only have to face this once in every 19 games with White.

My recommendation is the Panov-Botvinnik Attack. This tends to lead to IQP positions with a natural attack for White vs. a structural advantage for Black, a trade off which I'm perfectly happy to make.

Game Thirty-Four
Kunte – Prakash
Goodricke Open 2001

1 e4 c6 2 d4 d5 3 exd5 cxd5 4 c4 ♘f6 5 ♘c3 e6 6 ♘f3 ♗b4 7 cxd5

7 ♗d3 dxc4 8 ♗xc4 is the main alternative.

7 ... ♘xd5 8 ♕c2!

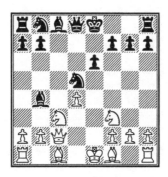

White players often go 8 ♗d2, which looks like and is a concession. Having played both moves, I think that 8 ♕c2 is more critical – White wants to set up a battery with ♗d3 (making it difficult for Black to castle) and develop the c1-bishop in one move to a decent square. The downside is that the move entails a pawn sacrifice, the acceptance of which is examined in this game.

8 ... ♘c6 9 ♗d3 ♗a5 10 a3

This is the move order used in the game, but I would recommend going 9 a3 ♗a5 (9 ... ♗e7 is the next game) 10 ♗d3 with the same position but giving Black fewer options along the way.

10 ... ♘xc3 11 bxc3 ♘xd4!

This is the point.

12 ♘xd4 ♕xd4 13 ♗b5+ ♗d7 14 0-0! ♕d5

14 ... ♕xc3 (untested to my knowledge) is really asking for it. There are several routes to good activity, but my preference would be for 15 ♕a4 ♖d8 (15 ... 0-0 16 ♗xd7 ♕xa1 17 ♕xa5 leaves rough material parity but in reality the two bishops will slaughter the rook and pawns; incidentally 15 ... ♕xa1? 16 ♗xd7+ wins since if 16 ... ♔e7 then 17 ♗g5+) 16 ♗xd7+ ♖xd7 17 ♗d2 ♕xd2 18 ♖ad1, picking up the queen. While Black will have more than enough on paper (a rook, a bishop and two pawns), his king will be confined to the centre and the white queen will always be able to pick up some material, for instance 18 ... a6 19 ♖xd2 ♗xd2 20 ♖d1 ♔e7 21 ♕g4

(threatening 22 ♖xd2 and 23 ♕g5+) 21 ... ♖hd8 22 ♕xg7 h5 23 g3 and personally I'd take White. If this isn't to your taste then you should take a more traditional route at move 15, for instance 15 ♗xd7+ ♔xd7 16 ♕a4+ ♔e7 17 ♖b1 with compensation.

15 c4 ♕f5 16 ♗xd7+ ♔xd7 17 ♕b2!

Topalov's preferred treatment, definitely one of the highest accolades a move can have in the Panov-Botvinnik. It looks a touch clumsy but the queen eyes the b7-and g7-pawns (the latter is likely to be too hot to handle for quite a while, but nevertheless this tension is an important factor in the position) and is ready to glide into checks on a3 or d4 if need be.

17 ... b6 18 a4!

18 c5?! prematurely closes the a3-f8 diagonal and so allows the black king to escape to comfort. After 18 ... ♔e7 19 cxb6 axb6 20 ♗e3 ♖hd8 21 ♖ad1 ♔f8 22 ♖xd8+ ♖xd8 a draw was agreed in Aronian-Asrian,Yerevan 2001.

18 ... ♔e7

18 ... f6 19 ♖d1+ ♔c6?! leads the king into peril – the excellently-titled Al Karpov acted with the precision of his namesake against Ovetchkin in the Russian Team Championship 2000, winning crisply after 20 c5! ♖ad8 (the attack is too strong after 20 ... ♕xc5 21 ♗e3!, for instance 21 ... ♕e5 22 ♕c2+ when blocking on the c-file costs a piece) 21 ♕b5+ (21 ♗e3 ♖d5 22 ♕b5+ ♔c7 23 ♕a6 ♖xd1+ 24 ♖xd1 ♖d8 25 cxb6+ ♔xb6 26 ♗xb6+ axb6 27 ♕a7+ ♔c6 28 ♖c1+ ♔d5 29 ♕b7+ was the equally terminal continuation of Ravi-Ramesh, Calcutta 2002) 21 ... ♔c7 22 ♗e3 ♔b8 23 ♕c6 ♕h5 24 ♖d6 ♖c8 25 ♕d7 ♖hd8 26 ♕xg7 ♕e5 27 ♗f4 ♕xf4 28 c6.

After 18 ... ♖ad8, instead of the routine 19 ♖a3?! (I would recommend 19 ♗e3!, preparing c5 and taking advantage of the weak a-pawn. ... ♔e8 runs into ♕xg7 while ... ♔e7 can still be met by ♕a3+) 19 ... f6 20 ♖g3 ♖hg8 21 ♖f3 ♕e4 22 ♕b5+ ♔c7 23 c5 ♕c6 24 cxb6+ axb6 25 ♕a6 e5 when White had nothing clear in Velikhanli-Maric,Varna 2002.

18 ... ♖hd8 significantly weakens the kingside: after 19 ♖a3! f6 20 ♖g3 g6 21 ♖h3 h5 22 c5 e5 23 ♕b3 ♕e6 24 ♕d3+ ♔c7 25 ♕c2 ♔b7 26 ♕xg6 White was clearly better in Calzetta Ruiz - Kachiani Gersinska, Istanbul 2000.

19 ♕a3+!

The start of an excellent co-ordinating manoeuvre. The queen is destined for g3, the bishop for b2, followed by random rook to the middle. I'd be hugely uncomfortable with Black here – note that he doesn't move his bishop for the rest of the game.

19 ... ♔f6 20 ♕g3 e5 21 ♗b2 ♔e6 22 ♖ad1 ♖hd8 23 ♖d5!

Very elegant.

23 ... ♖xd5 24 cxd5+ ♔d7 25 ♕b3

Interesting but risky.

Dautov recommends 25 ♕xg7 ♖e8 26 ♕g3 as leading to a slight White advantage.

25 ... ♖c8 26 h3 a6 27 ♕g3 ♖c5 28 ♗xe5 ♖xd5 29 ♗xg7 ♕g6 30 ♕f3 ♕f5 31 ♕e2 ♕d3 32 ♕b2 ♕e4 33 ♗h6 ♖d6 34 ♗e3 h5 35 ♕h8 ♕xa4 36 ♕xh5 ♕b3 37 ♗f4 ♖d3 38 ♖c1!

Black's exposed king and awful bishop are still major problems even though we're almost at move 40.

38 ... b5 39 ♕f5+ ♔e8 40 ♕e4+ ♔d7 41 ♕c6+ ♔e7 42 ♗g5+ ♔f8 43 ♕h6+ 1-0

Game Thirty-Five
Fedorowicz – Enhbat
US Championship 2003

1 e4 c6 2 d4 d5 3 exd5 cxd5 4 c4 ♘f6 5 ♘c3 e6 6 ♘f3 ♗b4 7 cxd5 ♘xd5 8 ♕c2 ♘c6

Black can also play more conservatively with 8 ... ♘d7, intending ... ♘7f6 to reinforce d5. After 9 ♗d3 ♘7f6 10 0-0 ♗d7 (Potkin-Vescovi, Anibal Open 2001 proceeded 10 ... ♗e7 11 a3 0-0 12 ♘e5 h6 13 ♕e2 ♕d6 14 ♖d1 b6 with a more traditional IQP position, and after 15 ♘xd5! ♕xd5 [15 ... ♘xd5 16 ♕e4 and ... ♘f6 is impossible] 16 ♗c4 ♕e4 17 ♕xe4 ♘xe4 18 d5 ♗d6 19 ♘d3 ♖e8?! 20 ♗b5 ♖d8 21 ♗c6 ♖b8 22 dxe6 ♘f6 23 e7 ♗xe7 24 ♗f4 White's overwhelming activity collected material) 11 ♘xd5 ♘xd5 12 ♘e5 ♗d6 13 ♗e4 ♖c8 14 ♕b3 ♗c6 15 ♕g3! g6 16 ♗h6 ♗f8 17 ♕f3 f5 18 ♗xf8 ♔xf8 19 ♖fe1 ♔g7 20 ♘xc6 ♖xc6 21 ♗xd5 exd5 22 ♖e5 was beautiful for White in Benjamin-Seirawan, US Championship Playoff 2000.

9 a3 ♗e7 10 ♗d3

10 ... ♗f6

After 10 ... ♘f6 11 0-0 0-0 the smart move is 12 ♖d1!. Now in Topalov-Gausel, Moscow 1994 Black completely missed White's threat and after 12 ... a6? (12 ... h6 13 ♗c4 ♕b6 14 ♗e3 ♕c7 occurred in Bruzon-Asrian, Yerevan 2000, when instead of Bruzon's 15 ♘b5 I like 15 ♖ac1!

with strong pressure. Baburin analyses 12 ... ♗d7 as leading to a White advantage after 13 d5! exd5 14 ♘xd5 h6 15 ♘xe7+) 13 d5!! exd5 14 ♘xd5 ♘xd5 15 ♗xh7+ ♔h8 16 ♗e4 ♗e6 17 ♗xd5 ♗xd5 18 ♕f5 g6 19 ♕xd5 ♕xd5 20 ♖xd5 ♖fd8 21 ♖d2! found himself a pawn down for nothing.

11 0-0 ♘xc3 12 bxc3 h6

Once again, White's battery on the b1-h7 diagonal forces Black to play this ugly move. The structure now occurring has been called the 'Isolated Pawn Couple'. It shares many characteristics of IQP positions, but has the advantage for White of extra stability (the d4-pawn is no longer weak). In this game we see the typical plan for White in these positions, namely the activation of his pieces coupled with a c3-c4 advance to create hanging pawns.

13 ♕e2!

The best square for the queen.

13 ... ♕d5

13 ... 0-0? runs into 14 ♕e4, but now Black's king is forced to stay in the centre.

14 ♖b1!

Taking advantage of the changed structure – the rook pressurises the b7-pawn (thus making the development of the c8-bishop a chore) and entertains notions of coming into play with lines like ♖b5-h5.

14 ... a6

14 ... 0-0 15 ♖b5! and ♕e4 is strong.

15 c4 ♕h5 16 ♕e4

This position has gone badly wrong for Black, and Fedorowicz's prosecution of the advantage is impressive.

16 ... ♔f8 17 ♖e1 ♘e7 18 ♗d2 ♕f5 19 ♕e3 ♕h5 20 ♕f4

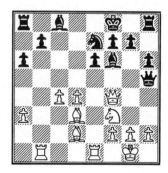

20 ♗b4 intending d5 is also very unpleasant but John has spotted a nice square for the white queen.

20 ... ♘g6 21 ♕c7 ♚g8 22 ♗e4 ♚h7 23 ♕xf7

Game over.

23 ... ♖d8 24 ♗e3 ♖d7 25 ♕e8 ♖e7 26 ♕a4 ♗d7 27 ♕d1 ♗e8 28 ♘g5+ 1-0

Game Thirty-Six
Kurajica – Scekic
Jahorina 2003

1 e4 c6 2 d4 d5 3 exd5 cxd5 4 c4 ♘f6 5 ♘c3 e6 6 ♘f3 ♗e7 7 cxd5 ♘xd5

John Richardson tried 7 ... exd5 against me in the 4NCL. It is a much less ambitious choice than the knight recapture, since by masking the d4-pawn Black sucks a load of tension out of the position. White has a pleasant choice. After 8 ♗b5+!? ♗d7 (8 ... ♘c6 leads to a menacing white initiative after 9 ♘e5 ♗d7 10 0-0, for instance Van Beers-Duvekot, Gent Open 2001 continued 10 ... 0-0 11 ♖e1 ♖c8 12 ♗g5 ♗e6 13 ♕a4 ♕b6 14 ♖ad1 with a clear advantage) 9 ♗d3 (now the d7-bishop is awkwardly placed) 9 ... ♘c6 10 h3 (playing against the d7-bishop) 10 ... ♕b6 11 0-0 0-0 12 a3 ♖fe8 13 ♗g5! (the pawn is taboo due to ♘a4 winning the queen) 13 ... ♗e6, 14 ♖e1 followed by ♘a4 and ♖c1 would have left White with a very pleasant edge (I'll leave it to more industrious readers to track down the 29 move rout I suffered after the move I actually chose!).

8 ♗c4 0-0 9 0-0 ♘c6 10 ♖e1

This position is a real tabiya. It frequently arises from the Queen's Gambit Declined rather than the Caro-Kann, and has been the stage for some of the most famous games in history.

10 ... ♘xc3

Strangely, a number of strong players persist in playing 10 ... b6?! even though the position after 11 ♘xd5! exd5 12 ♗b5 has been known to be good for White since the seminal Botvinnik-Alekhine, AVRO 1938. After 12 ... ♗d7 13 ♕a4 ♘b8 (13 ... ♖c8 14 ♗f4 ♗f6 15 ♖ac1 ♖e8 16 ♖xe8+ ♕xe8 17 ♖e1 ♕d8 18 h3 h6 19 a3 ♘b8 20 ♗xb8 ♗xb5 21 ♕xb5 ♖xb8 22 ♘e5 ♗xe5 23 ♖xe5 ♖c8 24 g3 ♕f6 25 ♕xd5 also lost in Hansen-Palo, Danish Championship 2003) 14 ♗f4 ♗xb5 15 ♕xb5 a6 16 ♕a4 ♗d6 17 ♗xd6 ♕xd6 18 ♖ac1 ♖a7 19 ♕c2 ♖e7 20 ♖xe7 ♕xe7 21 ♕c7 ♕xc7 22 ♖xc7 f6 23 ♔f1 ♖f7 24 ♖c8+ ♖f8 25 ♖c3 White was clearly better, and Black's alternatives aren't any better:

a) 12 ... ♘a5 13 ♘e5 ♗e6 14 ♗f4 ♗f6 15 b3 ♗f5 16 ♗a6 ♗e7 17 ♕h5 g6 18 ♕f3 ♗e4 19 ♕c3 f6 20 ♘g4 g5 21 ♗c7 ♕d7 22 f3 ♗g6 23 ♗g3 h5 24 ♘e3 h4 25 ♗f2 ♔g7 26 ♘xd5 ♗d6 27 b4 ♘b7 28 ♘e3 ♘d8 29 ♖ad1 ♘e6 30 ♘g4 ♖ad8 is recorded as '0-1' in Poluljahov-Slapikas, Bank Zachodni Open 1999, though I wouldn't be quite so despondent about White's extra pawn!;

b) 12 ... ♗b7 13 ♗f4 ♗d6 (13 ... a6 14 ♗d3 ♗f6 15 ♗c2 g6 16 ♕d2 ♖c8 17 ♗b3 ♘a5 18 ♗e5 ♘c4 19 ♕f4 ♘xe5 20 dxe5 ♗g7 21 h4! and White stood much better in Korneev-Roa Alonso, Pablo Gorbea Memorial 2002) 14 ♘e5 ♘e7 15 ♗d3 ♗c8 16 ♕h5 g6 17 ♕h6 ♗f5 18 ♖e3 f6 19 ♘c6 ♘xc6 20 ♗xf5 ♗xf4 21 ♗e6+ ♔h8 22 ♕xf4 g5 23 ♕g4 ♕d6 24 ♖c1 and White is too active: Korneev-Burmakin, 7th HIT Open, Nova Gorica 2002.

I feel comfortable with White after the 10th move options too:

10 ... ♗f6 11 ♘e4 ♘ce7 12 ♘xf6+ ♘xf6 13 ♗g5 ♘ed5 14 ♘e5 ♕d6 15 ♕f3 ♖b8 16 ♕g3 gave White a promising position on the kingside in Rotstein-Mufic, Triesen 2004;

10 ... a6 is best met by 11 ♗b3! as in Stanec-Ganaus, Poyntner Memorial 2002, when 11 ... b5 12 ♘xd5 exd5 13 ♘e5! would have been clearly better for White, whose pieces are far more active.

11 bxc3 b6 12 &d3! &b7 13 h4!

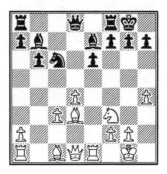

Taking control of the g5-square.

13 ... &xh4

Obviously the critical response, but conceding a dangerous attack.

13 ... ♘b8!? was an interesting attempt to swing the knight round to f6. Pelletier-Prie, 28th Rapid Open, Aubervilliers 2003 continued 14 h5 ♘d7 15 &c2 ♘f6 16 ♕d3 &xf3 17 ♕xf3 ♕d5 18 ♕d3 ♖ac8 19 h6 g6 20 &b3 ♕f5 21 ♕xf5 gxf5 22 c4 ♘e4 23 &f4 &f6 24 ♖ad1 ♖fd8 25 d5! with an advantage to White.

13 ... ♖c8 14 ♘g5 h6?! (14 ... g6 is more tenacious though White retains a very dangerous position with 15 ♕g4!, for example 15 ... e5 16 ♘xh7!? ♔xh7 17 h5! ♕d6 18 hxg6+ fxg6 19 ♕h3+ ♔g8 20 &c4+ ♖f7 21 &xf7+ ♔xf7 22 ♕h7+ ♔e8 23 dxe5 ♕e6 24 &a3! with good chances) fell foul of 15 ♘h7! in Kindermann-Schlosser, Austrian Team Championship 2002. 15 ... &xh4 (15 ... ♖e8 16 ♕g4! f5 17 ♕g6 &xh4 18 &xh6 &xf2+ 19 ♔xf2 ♕h4+ 20 ♔g1 ♕xh6 21 ♘f6+ ♔f8 22 ♕xh6 gxh6 23 ♘xe8 ♖xe8 24 ♖e3 is much better for White) 16 ♘xf8 ♔xf8 17 &e4 and White was clearly better.

Nikolaidis-Ruck, European Blitz Championship 2002 continued 13 ... ♕d5?! 14 c4 ♕d8 15 &b2 with an excellent position for White, who managed to snip a pawn after 15 ... &f6 16 ♕d2 ♘e7 17 &e4 &xe4 18 ♖xe4 ♖c8 19 ♖c1 ♘f5 20 ♖g4 ♕d7 21 ♕e2 ♖fe8 22 h5 h6 23 ♘e5 &xe5 24 ♕xe5 f6 25 ♕xf6 ♕f7 26 ♕xf7+ ♔xf7.

14 ♘xh4 ♕xh4 15 ♖e3 g6

15 ... ♕d8 16 ♕h5 g6 17 ♖g3 ♕d7 18 &h6 ♖fe8 19 ♖e1 ♕c7 20 ♖ee3 ♘e7 21 ♕g5 ♘d5 22 c4 f6 23 ♕h4 ♕f7 24 cxd5 was winning in Poluljahov-Volkov, Russian Team Championship 2001.

16 ♖g3 ♕e7

16 ... ♕f6 17 ♕g4 e5 18 ♗g5 ♕g7 19 ♕h4 f5 20 ♗c4+ ♔h8 21 ♗h6 ♕f6 22 ♗g5 ♕g7 23 ♗h6 ♕f6 24 ♗g5 was agreed drawn in Skytte-Malakhatko, Cappelle la Grande 2003, but I prefer 17 ♗h6 ♖fd8 18 ♕g4, when ♖f3 followed by ♗g5 is on the cards.

17 ♗h6!

Not allowing Black to use his rook defensively along the second rank, as was the case after 17 ♗g5 f6 18 ♗h6 ♖f7 as in Izoria-Golod, 2nd IECC 2001.

17 ... ♖fd8 18 ♕g4 f5 19 ♕e2 ♖e8 20 ♖e1 ♕d7 21 ♗c4 ♘d8 22 ♕e5 ♖c8 23 ♗b3 ♕c7 24 ♕xc7! ♖xc7 25 d5!

White's initiative and Black's back rank problems persist even after the exchange of queens. If the extra pawn is seen as the one on h7, it is obviously cold comfort for Black's suffering.

25 ... ♖c5 26 ♖d3 ♗a6 27 ♖d4 ♗c8 28 ♗g5 ♘f7 29 ♗f6 e5 30 f4 e4 31 ♖c1 ♖c7 32 d6! ♖d7 33 ♖cd1 ♔f8 34 ♗a4 ♘h6 35 ♖e1 ♘g4 36 ♗h4 a6 37 ♗c6 ♔f7 38 ♖b1 b5 39 a4 ♖e6 40 axb5 ♖dxd6 41 ♗d5 ♖b6 42 ♖c4 ♘e3 43 ♖c7+ ♔e8 1-0

Game Thirty-Seven
Marin – Engqvist
Rilton Cup 2002

1 c4 c6 2 e4 d5 3 exd5 cxd5 4 d4 ♘f6 5 ♘c3 ♘c6 6 ♘f3 ♗g4

Black intends 7 ... e6, after which White can only beg for a draw. So the b7-weakness must be quickly exploited:

7 cxd5 ♘xd5 8 ♕b3! ♗xf3 9 gxf3

Now it's decision time for Black.

9 ... e6

This line leads, more or less by force, to a very interesting endgame where White has a good initiative. The alternative is examined in the next game.

10 ♕xb7! ♘xd4 11 ♗b5+ ♘xb5 12 ♕c6+! ♔e7 13 ♕xb5 ♕d7

Fischer-Euwe, Leipzig Olympiad 1960 saw 13 ... ♘xc3 14 bxc3 ♕d7, when 15 ♖b1! was Bobby's novelty. Fischer then analyses 15 ... ♕xb5 16 ♖xb5 ♔d6! 17 ♖b7 f6 18 ♔e2 ♔c6 19 ♖f7 a5 20 ♗e3 "with an enduring edge."

14 ♘xd5+

As an aside, 14 ♕e2!? was a new one for me when I saw it appear in the all-Scottish clash Motwani-Grant, British Championship 2003. After 14 ... ♖d8 15 0-0 ♘xc3 16 bxc3 ♕d3 17 ♕xd3 ♖xd3 18 ♖b1 h6 19 ♖b8 ♖d8 20 ♗a3+ ♔e8 21 ♖fb1 ♗e7 22 ♖1b7 ♖xb8 23 ♖xb8+ ♗d8 24 ♖b7 h5 25 ♖xa7 ♖h6 26 ♗d6 ♖f6 27 c4 Black's passive handling had landed him in a hopeless position. Food for thought if you want a slight twist on the main variations.

14 ... ♕xd5

There are now several ways of going into the endgame – with or without ♗g5+, with or without queenside castling. For the sake of brevity I'll just present the best line!

15 ♗g5+!

Forcing a pawn to a dark-square, and more importantly preparing the e6-square for a later rook invasion.

15 ... f6 16 ♕xd5 exd5 17 ♗e3 ♚e6

17 ... ♚f7 effectively amounted to a loss of tempo after 18 0-0-0 ♖d8 19 ♖d3 ♖d7 20 ♖hd1 ♚e6 in Dolmatov-Lechtynsky, Hradec Kralove 1981, but the game is still instructive: 21 a3 ♗e7 22 ♖c3 ♖hd8 23 ♖c6+ ♗d6 24 h3. Already the parallels with the main game are apparent. Now Black decides on some risky activity. 24 ... ♚e5 25 f4+ ♚e4 26 ♖d4+ ♚f3 27 ♖xd5 ♗xf4 28 ♖f5 ♖d1+ 29 ♚c2 ♖8d2+ 30 ♚b3 ♖d3+ 31 ♚a4 g5 32 ♖cxf6 ♚g2 33 ♗xf4 gxf4 34 ♖xf4 and White eventually prevailed in the rook ending.

18 0-0-0!

I fully concur with Aagard here that this represents White's optimal treatment (some players go kingside or leave the king in the middle, occasionally without ♗g5+). I understand the confusion of anyone who, promised an 'attacking' repertoire, is scanning the board for a pair of queens and is offended that neither lady is present. However, despite the paucity of the respective forces, White has a very substantial initiative in this position, largely due to the weakness of the d5-pawn. The black monarch, at least in the short term, must play nursemaid to this weakling, which in turn will expose him to dangers once the white rooks get going on the central files. Of course, White's structure is no oil-painting either, but of the two obvious deficiencies (allowing the d-pawn to be passed and the shattered kingside pawns), the former is rarely a problem since a secure blockade can be errected on d4 while the latter affords a half-open g-file for a rook.

The queenside majority is very useful here too – having a necessarily winning position in king and pawn endgames gives White something to play around with. While most top-level outings for this variation end in draws (even Onischuk hasn't notched up a win in a while), the long-term and low-risk nature of White's initiative means that Black must play very accurately just to survive here, a task not relished by anyone, especially club players.

18 ... ♝b4 19 ♜d3!

The right square for this piece, invulnerable and with options of aggression against the d5-pawn or swinging across the third rank. I think this move is more flexible than 19 a3 or 19 ♚b1, though both have led to instructive White wins by masters of this variation:

19 a3 ♜hc8+ 20 ♚b1 ♝a5 21 b4 ♝b6 occurred in Dolmatov-Christiansen, Luzern 1993 and was a model example of how to handle this bishop redeployment: 22 ♜he1! ♚d6 23 ♜d3 ♝xe3 (very much an admission of defeat, but how else could Black meet the threat of doubling on the d-file?) 24 fxe3 a5 25 ♜ed1 axb4 26 ♜xd5+ ♚e6 27 axb4 ♜a4 28 ♜5d4 ♜c3 29 ♜e4+ ♚f7 30 ♜d7+ ♚f8 31 ♜d8+ ♚f7 32 ♜d7+ ♚f8 33 ♚b2 ♜aa3 34 ♜a7! was another winning rook endgame for White.

19 ♚b1 ♜hc8 20 ♜d3 ♜c7 21 ♜hd1 ♜d8 22 a3 ♝e7 23 b4 g5!? represented an interesting treatment in Onischuk-Gretarsson, Wijk aan Zee 1996. I suspect Black needs to try something like this in order to generate some chances. That said, there are pitfalls to his plan too, as was brilliantly demonstrated after 24 ♚a2 ♜cd7 25 ♜c1 d4 26 ♝d2 ♝d6 27 h4! gxh4 28 ♜h1 f5 29 ♜xh4 ♝e5 30 ♜h6+ ♚d5 31 ♚b3 ♜g8 32 f4 ♝b8 33 f3 ♜g6 34 ♜h1 a6 35 ♜e1 ♚c6 36 ♜e8 ♝c7 37 ♚c4 ♜gd6 38 a4 ♚b7 39 ♜f8 ♜d5 40 ♜f6 ♝b6 41 ♝e1 ♝c7 42 ♝f2 ♜7d6 43 ♜f7 ♜d7 44 ♜xh7 ♝xf4 45 ♜xd7+ ♜xd7 46 ♝xd4 when White's patience resulted in a pretty trivial endgame win.

19 ... ♜hd8 20 ♚b1 a5!

Black too plays thematically, here taking pre-emptive measures against the realisation of White's majority while freeing the a8-rook for less mundane defensive tasks.

21 a3

21 ... ♗e7

21 ... ♗f8 22 ♖e1 ♔f5!? is a more active treatment. Nielsen-Dominguez, North Sea Cup 2002 continued 23 ♖c1 ♖d7 24 ♖c6 a4 25 ♖b6 g5 26 ♖b5 ♔e6 27 ♖d4 ♖a6 28 h3 (28 h4!? is worth a go) 28 ... ♗e7 29 ♔c2 ♖c7+ 30 ♔d3 ♗c5 31 ♖g4 ♗d6 32 ♖d4 ♗c5 33 ♖g4 ♗d6 34 ♖d4 ♗c5 35 ♖g4 ♗d6 with a draw.

22 ♖e1! ♔f7 23 ♖c1!

A smart use of the white assets outlined above – by pushing the king away from the d5-pawn, White prevents any contest of the c-file.

23 ... ♖d7 24 ♖c6 a4 25 ♔c2 f5 26 ♗d4!

The next phase – this bishop clearly wasn't pulling its weight and seeks more productive pastures. Note how Black's pieces are fulfilling purely defensive roles, and at least two of his pawns (on the a- and d-files) are looking a little tender.

26 ... ♗g5 27 ♗e5 ♗h4 28 ♖d2 ♖aa7 29 f4 ♗e7 30 ♖d3 ♖a8 31 ♔d2 ♔g8

Marin's astute regrouping has the added benefit of opening up the kingside third rank for some swinging. As before, a little intermezzo poisons the dagger.

32 ♖dc3! ♖aa7

Otherwise ♖c7 comes, but now the back rank is weak.

33 ♖g3 ♗h4 34 ♖c8+ ♖d8 35 ♖xd8+ ♗xd8 36 ♖d3 ♗b6 37 ♔e2 ♖d7 38 ♖c3 d4 39 ♖c8+ ♔f7 40 ♔d3

One more tempo and Black would be fine, but with the blockade locked in it's game over.

40 ... &a7 41 &c4 &g6 42 &xa4 &h5 43 &c4 &g4 44 b4 &h3 45 &c7 &xc7 46 &xc7 &xh2 47 a4 &g1 48 a5 1-0

Keeping it Complicated: ... &c6 without an endgame

This is what happens when Black avoids the endgame in the 5 .... &c6 variation. White's pieces exert massive pressure on both flanks, but his structure is pretty bad. In a real game, Black also has some pieces, but you don't need to worry about them at this stage.

Game Thirty-Eight
Bagheri – Gozzoli
Breizh Masters 2004

1 e4 c6 2 d4 d5 3 exd5 cxd5 4 c4 &f6 5 &c3 &c6

This position actually arose via 1 c4 c5 2 &f3 &c6 3 e3 &f6 4 d4 cxd4 5 exd4 d5 6 &c3 – Panov positions can arise from a whole host of openings, so they merit study whatever your repertoire.

You should be aware of 5 ... ♗e6, which is pretty rare but can be confusing. 6 ♘ge2! dxc4 7 ♘f4 ♗g4 8 f3 ♗d7 9 ♗xc4 is probably best, when Arnason-Komarov, Cannes 1993 continued 9 ... e6 10 0-0 ♕c7 11 ♕e2 ♗d6 12 g3 0-0 13 ♗e3 ♘c6 14 ♖fd1 ♘e7 15 ♘e4! ♘xe4 16 fxe4 ♖ac8 17 ♖ac1 with a beautiful position for White.

6 ♘f3 ♗g4 7 cxd5 ♘xd5 8 ♕b3 ♗xf3 9 gxf3 ♘b6

This is the alternative to allowing the endgame we examined previously. The approach I'm recommending is based on very rapid development and an opening of the position.

10 ♗e3

10 d5 is a much sharper alternative, but Black tends to generate substantial play in this line, whereas the simpler text gives the same chances without the attendant risks.

10 ... e6 11 0-0-0! ♗e7 12 d5!

Definitely correct – why give Black the chance to blockade?

12 ... exd5 13 ♘xd5 ♘xd5 14 ♖xd5 ♕c7 15 ♔b1 0-0 16 f4!

So here we are. Again, what White's kingside pawns lack in long-term stability they provide in an open g-file and very useful central control.

White has the bishop pair, more active pieces and a very useful initiative. Here we examine a natural approach which falls short.

16 ♗d3?! commits the bishop prematurely and doesn't take control of the centre: 16 ... ♘b4 17 ♖h5 ♘xd3 18 ♕xd3 g6 19 ♖c1 ♕b8 20 ♗h6 ♖d8 21 ♕c3 ♗f8 22 ♗xf8 ♖xf8 23 ♕d4 was agreed drawn in Kharlov-Yevseev, 5th Russian Cup Final, Kazan 2001.

16 ... ♘b4

This is one of the more annoying possibilities, but there are at least two good responses.

Ormsby played 16 ... ♖fd8 against me in the Isle of Man 2002, but the game illustrates White's possibilities on both wings: 17 ♗g2 ♖xd5 18 ♗xd5 ♗f6 19 ♖c1 ♕d7 20 ♗e4 ♖d8 21 ♕b5 g6 22 f5 ♔g7 23 a3 ♕d6. The position has been improved about as much as possible, and I decided to go for a combination: 24 fxg6 hxg6 25 ♗xc6 bxc6 26 ♖xc6 ♕xh2 27 ♖xf6!? ♕g1+ 28 ♔a2 ♔xf6 29 ♕c6+ ♔g7 30 ♕c3+ ♔h7 31 ♕c7 ♕d1 32 ♕xf7+ ♔h8 33 ♗xa7 and the black king soon fell to the white attack.

16 ... ♖ad8 17 ♗g2 ♖xd5 18 ♗xd5 ♗f6 occured in Narciso Dublan - Matulovic, Belgrade 2001, and now I like 19 ♖c1! with pressure on the knight and the a-pawn.

17 ♖d4

As far as I can tell this is a novelty.

Berkes-Cornette, World U-18 Championship 2002 continued 17 ♖d1 ♕c6 18 ♗e2 ♕g6+, and now 19 ♗d3! ♘xd3 20 ♕xd3 ♖fd8 21 ♕xg6 hxg6 22 ♖xd8+ ♗xd8 23 ♖d1 a6 24 ♖d7 left White much more active.

17 ... ♘c6 18 ♕c2! ♕a5 19 ♖a4

This places Black in a quandry. If he retreats the queen, then the white pieces will develop naturally – ♗g2 and ♖c1, with possible kingside play later via ♖g1, f5 and ♗e4 (possibly swinging the a4-rook over to help).

19 ... ♕e1+ 20 ♕c1 ♕xc1+ 21 ♔xc1 ♖ac8 22 ♔b1!

However, the endgame is very unpleasant for Black. By exchanging queens he has exchanged the main defender of his queenside pawns, and the white build up is very natural and easy to play.

22 ... ♖fd8 23 ♗h3 ♖c7 24 ♖c1 ♗d6 25 ♗g2 f5 26 ♖ac4

More or less forcing the win of a pawn, since Black can't hold on to all his material without messing up his own position.

26 ... ♔f7

26 ... ♖dc8 27 ♗d5+ ♔h8 is horrible (27 ... ♔f8 28 ♗e6 wins material).

27 ♗xc6 bxc6 28 ♖xc6 ♖xc6 29 ♖xc6 ♗b8 30 ♔c2 h6

Preparing play with g5. Another reason I like this game is Bagheri's superb, calm technique, gradually taking care of all the kingside threats.

31 b4! ♖e8 32 ♖c4 ♔g6 33 ♔d3 ♔h5 34 f3! ♔h4 35 ♖c5! ♖f8 36 ♖b5! g5 37 ♖b7! g4

The last chance of counterplay, but White has it covered.

38 ♔e2 ♔h3 39 ♖h7 ♔xh2 40 ♖xh6+ ♔g3 41 ♖g6 ♖e8 42 fxg4! fxg4

42 ... ♗xf4 43 gxf5+ and 44 ♖e6 is elegantly decisive.

43 f5 ♖f8 44 f6 a6 45 ♗c5 ♖f7 46 ♗e7 ♗e5 47 ♔e3 1-0

Taking Pawns: The ... g6 Structure.

This is the characteristic structure from the 5 ... g6 variation. The first thing to note is that White has a big fat extra pawn. It's clear that this pawn (the one on d5, I guess), isn't that useful for the primary purpose of pawns, namely promotion – White can't generate a passed pawn in this structure. The value of White's extra pawn is more in its restrictive effect – black bishops and knights are respectively denied the c6- and e6-squares, while the fact that any ... e6 from Black will probably give White a d-file passer means that White can build up on the e-file against a relatively fixed target. However, White should be prepared to jettison this pawn if Black goes to great lengths to regain it – after a ... ♘a6-c7 manoeuvre, for instance, a break with d6! can leave Black's pieces misplaced in the new structure.

Game Thirty-Nine
Lalic – Sriram
Goodricke 2002

1 e4 c6 2 d4 d5 3 exd5 cxd5 4 c4 ♘f6 5 ♘c3 g6 6 cxd5!?

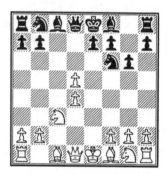

A little twist on the better-established 6 ♕b3. White hopes to do without this move, while inviting Black to capture on d5.

6 ... ♗g7

Probably the best move.

After 6 ... ♘xd5 7 ♗c4! Black is substantially behind in development. After 7 ... ♘xc3 (7 ... ♘b6 8 ♗b3 ♗g7 9 ♘f3 ♘c6 [Kostin-Burmakin, Russian Team Championship 2004 saw 9 ... 0-0 10 0-0 ♘c6 and now 11 d5 would have transposed] 10 d5 ♘a5 [10 ... ♘e5 is also possible, but after 11 ♘xe5 ♗xe5 12 ♗e3 I prefer White, who will build up behind the d-pawn] 11 0-0 0-0 12 ♖e1 looked like a good Grunfeld for White, and Black opted for a dubious treatment when 12 ... ♘xb3 13 axb3 e6?! 14 d6 ♗d7 15 ♗g5 f6 16 ♗e3 ♘c8 17 ♗c5 b6 18 ♗a3 ♖e8 19 ♘d5 was crushing in Glek-Szabolcsi, Parisian Championship 2000) 8 ♕b3 e6 9 bxc3 ♗g7 10 ♗a3 ♘c6 11 ♘f3 ♘e7 12 ♕b5+ ♕d7 13 ♘e5 ♗xe5 14 ♕xe5 ♖g8 15 ♗b5 ♘c6 16 ♕c5 ♔d8 17 d5 exd5 18 0-0-0 was game over in Khenkin-Ebenschwanger, Bad Wiessee 2000.

6 ... ♘bd7!? is Ian Rogers' clever move order. The idea is obviously to stop ♗c4, which will now be met with a quick ... ♘b6. In my game against him at the 4NCL 2004, after 7 ♗g5 ♗g7 8 ♗e2 ♘b6 9 ♗xf6 ♗xf6 10 ♗f3 0-0 11 ♘ge2 ♗g7, instead of castling (which allowed ... ♘c4), I should have played 12 ♕b3! and after Ian's intended 12 ... ♗f5 13 ♖d1! to prevent ... ♗d3. I prefer White, who will castle, put a rook on the e-file and perhaps

play d6 to unleash the f3-bishop, while Black still needs to show compensation for the pawn.

7 &c4 0-0 8 ♘ge2 ♘bd7

8 ... ♘a6 9 0-0 ♘c7 is an alternative development, after which I think the typical 10 ♕b3 b6 (after 10 ... a6, instead of Ftacnik's 11 d6 I'd prefer 11 a4! when Black has difficulties with his c8-bishop) 11 d6! exd6 12 &g5 gives White a nice advantage – his bishops are very active and ♘f4 is coming.

9 &g5 ♘b6 10 &xf6 &xf6 11 &b3 &g4 12 f3 &f5 13 ♘g3 ♕d7 14 0-0

Compared to the ♕b3 lines, White's position is much better co-ordinated.

14 ... ♖ac8 15 ♘ge4 &g7 16 ♔h1 ♘c4 17 ♘c5!?

17 ♕e2 is fine, but the text is even better.

17 ... ♘xb2 18 ♕d2 ♕c7 19 ♖ac1 b6

19 ... &xd4 fails to 20 ♘b5.

20 ♘b5 ♕d8 21 ♘e4 ♕d7 22 ♕e2 &h6 23 ♖xc8

23 ♖c6 also does the trick, for instance 23 ... ♖xc6 24 dxc6 ♕xc6 25 ♕xb2!.

23 ... ♖xc8 24 d6! ♖c1 25 ♖xc1 &xc1 26 ♘bc3 ♔g7 27 ♕c2 &xe4 28 ♘xe4 1-0

CHAPTER SEVEN
The Pirc/Modern Defence

"I only play one opening."

GM David Norwood (who uses 1 g3 and 1 ... g6 in every game).

1 e4 d6 2 d4 ♘f6 3 ♘c3 g6

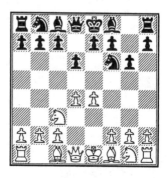

These moves (and 1 ... g6) introduce the Pirc/Modern complex (hereafter 'the Modern' for brevity). An invention of the hypermodern school, this system gives White a completely free hand in both his central structure and piece deployment, hoping to strike later once we've revealed our intentions. White's approach to this line has changed with time.

The solid Classical variation (♘f3, ♗e2 and 0-0) has been a perpetual favourite with solid positional players. For the more aggressively-inclined, the Austrian Attack (f4, ♘f3, ♗d3) has provided some good times but recently has fallen out of fashion somewhat. Most top players now opt for the '150 Attack', which is based on ♗e3 and ♕d2 followed by trading off dark-squared bishops with ♗h6. This can be coupled with either kingside or queenside castling, and is both solid and aggressive.

My recommendation is basically the same thing, but with ♗g5 instead of ♗e3. This is clearly a more aggressive post for the bishop, and can be coupled with either a rapid f4 and e5, or a more sedate ♕d2, as in the 150 Attack. The only way Black can seek to take advantage of this is through a ... h6, ... g5 and ... ♘h5 advance, which is very double edged and often runs into e5! with advantage.

The Modern is notoriously difficult to study and even harder to classify. This is because Black's unambitious development (all occurring within his first three ranks) gives him a lot of flexibility as regards both piece placement and move order. There is always the move ... g6, and the move ... d6 (some systems involve ... c6 and ... d5, but these are ineffective against ♗g5 systems), but other than that he can play with or without: ... ♘f6, kingside castling, ... a6 + ... b5, ... c6 + b5, etc. And each line can easily transpose into another.

Faced with such an opening, the best practice is to have a good understanding of what one wants to do with one's own forces, and not radically change plan when Black throws in something erratic. Broadly, I've broken the Modern down into three sections, each of which is covered by an illustrative game:

I.   Black castles early. Against this I'm recommending the most aggressive approach of ♕d2, 0-0-0, f3, g4, h4 and (hopefully) 'sac, sac, mate!' down the h-file as Bobby Fischer once said.

II.   Black plays ... ♘f6, but delays castling. Given that these lines involve very early queenside pawn play with ... b5, castling queenside is inadvisable for White. Instead I'm recommending an approach based on kingside castling, followed by f4 (with threats of e5 hitting the knight or f5 attacking down the f-file).

III.   Black foregoes both early castling and an early ... ♘f6. Against these systems, castling queenside runs into substantial counterplay, while f4 loses some of its bite because there is no f6-knight to attack. The downside of these systems for Black, however, is chronic underdevelopment – leaving your g8-knight at home for the first few moves isn't too advisable. So I've recommended a very classical approach based on quick development with ♘f3.

Perhaps it would have been more prudent to recommend 'f4 and 0-0 against everything', but I think it's no harm to have several techniques in one's repertoire so as to be able to react in the best way to any chosen formation. Hopefully I've made clear why I've picked each formation against each of the three Black setups within the Modern.

Finally, we'll have a look at early ... c6 systems which are rather aberrational and give White good chances.

Game Forty
Motylev – Sturua
Dubai Open 2003

1 e4 d6 2 d4 ♘f6 3 ♘c3 g6 4 ♗g5

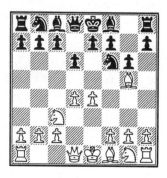

One of the nice things about this system for White is that the f6-knight is attacked, which means that Black always has to watch out for ♗xf6, and so to some extent his flexibility is reduced. I certainly think that early ... b5 systems are more dubious here than in the 150-Attack.

4 ... ♗g7

4 ... a6 is very rarely tried. After 5 ♘f3 ♗g7 6 ♕d2 we transpose into a note to the next game, but Volzhin-Davies, Gausdal 2000 saw an independent approach with 5 ♕e2!?. After 5 ... ♗g7 6 e5 ♘fd7 7 0-0-0 ♘c6 8 f4 0-0 9 d5 ♘a5 10 exd6 cxd6 11 ♗xe7 ♕b6 12 ♗xf8 ♔xf8 13 ♖e1 ♘f6 14 ♕e3 ♕c7 15 ♘f3 b5 16 a3 White amazingly agreed a draw. Call me old-fashioned, but I've always prefered a rook and a pawn to a knight. Black has a little compensation but most definitely not enough.

4 ... c6 5 ♕d2 b5 (5 ... h6 6 ♗h4 g5 7 ♗g3 ♘h5 is possible here as everywhere else, but Yakovich-Kuzmin, Swidnica 1999 showed an interesting method of playing against the early kingside advances: 8 ♘ge2 ♕a5 9 h4 g4 10 ♗h2! ♘d7 11 ♘g3 ♘hf6 12 ♗c4 h5 13 0-0 ♗h6 14 ♕e1 ♕b4 15 b3 b5 16 a3 ♕a5 17 ♗d3 ♗f4 18 b4 ♕b6 19 ♘ce2 ♗xg3 20 ♗xg3 and Black's activity had petered out, leaving him underdeveloped and with neither central control nor a dark-squared bishop; Van der Wiel played 5 ... ♘bd7 against Afek at the Dieren Open 2000. After 6 f4 ♕a5 7 ♘f3 b5 8 ♗d3 b4 9 ♘e2 ♗a6 10 0-0 d5 11 e5 ♘e4 12 ♕e3 f5 13 a3 ♗b7 14 axb4 ♕xb4 15 c3 ♕b6 16 b4 White was well on top) 6 e5!? dxe5 7 dxe5 ♕xd2+ 8 ♗xd2 ♘g4 9 f4 h5 10 ♘e4 ♗f5 11 ♗d3 a5 12 ♘f3 and White had a pleasant endgame in Ulibin-Himdan, Abu Dhabi 2002.

5 ♕d2!

This is how I recommend handling this system – now the ♗g5 has options of going to h6, while queenside castling is just a move away. Some players forego ♕d2 in favour of an immediate 5 f4, but this is riskier (I don't like creating such a huge centre before when I've only developed two pieces) and less flexible (since the pawn might want to go to f3 to support g4, as in the text).

5 ... 0-0

Motylev-Marin, Bucharest 2001 continued 5 ... h6 6 ♗h4 g5 7 ♗g3 ♘h5, which is riskier than the last note because Black has already committed his king to the kingside. After 8 0-0-0 ♘d7 9 e5 dxe5 10 dxe5 e6 (White has ample compensation after 10 ... ♘xg3 11 hxg3 ♗xe5, for instance 12 f4 gxf4 13 gxf4 ♗g7 and now Bruzon-Cavatorta, Aosta Open 2004 continued 14 ♘f3 c6 15 ♘e5 ♕c7 16 ♗c4 ♘xe5 17 fxe5 ♗e6 18 ♗xe6 fxe6 19 ♖de1 ♖d8 20 ♕e3 with absolutely tremendous compensation, but I also like 14 ♘ge2 c6 15 ♖h3! intending ♖d3) 11 ♕e2 ♘xg3 12 hxg3 ♕e7 13 f4 ♘b6 14 ♕f3 f5 15 exf6 ♕xf6 16 ♕h5+ ♔e7 17 ♘f3 ♗d7 18 ♘e5 ♗e8 19 ♕f3 gxf4 20 gxf4 ♖f8 21 ♘e2 ♖d8 22 ♖xd8 ♔xd8 23 ♕xb7 ♕e7 24 ♕b8+ ♘c8 25 ♘d4 ♗xe5 26 fxe5 ♗d7 27 ♗a6 ♕g5+ 28 ♔b1 ♕xg2 29 ♖d1 ♕g4 30 ♗e2 Black resigned since 31 ♘c6+ is crushing.

5 ... c6 6 ♗h6 is an important position which can also arise from a 4 ♗e3 move order. 6 ... ♗xh6 (6 ... 0-0 7 f3 b5 8 g4 followed by h4-h5 and 0-0-0 gives similar play to the main game) 7 ♕xh6 ♕a5 (7 ... e5 8 0-0-0 ♕e7 9 ♘f3 ♘bd7 10 ♗c4 is comfortably better for White: Ziatdinov-Chapman, Continental Open 2000) and White has several continuations of varying aggression, but since Black's most important piece has been exchanged I think we can afford to consolidate our spoils with 8 ♕d2 ♘bd7 9 ♘f3 b5 10 ♗d3 b4 11 ♘e2 ♗a6 12 0-0 ♗xd3 13 ♕xd3 0-0 14 ♘g3 and White had a risk-free advantage in Pavasovic-Ciglic, Ljubljana Open 2001.

6 0-0-0 c6 7 ♔b1! b5 8 f3 ♘bd7 9 e5! ♘e8 10 h4

10 ... f6

Accepting the pawn with 10 ... dxe5 11 dxe5 ♗xe5 is too dangerous after 12 h5!, for example: 12 ... ♘d6 13 hxg6 fxg6 (13 ... hxg6 14 ♗f4 ♗f6 15 g3) 14 ♘xb5! is better for White.

11 exf6 exf6 12 ♗e3 d5 13 h5 ♖f7 14 hxg6 hxg6 15 g4 ♘f8 16 ♘h3 ♖e7 17 ♘f4 ♘c7 18 ♗d3 ♕e8 19 ♖de1 a5 20 ♗xb5!?

Typically attentive play from Motylev. The subsequent opening of the black king seems objectively sound and leads to huge practical chances.

20 ... cxb5 21 ♘fxd5 ♘xd5 22 ♘xd5

22 ... ♖b7 23 ♗h6 ♕d8 24 ♗xg7 ♖xg7

24 ... ♔xg7 25 ♕h6+ ♔f7 (25 ... ♔g8 26 ♖e8!) 26 ♕h8! is decisive.

25 ♖e8! ♕xd5 26 ♖h8+ ♔xh8 27 ♖xf8+ ♕g8 28 ♕h6+ ♖h7 29 ♖xg8+ ♔xg8 30 ♕xg6+ ♔h8 31 ♕xf6+ ♖g7 32 ♕f8+ ♔h7 33 a3!

A fitting end to Motylev's enterprising play. While material is nominally equal, it is clear that with Black's pieces unco-ordinated, two weak black pawns and three white passers, White must win.

33 ... ♗b7 34 ♕f5+ ♔g8 35 f4 ♖d8 36 ♕e6+ ♔h7 37 ♕e5 ♖d5 38 ♕e4+ ♔g8 39 f5 ♖f7 40 ♕e6!

Necessary to get the g-pawn rolling.

40 ... ♖xd4 41 ♕e8+ ♖f8 42 ♕e6+ ♖f7 43 ♕e8+ ♖f8 44 ♕g6+ ♔h8 45 ♕h5+ ♔g8 46 ♕g5+ ♔h8 47 ♕e7 ♖d1+ 48 ♔a2 ♖f7!

Smart, but it doesn't really make a difference.

49 ♕e8+ ♔g7 50 ♕e5+ ♔g8 51 ♕xb5 ♗d5+ 52 c4 ♗f3 53 ♕e8+ ♖f8 54
♕g6+ ♔h8 55 ♕h5+ ♔g8 56 ♕g5+ ♔h8 57 ♕e3 ♗h1 58 ♕h6+ ♔g8 59
♕g6+ ♔h8 60 f6 ♖d7 61 ♕h6+ 1-0

Game Forty-One
Sutovsky – Azmaiparashvili
FIDE Grand Prix 2002

1 e4 d6 2 d4 g6 3 ♘c3 ♗g7 4 ♗g5

This is fully playable even without ... ♘f6 thrown in. To avoid
transposition to the Pirc lines considered in the previous game, Black needs
to start getting fancy, which always carries the risk of an accident.

4 ... a6

The previous comment is thrown into sharp relief by Rublevsky-
Chepukaitis, Korchnoi tournament 2001. After 4 ... h6 5 ♗h4 a6 6 ♘f3
♘d7 7 a4 b6 8 ♗c4, Black crowned his already provocative play with 8 ...
g5?. Rublevsky didn't need to be asked twice: After 9 ♗xg5! hxg5 10
♗xf7+! ♔xf7 11 ♘xg5+ ♔g6 (11 ... ♔e8 12 ♘e6 is a very typical tactic
when Black plays an early ... ♘d7; 11 ... ♔f6 12 ♕g4 was Rublevsky-
D'Amore Istanbul Olympiad 2000, which continued 12 ... ♘e5 13 ♘d5+
♔g6 14 ♘f4+ ♔f6 15 dxe5+ dxe5 16 ♘h7+) 12 ♘e6 ♘h6 (12 ... ♕e8 13
♕g4+ ♔f7 14 ♕xg7+ ♔xe6 15 d5 mate is the point) 13 ♘d5 ♘f6 14 ♘xd8
♖xd8 15 ♘xe7+ ♔f7 16 ♘xc8 ♖dxc8 17 f3 it was time to resign (not that
Black did).

Rublevsky-Gofshtein, Ordix Open 2000 continued 4 ... ♘d7 5 ♘f3 a6 6
a4 h6 7 ♗e3 (7 ♗h4 transposes to Rublevsky-Chepukaitis above and so
would probably be his choice today, but I like 7 ♗e3 just as much – with
the protruding pawn on h6, Black will find it difficult to castle) 7 ... e6 8
♕d2 b6 9 ♗d3 ♗b7 10 0-0 ♘gf6 11 h3 c5 12 ♖fe1 cxd4 13 ♘xd4 ♘c5 14

f3 d5 15 e5 ♘fd7 16 f4 0-0 17 b4 ♘e4 18 ♗xe4 dxe4 19 ♗f2 (19 ♖ad1 is also strong) 19 ... g5 20 ♘xe4 gxf4 21 ♘d6 ♗d5 22 ♘4f5 ♗xe5 (22 ... ♘xe5 fails to 23 ♗h4 ♕c7 24 ♘xg7 ♔xg7 25 ♕xf4 f6 26 ♗xf6+ ♖xf6 27 ♕xe5) 23 ♖xe5 ♘xe5 24 ♕xf4 ♘g6 (24 ... exf5 25 ♕xe5 ♗e4 26 ♘xe4 fxe4 27 ♗d4 f6 28 ♕xe4 is much better for White) 25 ♕xh6 ♕f6 26 ♗d4 e5 27 ♗xb6 ♗e6 28 ♖f1 ♖ac8 29 ♘h4 ♗g4 30 ♘hf5 ♗xf5 31 ♗c5 and Black resigned.

4 ... ♘c6 doesn't achieve much after 5 d5 ♘d4 6 ♘ge2 c5 7 dxc6 ♘xc6 8 ♕d2 ♘f6 9 0-0-0. Teske-Hidalgo Begines, Seville Open 2004 continued 9 ... 0-0 10 f3 ♗d7 11 h4 ♘e5 12 ♘g3 h5 13 f4 ♘eg4 and now 14 f5 would have given a strong attack.

4 ... c6 5 ♕d2 b5 is possible, and now either 6 ♘f3 or 6 0-0-0!? looks promising – I don't think the b-pawn constitutes a roaring attack, while White has five pieces optimally placed and is ready to develop the remaining ones.

4 ... c5 5 dxc5 ♕a5 6 ♕d2 ♗xc3 7 ♕xc3 ♕xc3+ 8 bxc3 dxc5 9 a4 ♗d7 10 ♘f3 ♗c6 11 ♘d2 ♘d7 12 ♗b5 ♖c8 13 ♔e2 f5 14 ♖hb1! and White had the better endgame in Motylev-Inarkiev, Tomsk 2004.

5 ♘f3

5 ... ♗g4

With hindsight this looks a little dubious, but the game is so deliciously violent and the two competitiors are so strong that I couldn't resist its inclusion. That said, I'm very happy with White's resources in general here.

5 ... b5 is also a major continuation, of course. Magem Badals-Tkachiev, FIDE WCh KO 1999 continued 6 ♗d3 ♗b7 7 a4 b4 8 ♘e2 ♘d7 9 0-0 ♘gf6 10 ♘g3 0-0 11 ♖e1 c5 12 e5! dxe5 13 dxe5 ♘d5 14 ♗e4 ♘7b6 15 a5 ♘c8 16 ♕d2 ♕d7 17 c4 bxc3 18 bxc3 c4 19 ♗h6 ♖d8 20 ♗xg7 ♔xg7 21 ♘d4 e6 22 h4! ♘ce7 23 h5 ♘g8 24 ♖ab1 ♖ab8 25 hxg6 hxg6 26 ♗f3 and White was doing well, even before 26 ... ♘de7? 27 ♗xb7 ♖xb7 28 ♖xb7 ♕xb7 29 ♘xe6+! fxe6 30 ♕xd8.

5 ... ♘d7 6 ♕d2 and I prefer White – I'm not entirely sure what Black's doing.

5 ... h6 6 ♗h4 b5 was essayed in Smirnov-Tseshkovsky, Russian Ch 2003. Again Black's creeping pawn play doesn't look too convincing. After 7 a4 b4 8 ♘d5 a5 9 e5 dxe5 10 dxe5 ♗b7 11 ♗c4 g5 12 ♗g3 e6 13 ♘e3 ♕xd1+ 14 ♖xd1 ♘d7 15 ♗b5 0-0-0 16 ♘c4 ♘e7 17 ♘xa5 ♗xf3, the simplest was 18 ♗xd7+ ♖xd7 19 gxf3 with an extra a-pawn for not-very-much.

I've been wondering why so few people play 5 ... ♘f6 here. After all, with a white knight on f3, two of White's most aggressive setups (f4-f5, and f3 with g4) are ruled out. I think that the point might be 6 ♕d2!, when the f6-knight doesn't sit well with an ... a6-advance. White plans to castle queenside and push e5 (with tempo after Black's last move), and Black really doesn't have time to be creeping round the edges in the face of this. In general in Modern positions, Black's ... a6 and ... b5 plan is rarely coupled with an early ... ♘f6.

6 ♗c4 ♘c6 7 h3 ♗xf3 8 ♕xf3 ♗f6 9 ♗e3 e6

Finkel analyses 9 ... e5 10 d5 ♘d4 11 ♕d1! ♘e7 12 ♘e2! ♘xe2 13 ♗xe2 with an excellent position.

10 0-0-0

10 ... ♗g7 11 h4!

Central pawn play is problematic at the moment, so Sutovsky correctly looks to the kingside to extend his operations.

11 ... h6 12 ♕g3 h5

I guess Black could argue that ♕g3 has stopped a g4-break, but the distinction seems lost on Sutovsky who breaks through rapidly.

13 ♗g5 ♘ce7 14 ♘e2 ♕d7 15 ♘f4 c6 16 ♖he1 d5 17 ♗b3 ♘f6 18 f3 dxe4?!

Black really can't afford to open the position like this, but his setup is already completely devoid of quality. White has two bishops, more space and better pieces, so I'm not going to blame Azmai for walking into a haymaker.

19 fxe4 ♘g4 20 d5! cxd5 21 exd5 e5 22 ♗xe7 ♕xe7 23 d6 ♕d8 24 ♗xf7+!!

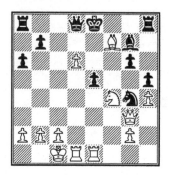

1-0

25 ♕b3+ follows, so the clocks were stopped.

Game Forty-Two
Motwani – Summerscale
Scottish Championship 1999

1 e4 d6 2 d4 ♘f6 3 ♘c3 c6 4 f4

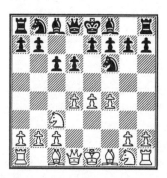

4 ... ♕a5

4 ... ♕b6 isn't too scary either: White was clearly better after 5 e5 ♘d5 6 ♘xd5 cxd5 7 ♗d3 g6 8 ♘e2 ♘c6 9 c3 ♗f5 10 ♗xf5 gxf5 11 ♘g3 e6 12 0-0 in Leko-Hodgson, Cacak 1996.

4 ... g6 5 ♘f3 ♗g7 is a poor version of the Austrian Attack for Black: 6 ♗d3 0-0 7 0-0 b5 8 e5 dxe5 9 dxe5 ♘d5 10 ♘xd5 ♕xd5 11 ♕e2 ♗g4 12 ♗e4 ♕d7 and White was better in Sturua-Velikhanli, Dubai Open 2004.

5 e5 ♘e4 6 ♕f3 d5

Motwani-Adams, Moscow 1994 continued 6 ... ♘xc3 7 ♗d2 ♗f5 8 ♗d3! ♗xd3 9 cxd3 ♕d5 10 bxc3 dxe5 11 fxe5 ♕xf3 12 ♘xf3. This game is the main reason why players have turned to 6 ... d5. With two half-open files to work on, White is much better here, as was demonstrated after 12 ... e6 13 ♔e2 ♘d7 14 ♖hb1 b6 15 a4 ♗e7 16 a5 b5 17 c4! a6 18 ♖c1! 0-0 19 cxb5 cxb5 20 ♖c7 ♖fd8 21 ♖ac1 with a clear advantage.

7 ♗d3 ♘a6

7 ... f5?! 8 exf6 exf6 occured in Shaw-Miles, British Championship 2001, when White should just take the pawn: 9 ♗xe4 dxe4 10 ♕xe4+ and Black's compensation is dubious, for instance 10 ... ♔d8 11 ♕f3 ♗f5 12 ♔d1.

8 ♘ge2

8 ... ♘b4

Whatever about move 7, 8 ... f5? is clearly wrong. In Motwani-Redpath, Scottish Championship 2003, Black got slaughtered after 9 exf6 exf6 10 ♗xe4 dxe4 11 ♕xe4+ ♔f7 12 0-0 ♗f5 13 ♕f3 ♘b4 14 g4! ♘xc2 15 gxf5 ♘xa1 16 ♗d2 ♘b3 17 axb3 ♕xf5 18 ♘g3 ♕c2 19 ♘ce4 ♕xb2 20 ♘g5+! fxg5 21 fxg5+ ♔e8 22 ♕e2+ ♗e7 23 ♘f5.

9 0-0 ♘xd3 10 cxd3 ♘xc3 11 bxc3 g6 12 a4 h5 13 h3 h4 14 ♗a3 ♗f5 15 ♖fb1 ♕c7

16 ♛e3

Motwani's improvement 16 a5! e6 17 ♗c5! leads to a clear advantage, since Black has no compensation for the weaknesses on h4 and b7.

16 ... e6 17 a5 ♗xa3 18 ♖xa3 0-0 19 ♔h2 b6 20 ♖ba1 ♖ab8 21 axb6 axb6

Here Rowson suggests ♖1a2, ♘c1-b3 and pushing c4-c5.

22 ♘g1 ♔g7 23 ♘f3 ♖h8 24 ♖a7 ♖b7 25 ♖a8 ♖bb8 26 ♖8a7 ♖b7 27 ♖a8 ½-½

CHAPTER EIGHT
The Scandinavian Defence

"Nowadays 6 ♘e5 is more popular, but during my preparations for the World Championship, I noticed that the lines with 6 ♗c4 were very dangerous for Black to navigate. Since Joel didn't have a great deal of experience with the Centre Counter, I decided to test him in this line."

GM Vishy Anand

1 e4 d5

Formerly a rather offbeat variation, the Scandinavian (or Centre Counter) has used the fame which its regular practitioners Larsen and Rogers lent it, and is now more popular than ever. A high point for the variation came when Anand used it against Kasparov in their 1995 World Championship match – a surprised Gazza couldn't make a dent. There have also been some books published on this opening in the past few years, a factor which always leads to more adherents, particularly at club level.

So we need to take it seriously, of course, but objectively this line looks less adequate than mainstream defences to 1 e4. Whether Black likes it or not, White's first move took control of d5, and the cost of the Scandinavian is the time Black must lose in recapturing the pawn, whether with the knight or the queen. Amongst top players, no one uses this line on a regular basis for precisely this reason. Black risks a lot without gaining much in return.

A word about the recommendations. 2 ... ♘f6 leads to solid but cramped positions for Black, and here White has few problems in maintaining a pleasant edge. 2 ... ♕xd5 has always been the most popular move. After 3 ♘c3 ♕a5 (alternative queen moves are worse) I've recommended a very aggressive line, which I feel is fully justified by Black's time wasting antics.

Game Forty-Three
Volokitin – Vovsha
Biel 2000

1 e4 d5 2 exd5 ♕xd5 3 ♘c3 ♕a5 4 d4 ♘f6 5 ♘f3 c6 6 ♗c4 ♗f5

6 ... ♗g4 gives an easier time: 7 ♗d2 e6 8 h3 ♗h5 9 g4 ♗g6 10 ♘e5 ♘bd7 11 ♘xg6 hxg6 12 g5 ♘h5 13 ♘e4 ♕c7 14 ♕f3 and White was better in Almasi-Magem Badals, Pamplona 2000.

7 ♘e5 e6 8 g4!

While opinion is divided on this issue, I feel that this aggressive approach is White's best against the Scandinavian. The main commodity gambled by Black's opening is time – given the chance to play ... ♘bd7, ... ♗b4 and ... 0-0, there will be no reason for him to stand worse. In addition, most Black players of this line are trying to avoid theory, so it's probably worthwhile to sharpen things up.

8 ... ♗g6

8 ... ♗e4 9 0-0 ♗d5 is a safer approach for Black. White's kingside space is still handy though, and after 10 ♗d3! I like his chances. 10 ... ♘bd7 (10 ... ♘fd7 appears less logical: 11 f4 ♗e7 12 g5 g6 13 ♗e3 ♕d8 14 ♕g4 h5 15 ♕h4 ♘xe5 16 fxe5 ♕b6 17 b3 ♕a5 18 ♘e4 ♘d7 19 c4 ♗xe4 20 ♕xe4 ♖h7 21 ♖f2 with a huge plus for White in Mortensen-Johansen, Denmark 1996) 11 ♗f4 ♘xe5 12 dxe5 ♕b4 13 ♗g3 ♘d7 (13 ... ♘xg4?? doesn't work: 14 a3 ♕d4 15 ♘xd5 exd5 16 c3) 14 ♘xd5 cxd5 15 a3 ♕c5 16 ♕e2 ♗e7 17 ♔h1 g6 18 f4 0-0 19 f5! with a big kingside initiative in Hossain-Johansen, Gausdal Troll Masters 2002.

9 h4!

The most ambitious. White takes advantage of the fact that, due to the e5-knight, Black can't move his h-pawn to cope with the threatened h4-h5.

9 ... ♘bd7

Given as best by Anand, who prepared this line for a World Championship and so should be trusted on such matters.

Amazingly, 9 ... ♗d6 has a 100% score on my database. Koenig-Kleinegger, Ruhrgebiet 1998 continued 10 ♗f4 ♗xe5 11 ♗xe5 ♘bd7 12 ♗xf6 ♘xf6 13 h5 ♗e4 14 0-0 0-0-0 15 ♘xe4 ♘xe4 16 c3 ♕g5 and now I like 17 ♕e2.

9 ... ♗b4 10 ♗d2 ♘e4 11 f3!, as in Campora-Curt Hansen, Palma de Mallorca 1989 is good for White, for instance 11 ... ♗xc3 12 bxc3 ♘xc3 13 h5 ♘xd1 14 ♗xa5 ♗xc2 and even the simple 15 ♖xd1 ♗xd1 16 ♔xd1 is enough for an advantage.

10 ♘xd7 ♘xd7 11 h5 ♗e4 12 ♖h3!

12 ... ♗g2

This idea has retained its popularity even though its main idea (to force the rook to g3, thus gaining a tempo with an eventual ... ♗d6) is frustrated by Volokitin's next move, and leaving the bishop on g2 is risky due to prospects of f3.

12 ... ♗d5 has scored quite well for Black in practice. White players have tried 13 ♗xd5?!, which looks clearly wrong, and 13 ♗d3, in which Rublevsky lost a very complicated game with White. As I have failed to find a significant improvement on this game, I've had to look elsewhere for White approaches, and luckily he has 13 ♗e2!?. According to my sources this has only been essayed once, in Feygin-Woerdemann, Germany 1998, but the move looks very logical to me. While ♗d3 has the benefit of hitting the h7-pawn and hence making it difficult for Black to use his h8-rook or play ... g6, ♗e2 is much more harmonious. It leaves the third rank free for the rook, either to swing into an attack against the black king or, more mundanely, to protect the c3-knight. The bishop also blocks the e-file,

making ♘xd5 a more tempting prospect for White. The d4-pawn is now protected by the white queen, making ... ♕b6 less effective. Finally, it should be noted that the bishop can, of course, relocate to d3 at a moment's notice – with White pushing cross-board space advantages, the most important thing right now is to consolidate and that's what the quiet bishop retreat seems to do. The above-mentioned game continued 13 ... c5 14 ♔f1!? cxd4 15 ♕xd4 ♗c6 16 h6 ♖g8 17 ♗e3 ♗c5 18 ♕d3 ♗xe3 19 ♕xe3 gxh6 20 ♖xh6 0-0-0 21 ♖h5 ♕b4 22 ♘b5 ♗xb5 23 ♖xb5 ♕a4 24 ♕c3+ ♔b8 25 ♖b4 and Black resigned as he is dropping his queen.

13 ♖e3 ♘b6 14 ♗d3 ♘d5 15 f3!

15 ... ♘xc3

15 ... ♗b4 was Lautier's choice in the stem game against Anand in Biel 1997. After 16 ♔f2! ♗xc3 17 bxc3 ♕xc3 18 ♖b1 ♕xd4 19 ♖xb7 ♖d8 the Indian devised a fiendish tactical plan: 20 h6!! gxh6? 21 ♗g6!!, winning after 21 ... ♘e7 (21 ... ♕xd1 22 ♖xe6+ ♔f8 23 ♗xh6+ ♔g8 24 ♗xf7 mate) 22 ♕xd4 ♖xd4 23 ♖d3 ♖d8 24 ♖xd8+ ♔xd8 25 ♗d3!.

16 bxc3 ♕xc3+ 17 ♗d2 ♕xd4 18 ♖b1 ♗c5 19 ♕e2 ♗h3 20 ♕h2 ♗xg4 21 ♖e4 ♕d5 22 fxg4 0-0-0

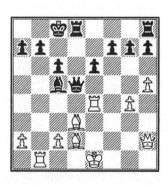

Black's three pawns are insufficient compensation for the piece, since he only has one passer and can't use his extra foot soldiers dynamically. White's central control provides sufficient protection for his king. Volokitin wraps things up nicely:

23 ♖b3 g6 24 ♗c3 f5 25 ♖e5 ♕d6 26 ♖e2 ♖he8 27 ♕xd6 ♗xd6 28 ♗f6 ♗g3+ 29 ♔f1 ♖d6 30 gxf5+- e5 31 ♗g5 gxh5 32 f6 h6 33 f7 ♖f8 34 ♗c4 b5 35 ♗e7 ♖d1+ 36 ♔g2 bxc4 37 ♗xf8 cxb3 38 axb3 ♖d7 39 ♗e7! 1-0

Game Forty-Four
Lutz – Adams
Frankfurt 1999

1 e4 d5 2 exd5 ♕xd5 3 ♘c3 ♕d8

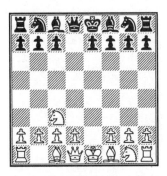

This is the most respectable of the alternatives to 3 ... ♕a5. A few GMs keep it as a surprise weapon – Israeli GM Artur Kogan, for instance, has a ridiculous score with Black here. The move has no great pretensions, it just attempts to get out of the opening with a playable slight disadvantage. I'm recommending that we proceed much as against 3 ... ♕a5.

3 ... ♕d6?! is a little more dodgy. Sermek has tried it out a few times, but personally I think the queen gets in the way here. A good, aggressive treatment is 4 d4 c6 5 ♗g5!? (I've successfully tried a ♗c4, ♘ge2 and ♗f4 setup, which looks very logical to me. The problem seems to be that, if Black uses the 2 ... ♘f6 3 ♘f3 ♕xd5 4 ♘c3 ♕d6 5 d4 c6 move-order, the option is no longer available. In any event, Svidler's opening choices are always fascinating and I think his setup is just as good) 5 ... ♘f6 6 ♕d2 ♗f5 7 0-0-0 e6 8 ♘f3 ♘bd7 9 a3 ♕c7 10 ♘e5 ♗e7 11 f4 h6 12 ♗xf6 ♘xf6 13 ♗d3 ♗xd3 14 ♕xd3 ♗d6 15 ♕f3 0-0-0 16 ♖d3 ♔b8 17 ♔b1 a6 18 ♖hd1 with an excellent game, as in Svidler-Cicak, European Club Cup 2003.

3 ... ♕e5+? is rubbish, and was exposed as such after 4 ♗e2 c6 5 d4 ♕c7 6 ♘f3 ♗f5 7 ♘e5 ♘d7 8 ♗f4 ♘xe5 9 ♗xe5 ♕b6 10 ♘a4 ♕d8 11 ♘c5 ♕b6 12 0-0 e6 13 b4 ♘f6 14 ♖b1 a6 15 a4 ♗xc5 16 bxc5 ♕a5 17 ♖xb7 ♕xa4 18 ♗d3 ♗xd3 19 ♕xd3 0-0 20 ♖fb1 1-0 in Skripchenko-Tolhuizen, Aosta Open 2003.

4 d4 ♘f6

More for entertainment than anything else, take a peek at the unfeasibly violent Smirin-Kaganskiy, Israeli Championship 2002, which continued 4 ... c6 5 ♗c4 ♗f5 6 g4! ♗g6 7 f4! e6 8 ♘f3 ♗b4 9 0-0 ♘e7 10 ♘e2 h5 11 f5! exf5 12 gxf5 ♗xf5 13 ♘e5 0-0 14 ♗g5 ♕c8 15 c3 ♗d6 16 ♗xe7 ♗xe7 17 ♘f4 b5 18 ♘fg6 ♗g5 19 ♕xh5 ♗e3+ 20 ♖f2 ♗xg6 21 ♘xg6 ♗xf2+ 22 ♔h1 bxc4 23 ♘e7 mate. Painful stuff.

5 ♘f3 c6 6 ♗c4 ♗f5 7 ♘e5 e6 8 g4 ♗g6 9 h4

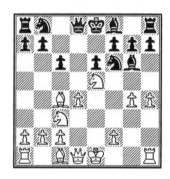

The parallels with the main line are obvious. The only difference is that here the queen is on d8 rather than a5, a factor whose importance is often hard to judge but seems detrimental here since the c3-knight is free to capture anything which lands on e4.

9 ... ♘bd7

Kotronias-Candela Perez, Linares Open 2003 continued 9 ... ♗b4 10 f3 ♘d5 11 ♗xd5 cxd5 12 ♕e2 ♕c8 13 ♗d2 ♘c6 14 ♘b5! ♗e7 15 ♗f4 ♘xe5 16 ♗xe5 and White's pieces were superbly placed. After 16 ... f6 17 ♘c7+ ♔f7 18 ♗f4 e5 19 dxe5 fxe5 20 ♕xe5 ♖d8 21 0-0-0 ♗f6 22 ♕e2 ♕d7 23 h5 ♗xc2 24 ♕xc2 ♖ac8 25 ♔b1 Black resigned.

10 ♘xd7 ♕xd7 11 h5 ♗e4 12 ♘xe4 ♘xe4 13 ♗e3 0-0-0 14 ♕f3

Facing the prospect of White castling long with two bishops and nursing kingside and central space advantages, Adams decides to roll the dice:

14 ... ♗b4+ 15 c3 ♘xc3 16 bxc3 ♗xc3+ 17 ♔e2 ♗xa1 18 ♖xa1

Black really doesn't have enough to match the bishops here, but Lutz's handling of the advantage is flawless.

18 ... f5 19 gxf5 exf5 20 d5!!

This is just superb. A move like this can have three benefits, and all of them are visible here:

1 The d4-pawn disappears, allowing White to play on the g1-a7 diagonal.

2 The c-file is opened, exposing the black king (though White must be careful, since obviously Black can use this file too, and with more pieces).

3 A black pawn appears on d5, killing his play on the d-file once it's blockaded.

20 ... cxd5 21 ♗d3 ♔b8 22 ♕f4+ ♔a8 23 ♕d4

Perfect play, and now the evaluation is clear.

23 ... b6 24 a4 f4 25 ♕xf4 ♖he8 26 ♗b5 ♕c8 27 ♗xe8 ♖xe8 28 ♕d4 ♕c2+ 29 ♔f1 ♕f5 30 ♖d1 ♕h3+ 31 ♔g1 ♕xh5 32 ♕xd5+ ♕xd5 33 ♖xd5

It is to Adams' credit that he managed to hang on for so long here, but the position is quite hopeless.

33 ... ♖e7 34 ♔g2 ♔b7 35 ♔g3 ♔c6 36 ♖d4 ♖e5 37 ♖c4+ ♔d7 38 ♗f4 ♖e7 39 ♖c7+ ♔e6 40 ♖xe7+ ♔xe7 41 ♗e5 g6 42 ♔f4 ♔e6 43 ♗c7 h6 44 ♔e4 g5 45 f3 ♔d7 46 ♗b8 h5 47 ♗xa7 ♔c7 48 ♔f5 g4 49 f4 g3 50 a5 bxa5 51 ♔g5 a4 52 ♔h4 g2 53 ♔g3 a3 54 ♔xg2 a2 55 ♗d4 ♔d6 56 f5 ♔e7 57 ♔g3 ♔f7 58 ♔h4 ♔e7 59 ♔xh5 ♔f7 60 ♔g5 ♔e7 61 ♔g6 ♔d6 62 f6 ♔d5 63 ♗a1 1-0

Game Forty-Five
Timofeev – Bryson
Capelle la Grande 2003

1 e4 d5 2 exd5 ♘f6 3 ♘f3!

3 d4 allows Black the option of 3 ... ♗g4!? with interesting gambit play (for him!).

3 c4 transposes into a Panov-Botvinnik after 3 ... c6 4 d4 cxd5 5 ♘c3, but the problem is 3 ... e6, the Icelandic Gambit, which is meant to be dubious but has always struck me as somewhat nasty. Besides, I don't think we should rush to allow Black a Panov-Botvinnik here – I certainly have more respect for the Caro-Kann than the 2 ... ♘f6 Scandinavian, so let's keep the game in these channels and see if we can rustle up some attacking chances.

3 ... ♘xd5

3 ... ♕xd5 4 ♘c3 transposes to 2 ... ♕xd5.

4 d4 ♗g4

4 ... g6 was Malakov's choice against Grischuk in the Lausanne Young Masters 2000. After 5 c4 ♘b6 6 ♘c3 ♗g7 7 ♗e3 0-0 8 h3 ♘c6 9 ♕d2 e5 10 d5 ♘a5 11 b3 e4 12 ♘d4 f5 13 ♗g5 ♕e8 14 0-0-0 c5 15 ♘de2 White was clearly better. Malakov tried the piece sac 15 ... ♘axc4?! 16 bxc4 ♘xc4 17 ♕c2 ♘e5 18 d6 ♘d3+ 19 ♖xd3 exd3 20 ♕xd3 f4 21 ♗e7 ♖f7 22 ♕c4 b5 23 ♘xb5 ♖b8 24 ♘ec3 ♖b7 25 ♘d5 a6 26 ♘bc7 ♕c6 27 ♗d3 and Black barely controlled a square.

4 ... ♗f5 5 ♗d3 ♗g6 (5 ... ♗xd3 6 ♕xd3 c6 7 c4 ♘f6 8 0-0 e6 9 b3 ♗e7 10 ♗b2 0-0 11 ♘c3 ♘bd7 12 ♖ad1 ♕c7 13 ♖fe1 also gives White easy activity: Caldeira-Cubas, Brasilia 2002) 6 0-0 e6 7 c4 ♘f6 8 ♘c3 ♗e7 9 ♗f4 0-0 10 ♗xg6 hxg6 11 ♕e2 ♘bd7 12 ♖ad1 c6 13 a3 ♖e8 14 ♖d3 ♕a5 15 ♘e5 ♖ad8 16 ♖fd1 ♕a6 17 ♗g5 and White was enormously active, even before the unfortunate 17 ... ♘d5 18 cxd5 ♗xg5 19 ♘e4 ♗f6 20 ♘xd7 1-0 of Korneev-Cubas, 6th Itau Cup 2002.

5 h3 ♗h5 6 c4 ♘b6 7 ♘c3

7 ... e5

Bryson also lost in this line to Conquest in the 4NCL 2001. A positional squeeze was the order of the day after 7 ... e6 8 ♗e3 ♘c6 9 d5 exd5 10 cxd5 ♘b4 11 ♗xb6 axb6 12 ♗e2 ♗d6 13 a3 ♗xf3 14 ♗xf3 ♘a6 15 0-0 0-0 16 b4! ♘b8 17 ♘b5 ♘d7 18 ♖c1 ♘f6 19 ♖c4 ♕d7 20 a4 ♖fe8 21 ♕c2 ♖e7 22 h4 ♖f8 23 g3 ♘e8 24 ♗g4 ♕d8 with a clear advantage for White.

8 g4! exd4 9 ♘xd4 ♗g6 10 ♗g2 c6 11 0-0

I love White's position! The wide open g2-bishop, the big lead in development – a clear advantage.

11 ... ♗e7 12 c5!

12 ... ♘6d7

12 ... ♗xc5 is very dangerous: 13 ♖e1+ ♗e7 14 ♗g5 ♘c8 (14 ... f6 is no improvement after 15 ♗f4 when 15 ... 0-0?! 16 ♘e6 ♕xd1 17 ♖axd1 wins the exchange) 15 ♕b3! ♕b6 16 ♕c4 and Black is on the edge of the abyss, for instance 16 ... f6 17 ♘d5!.

13 f4! h5 14 f5 ♗h7 15 g5!

Obviously Timofeev is in a foul mood. Already Black's position is hopeless – where did he go wrong?

15 ... ♘xc5

15 ... ♗xg5 runs into 16 ♘e6!! with carnage after 16 ... fxe6 17 ♕xh5+.

16 b4 ♘ca6 17 ♗e3

17 ... ♗xg5?

17 ... 0-0? 18 ♕xh5 ♗xb4 is far too dangerous: 19 g6 fxg6 20 fxg6 ♗xg6 21 ♕xg6 ♗xc3 22 ♗e4 and White wins.

17 ... ♗xb4 looks like the only way to try to complicate. Nonetheless, even here it looks like White is much better, for instance 18 ♘e4 ♘c5 19 ♘xc6! ♘xc6 20 ♗xc5 ♗xc5+ 21 ♘xc5 0-0 22 ♕xd8 ♖axd8 23 ♘xb7 ♖c8 24 ♘d6 ♖cd8 25 ♖ad1 with an overwhelming advantage.

18 ♗xg5 ♕xg5 19 ♖e1+ ♔f8 20 ♘f3 ♕f6 21 ♘e4 ♕e7 22 ♘d6 ♕d8 23 ♖e8+ ♕xe8 24 ♘xe8 ♔xe8 25 ♕d2!

Black's responses have all been forced since move 18, and now we can take stock. While Black is okay on a material count, his piece co-ordination is obviously insufferable.

25 ... ♗xf5 26 ♖e1+ ♗e6 27 ♘g5 1-0

CHAPTER NINE
The Alekhine Defence

"Alekhine was everything a chessplayer ought to be: an arrogant, selfish, alcoholic womanizer, with a talent for making enemies and a liking for cats."

William Hartston

1 e4 ♘f6 2 e5 ♘d5 3 d4 d6

At the time of its adoption by Alekhine, 1 ... ♘f6 was truly revolutionary, the most brash of the hypermodern openings. It should be pointed out that, as often happens, it isn't the inventor of the system but rather its chief protagonist who gets remembered – the earliest game I've found with the system is a sweet 1802 effort from Napoleon!

After such grand beginnings I guess the only way is down, and indeed the Alekhine, while undoubtedly sound, has never received the acclaim or popularity of the main defences to 1 e4.

The line which I'm recommending, 4 ♘f3, is the near-universal choice of top players when faced with the Alekhine. By contrast, the Four Pawns Attack (4 f4) gives Black a great deal of counterplay, while the Exchange Variation (4 exd6) is a little wet. This is an opening which everyone who plays 1 e4 should be happy to face, since its provocative nature inherently gives attacking chances.

Game Forty-Six
Zapata – Baburin
Bled Olympiad 2002

1 e4 ♘f6 2 e5 ♘d5 3 d4 d6 4 ♘f3 ♗g4

This is the classical way to handle the Alekhine. It is well explored and allows White several routes to an advantage, however, and so has declined in popularity.

5 ♗e2

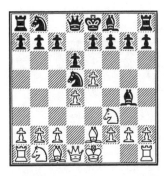

5 ... e6

The alternative 5 ... c6 6 c4 ♘b6 (6 ... ♘c7 was given short shrift in Rowson-Crouch, 4NCL 2002 after 7 0-0 ♗xf3 8 exd6! ♗xe2 9 dxc7 ♗xd1 10 cxd8=♕+ ♔xd8 11 ♖xd1 ♘d7 12 ♘c3 g6 13 b4 ♗g7 14 b5 ♖c8 15 c5 b6 16 a4!! bxc5 17 dxc5 cxb5 18 axb5 ♗xc3 19 ♖xa7 ♖c7 20 ♖a8+ ♖c8 21 ♖a3 ♗b4 22 ♖ad3 ♗xc5 23 ♖xd7+ ♔e8 24 ♗e3 ♗xe3 25 fxe3 with a clearly better endgame for White due to his active rooks and outside passed pawn) is best met by 7 ♘bd2! and now:

7 ... ♘8d7 8 0-0 ♗xf3 (8 ... dxe5 9 ♘xe5 ♘xe5 10 dxe5 ♗f5 11 ♗g4 e6 12 ♗xf5 exf5 13 ♕c2 ♕d7 14 ♘f3 0-0-0 15 ♗g5 ♕d3 16 ♕c1 ♖e8 17 b3 h6 18 ♖d1 ♕e4 19 ♗e3 c5 20 ♕a3 g5 21 ♕xa7 g4 22 ♕xb6 gxf3 23 g3 ♕g4 24 ♖d7 was Polgar-Fernandez Garcia, Basque Country vs. World Rapid 2003) 9 ♘xf3 dxe5 10 dxe5 e6 11 ♗d2 ♘c5 12 ♕c2 ♗e7 13 b4 ♘cd7 14 ♕e4 ♕c7 15 ♗c3 ♘a4 16 ♗d2 0-0 17 ♗d1 ♘ab6 18 ♗c2 g6 19 h4 ♖fd8 20 h5 and the white attack soon crashed through in Grischuk-Szmetan, Blitz Game 2000;

7 ... dxe5 8 ♘xe5 ♗f5 (8 ... ♗xe2 9 ♕xe2 ♘8d7 10 0-0 e6 11 ♘df3 ♘xe5 12 dxe5 ♗e7 13 ♖d1 ♘d7 14 ♖d4 ♕b6 15 ♖g4 g6 16 ♗h6 and there's nothing good about the black position: Dgebuadze-Popov, Wijk aan Zee 2001) 9 ♘ef3! e6 10 0-0 ♘8d7 11 b3 ♗e7 12 ♗b2 0-0 13 ♖e1 ♖e8 14 ♗f1 h6 15 ♕c1 ♕c7 16 ♗c3 ♘c8 17 ♕b2 ♗f6 18 b4 ♘e7 19 a4 and White

had quietly built up a beautiful position with both central and queenside space advantages in Vescovi-Malbran, Buenos Aires 2000.

6 c4 ♘b6 7 h3 ♗h5

7 ... ♗xf3?! is a premature sac of the 'minor exchange', White has a few routes to an edge, but I quite like the treatment of Agdestein against Kopylov from the Kiel Open 2000: 8 ♗xf3 ♘c6 9 exd6 cxd6 10 d5!? exd5 11 ♗xd5 ♘xd5 12 ♕xd5 ♕h4 13 0-0 ♗e7 14 ♖e1 0-0 15 ♘c3 and White had advantages in both structure and more purposeful piece placement, even before Black chucked the game with 15 ... ♘b4? 16 ♕xb7 ♘c2 17 ♖e4 ♕h5 18 ♖b1 ♗f6 19 ♕d5 ♗e5 20 c5 with a clear extra pawn.

8 exd6 cxd6 9 ♘c3

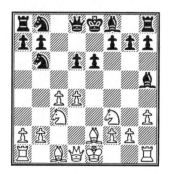

9 ... ♗e7

9 ... d5 runs into some difficulties after 10 cxd5 exd5 11 ♘e5!, for instance Vazquez-Almeida, Capablanca Memorial Premier II 2002 which continued 11 ... ♗xe2 12 ♕xe2 ♗e7 13 ♕b5+ ♘8d7 14 ♘xd5 a6 15 ♕b3 ♘xe5 16 ♘xb6 ♗b4+ 17 ♔f1 ♕xb6 18 dxe5 0-0 19 ♗e3 ♕b5+ 20 ♔g1 ♖fe8 21 a3 ♗f8 22 ♕xb5 axb5 23 f4 f6 24 ♔f2!? fxe5 25 f5 when, even after a ... b4 break, Black's structure is messy.

10 d5 e5 11 g4! ♗g6 12 h4

After the game, GM Baburin told me that Black faces serious dangers in this line, and indeed Zapata's treatment appears very effective.

12 ... h6

In a previous enocunter, Baburin preferred a more aggressive defence of the kingside with 12 ... h5 and after 13 g5 Black has a few options: 13 ... ♘8d7 14 ♗e3 ♖c8 15 b3 ♘c5 16 ♖g1 ♘bd7 17 b4 e4 18 ♘d2 ♘d3+ 19 ♔f1 (Fritz prefers the materialistic 19 ♗xd3 exd3 20 ♗xa7?!, but after 20 ... b6 the sidelined dark-squared bishop and awkward white king provide excellent compensation) 19 ... ♘xb4 20 ♘dxe4 0-0 21 ♗d4 ♖e8 22 a3 ♘a6 23 ♗xh5 ♖xc4 24 ♗e2 and with a dangerous kingside pawn roller White has a big attack, though Black managed to draw in Hamdouchi- Baburin, Saint Vincent 2000;

13 ... ♗f5 does nothing to compete for the crucial e4-square, and after 14 ♘d2! g6 15 ♘de4 ♕c8 16 ♗e3 ♘8d7 17 b3 a6 18 ♖c1 ♗xe4 19 ♘xe4 ♘c5 20 ♘g3! a5 21 a3 ♘bd7 22 b4 ♘a6 23 c5! dxc5 24 b5! ♘ab8 25 d6 ♗d8 26 ♕d5 0-0 27 ♘e4 White had a bind in Nevednichy-Loviscek, Nova Gorica 2002;

13 ... ♘a6 14 ♗e3 ♘b4?! was an over-ambitious plan in Delgado-Almeida, Cuban Championship 2002. White gained the advantage after 15 ♖c1 e4 16 ♘d4 ♘d3+ 17 ♗xd3 exd3 18 b3 ♕d7 19 f4 0-0 20 ♕f3 ♗f5 21 ♘xf5 ♕xf5 22 ♕e4 ♕g4 23 f5!.

Note that 12 ... e4? 13 ♘g5 h6 14 ♘gxe4 0-0 15 g5! is horrible for Black: Vozovic-Le Thanh Tu, World U-16 Championship 2001.

13 ♗e3 ♘8d7 14 b3 a6 15 ♗d3!

This is the main point which gives me confidence in this variation – Black can't adequately compete for the e4-square (note that an immediate ... ♘c5 would hang the e-pawn), and indeed it's unclear where his counterplay is going to come from.

15 ... ♗xd3 16 ♕xd3 ♘c8 17 ♔e2!

The king is perfectly safe in the middle, meaning that this is the most efficient way to connect the rooks.

17 ... ♘f8 18 ♘e4 ♘g6 19 h5 ♘f4+ 20 ♗xf4 exf4 21 ♖ag1! b5

Desperation, but there was no way to blockade.

21 ... ♗g5 22 ♘exg5 hxg5 23 ♕f5! is great for White: 23 ... ♕f6 24 ♕xf6! gxf6 25 ♘d4 and despite having the majority, Black is losing on the kingside.

22 cxb5 axb5 23 ♕xb5+ ♔f8 24 a4

The rest requires no comment.

24 ... ♖a5 25 ♕b7 ♕e8 26 ♖c1 ♘a7 27 ♖he1 f5 28 gxf5 ♗d8 29 ♔f1 ♕xh5 30 ♘xd6 ♔g8 31 ♖e8+ ♔h7 32 ♕f7 ♕h3+ 33 ♔e2 ♖xe8+ 34 ♕xe8 ♗f6 35 ♕g6+ 1-0

Game Forty-Seven
Grischuk – Ponomariov
Torshavn 2000

This was the first game I saw which indicated that Grischuk could fight for the World Championship one day.

1 e4 ♘f6 2 e5 ♘d5 3 d4 d6 4 ♘f3 g6 5 ♗c4 ♘b6 6 ♗b3 ♗g7

7 a4

7 ♕e2 ♘c6 8 0-0 0-0 9 h3 a5 10 a4 dxe5 11 dxe5 ♘d4 12 ♘xd4 ♕xd4 13 ♖e1 e6 14 ♘d2 ♘d5 15 ♘f3 ♕c5 16 ♕e4 was a nice position which led to a hilarious checkmate in Short-Timman, Tilburg 1991, but as this game has been published to death I've decided to plump for a more aggressive modern line which has been essayed by several very dangerous super-GMs. Indeed, if you want to make the most of any attacking positions you get as a result of this repertoire, you could do a lot worse than a religious study of the games of Grischuk, Sutovsky and Motylev.

7 ... a5

7 ... dxe5!? is a relatively new move. The critical position arises after 8 a5 ♘6d7 (8 ... ♘d5 is much more compliant, and after 9 ♘xe5 0-0 10 0-0 White is slightly better, for instance Hracek-Varga, Odorheiu Secuiesc 1995 which continued 10 ... e6 11 ♘f3 c5 12 c4 ♘b4 13 ♗g5 ♗f6 14 ♗xf6 ♕xf6 15 ♘c3 cxd4 16 ♘e4 ♕g7 and now 17 ♕xd4 would maintain the advantage) 9 ♗xf7+!? ♚xf7 10 ♘g5+ ♚g8 11 ♘e6 ♕e8 12 ♘xc7 ♕d8 (12 ... ♕f7?! is very risky: *NCO* believes White is clearly better after 13 dxe5! – as yet untested, as far as I know) 13 ♘xa8 (13 ♘e6 repeats) 13 ... exd4 14 c3 ♘c5 15 cxd4 ♗xd4 16 0-0 e5 17 ♗e3 ♘ba6 (17 ... ♘c6 18 ♗xd4 exd4 19 ♕c2 ♘e6 occurred in Cooper-Smith, Walsall 1992, and now I like 20 f4!? trying to open lines) 18 ♘c3 ♗f5 19 ♘a4, and now 19 ... ♕xa8 (Gutman analyses 19 ... ♘e6 20 ♖e1 ♕xa8 21 g4! as clearly better for White) 20 ♗xd4 exd4 21 ♘xc5 ♘xc5 22 ♕xd4 ♘e6 23 ♕d5 results in a balanced position. Black has a slight material advantage but major problems with major piece co-ordination and king safety. White will endeavour to bring his rooks into play to force some concessions.

8 ♘g5!?

With a threat!

8 ... e6 9 f4!

This is the point – due to Black's somewhat retarded queenside development, White can generate play against f7 quite quickly.

9 ... dxe5

9 ... ♘c6 10 c3 ♗d7 11 0-0 ♕e7 12 ♘e4! d5 13 ♘c5 ♘d8 14 ♗c2 ♘c8 15 b3 b6 16 ♘d3 f5 17 exf6 ♗xf6 18 ♗a3 ♘d6 19 ♘e5 ♘8f7 20 c4 c6 21 ♕g4 ♘h6 22 ♕h3 ♗g7 23 ♘d2 0-0 24 ♖ae1 resulted in a gorgeous position for White in Sutovsky-Reinemer, Isle of Man 2000.

10 fxe5 c5 11 c3 cxd4 12 0-0!

An important finesse.

12 ... 0-0 13 cxd4 ♘c6 14 ♘f3 f6 15 ♘c3!

15 ... fxe5

15 ... ♘d5 16 exf6 ♘xf6 leads to an IQP position with an open f-file and excellent attacking chances. After 17 ♔h1 ♔h8 18 ♗g5 h6 19 ♗h4 g5 20 ♗f2 ♘d5 21 ♗c2 ♘db4 I like 22 ♗e4!, preventing the equalizing 22 ♗b1 e5 23 d5 ♘d4 24 ♘xd4 exd4 25 ♘b5 d3 26 ♗xd3 ♕xd5 27 ♗e2 ♗f5 of Motylev-Janev, Ubeda 2001.

16 ♗g5! ♕d7 17 dxe5 ♘xe5 18 ♘xe5 ♖xf1+ 19 ♕xf1 ♕d4+ 20 ♔h1 ♕xe5

So White has sacrificed a pawn. Given one more move, Black will play ... ♗d7 and consolidate.

21 ♗d8!!

This is just superb – the gain of tempo from this bishop's adventures leaves Black with no time to develop his queenside.

21 ... ♕c5 22 ♘e4 ♕b4

Also 22 ... ♕d4 23 ♖d1 ♕xe4 24 ♗xb6 gives White a huge attack – he has ♖d8+ and ♕f7 in the pipeline (♗g1 can cover the back rank) while Black is playing without his queenside pieces.

23 ♘g5 ♔h8 24 ♕f7 ♗d7 25 ♗xe6 ♖xd8

26 ♕g8+ ♖xg8 27 ♘f7 mate

Game Forty-Eight
Iordachescu – Wohl
Vins du Merdoc Open 2002

1 e4 ♘f6 2 e5 ♘d5 3 d4 d6 4 ♘f3

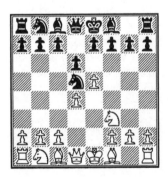

4 ... dxe5

4 ... ♘c6 was essayed in the final game of the Ponomariov-Ivanchuk FIDE World Championship match in 2002, where it fell victim to a model treatment by White. 5 c4 ♘b6 6 e6!!. One '!' is objective; this pawn sac is the strongest way to handle the position and greatly frustrates Black's development. The second '!' is for courage – needing only a draw to become FIDE World Champion, Ponomariov could be forgiven for treating

the position in a more conservative fashion, but instead trusts his judgement and goes for the critical line. 6 ... fxe6 7 ♘c3 g6 8 ♗e3 ♗g7 9 h4!. Much more purposeful than simple development – at a stroke White gives life to his h1-rook and prepares to weaken Black's kingside. 9 ... 0-0 10 h5 e5 11 d5 ♘d4 12 ♘xd4 exd4 13 ♗xd4 g5 14 ♗xg7 ♔xg7 15 h6+ ♔g8 16 ♕d2 e5 17 ♖h5! g4 18 ♕g5+! ♕xg5 19 ♖xg5+ ♔h8 20 ♖g7 ♖f6 21 ♖xc7 ♖xh6 22 b4. With c5 on the cards, White is winning here, but Ponomariov understandably took the draw and secured his place in chess history.

4 ... c6 5 ♗e2 dxe5 6 dxe5 ♗g4 7 0-0 ♗xf3 8 ♗xf3 e6 is solid but passive, and with his two bishops White can claim an enduring edge, for instance 9 ♘d2 ♘d7 10 ♖e1 ♕c7 11 ♘c4 ♘7b6 12 ♘xb6 axb6 13 c4 ♘e7 14 ♗d2 ♖d8 15 ♕c1 ♘g6 16 ♗c3 ♗e7 17 ♕e3 ♗c5 18 ♕e4 ♕e7 19 a3 ♕h4 20 g3 ♕xe4 21 ♖xe4 ♔d7 22 b4 with a clearly better endgame in Socko-Zilberman, Aeroflot Open 2002.

5 ♘xe5 c6

5 ... g6 6 ♗c4 c6 7 0-0 ♗g7 8 ♖e1 0-0 9 ♗b3 ♗f5 (9 ... ♘d7 10 ♘f3 ♘7f6 11 c4 ♘c7 12 ♘c3 ♗g4 was seen in Rowson-Baburin, Torshavn 2000, and now Rowson played 12 ♗e3 but I quite like the immediate 13 h3 ♗xf3 14 ♕xf3 ♕xd4 15 ♖xe7 ♕d6 16 ♖e1 when White's two bishops give him an edge) 10 ♘d2 ♘d7 11 ♘df3 ♘xe5 12 ♘xe5 a5 13 a4 ♕c7 14 c3 ♖ad8 15 ♕f3 ♕c8 16 h3 ♗e6 17 ♗d2 c5 18 c4 ♘b4 19 d5 ♗f5 20 g4 ♗d7 21 ♗c3 ♗e8 22 ♖e3 e6 23 g5 f6 24 gxf6 ♖xf6 25 ♕e4 ♖f5 26 ♖ae1 and White had a perfect attacking setup in Shirov-Agdestein, Radisson SAS Challenge 2001.

6 ♗c4 ♘d7

6 ... ♗e6 7 0-0 ♘d7 8 ♘f3 ♘c7 9 ♗d3 ♗g4 10 h3 ♗h5 11 ♗g5 ♗g6 12 ♗e2 h6 13 ♗h4 ♘d5 14 ♖e1 ♕c8 was Golubev-Kasimdzhanov, ACP Blitz Prelim 2004, and now I like 15 a3! preparing 16 c4.

7 ♘f3 e6 8 0-0 b5

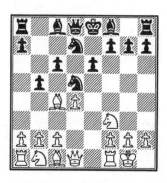

8 ... ♗e7 9 ♘bd2 0-0 10 ♘e4 b5 11 ♗d3 a6 12 c3 ♗b7 13 a4 ♕c7 14 ♖e1 gave a similar setup in Quezada-Ramirez, Capablanca Memorial 2004.

9 ♗d3!?

Joe Gallagher and Viktor Bologan have both dropped the bishop back to b3 in this and similar positions, but I quite like the directness of ♗d3 – White points at the kingside and runs little risk of the bishop looking at the d5-knight for the rest of the game.

9 ... ♗b7

9 ... a6 10 b3 ♗e7 11 c4 ♘5b6 12 ♘c3 b4 13 ♘e4 ♘f6 14 ♕c2 ♗b7 15 ♗f4 ♘xe4 16 ♗xe4 was beautiful for White in Kasimdzhanov-Brochet, French Team Championship 2004.

10 a4

This is often a useful move to flick in, but White can of course also play without generating queenside pressure. Other instances are instructive:

10 ♖e1 ♗e7 11 ♘bd2 0-0 12 ♘e4 a6 13 ♗g5 (13 c3 c5 14 dxc5 ♘xc5 15 ♘xc5 ♗xc5 16 ♕e2 ♕c7 17 ♘e5! f6 18 ♕h5 ♗xf2+ 19 ♔xf2 fxe5+ 20 ♔g1 e4 21 ♖xe4 ♕b6+ 22 ♗e3 ♘f6 23 ♕h3 ♕c7 24 ♖h4 ♕c6 25 ♗d4 h6 26 ♕g3 ♖ad8 27 ♖e1 ♖d5 28 ♗e4 and White was winning in Murdzia-Luther, Cappelle la Grande 2003) 13 ... ♗xg5 14 ♘fxg5 h6 15 ♘f3 c5 16 c4 bxc4 17 ♗xc4 ♕e7 18 ♖c1 cxd4 19 ♕xd4 ♖fd8 20 ♗f1 a5 21 ♘e5 ♘xe5 22 ♕xe5 ♗a6 23 ♗xa6 ♖xa6 24 ♖ed1 ♖aa8 25 g3 gave White a positional edge in Lutz-Luther, Essen 2002.

10 ... a6 11 ♖e1 ♗e7 12 ♘bd2 ♕b6 13 c4!

A good positional decision. At the cost of an IQP, White gains control over e5 with tempo.

13 ... bxc4 14 ♘xc4 ♕c7 15 ♗g5!

White's attack will be based mainly on dark squares, so this black bishop is of vital importance. Ensuring its exchange cements White's advantage.

15 ... c5 16 ♖c1 0-0 17 ♗xe7 ♘xe7 18 ♘ce5 ♖ad8 19 b4!

Not quite winning a pawn, but forcing a favourable transformation.

19 ... ♘xe5 20 ♘xe5 f6 21 ♖xc5 ♕d6 22 ♕h5 ♘f5 23 ♘f3 g6 24 ♕h3 ♗xf3 25 ♗xf5 exf5 26 ♕xf3 ♕xd4 27 ♕b3+ ♔h8 28 g3!

Despite appearances, Black is really struggling here. White's b-pawn is very fast, his pieces are more active and the black king will be a constant worry.

28 ... ♖fe8 29 ♖cc1 f4 30 b5 axb5 31 axb5 fxg3 32 hxg3 ♖xe1+ 33 ♖xe1 ♕d2 34 ♖b1 ♕d3 35 ♕xd3 ♖xd3 36 b6

This position is a trivial win. White simply marches his king to the queenside, and Black's kingside counterplay is much too slow.

36 ... ♖d8 37 b7 ♖b8 38 ♔g2 ♔g7 39 ♔f3 g5 40 ♔e4 ♔g6 41 ♔d5 ♔f5 42 ♖b4 h5 43 ♔c6 g4 44 ♔c7 1-0

CHAPTER TEN
Garbage

"Should a professional player learn by heart how to refute dubious opening schemes? The Greco Counter-Gambit, the Albin Counter-Gambit, the Schara-Hennig Gambit, the Canal Variation... In principle, learning by heart is not harmful – any exercise develops the capability of the organ being trained, in this case the brain. But one might ask, what for?"

GM Victor Korchnoi

These lines are not very good, but you should still have some idea of how to face them. In most cases, simple development should suffice for an advantage.

Game Forty-Nine
Rowson – Filipovic
Pula Open 2002

1 e4 b6

1 ... a6?!, the St.George, isn't very good either. White can proceed as against the Owen's, for instance 2 d4 b5 3 &d3 e6 4 ♘f3 &b7 5 0-0 c5 6 c3 ♘f6 7 ♕e2 with an excellent position in Shabalov-Gagnon, National Open 2002.

2 d4 &b7

This is Owen's Defence. It has had a few supporters at GM level – Kengis and Glek, for instance. English prodigy Luke McShane played it all the time a couple of years ago – since ditching it he's gone up 100 rating points, so I guess his attachment isn't too strong.

3 &d3!

I think this is best. 3 ♘c3 allows systems with ... &b4, when Black gains more central pressure.

3 ... e6 4 ♕e2

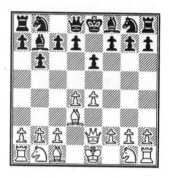

4 ... d5

The alternatives allow White a huge space advantage – while Black remains quite solid, his position requires very precise handling just to survive, and everyone should be more than happy taking a crack from the white side.

4 ... d6 5 ♘f3 ♘d7 6 c4 g6 7 b3 ♗g7 8 ♗b2 ♘e7 9 ♘c3 h6 10 ♖d1 0-0 11 0-0, Summerscale-McShane, Redbus KO 2002.

4 ... g6 5 f4 ♗g7 6 ♘f3 ♘e7 7 ♗e3 d6 8 c4 ♘d7 9 ♘c3 a6 10 0-0, Nascimento-Lima, Brasilia 2002.

4 ... ♘e7 5 ♘f3 c5 6 c3 d5 was Ivanov-Sharafuddin, World Open 2003, and now 7 e5 is the simplest.

4 ... f5?! is a bit dodgy after 5 ♘d2 ♘f6 6 ♘gf3 fxe4 7 ♘xe4 ♗e7 8 ♘fg5!, even before the 8 ... ♘xe4? 9 ♗xe4 ♗xe4 10 ♕xe4 ♘c6 11 ♘xe6! dxe6 12 ♕xc6+ of Babula-Odesskij, Czech Open 2003.

5 e5 c5 6 c3 ♕c8 7 ♘f3

This is like a very poor French for Black. He now tries exchanging off his bad bishop, but Rowson astutely starts a central fight which ends in a substantial advantage.

7 ... ♗a6 8 c4!

8 ... cxd4 9 ♘bd2 dxc4 10 ♘xc4 ♗xc4 11 ♗xc4 ♗b4+ 12 ♔f1 a6 13 g3!

Black temporaily has an extra pawn, but his position is unhealthy.

13 ... ♘c6 14 ♔g2 b5 15 ♗d3 ♘ge7 16 a3! ♗a5 17 a4! b4?!

17 ... bxa4 is a better defensive try, chopping off the dangerous a-pawn, but White is still better after 18 ♖xa4 ♕b7 19 ♗e4.

18 ♗g5 h6 19 ♗xe7 ♘xe7 20 ♖hc1 ♕d8 21 ♗xa6 0-0 22 ♗d3

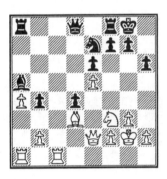

This is much better for White, whose co-ordination is superb.

22 ... ♕d7 23 ♕e4 g6 24 h4! ♗b6 25 h5! ♖xa4 26 ♖xa4 ♕xa4 27 ♕f4!

27 ... ♕b3 28 ♗c2 ♕d5 29 ♗e4 ♕d7 30 ♕xh6 ♘f5 31 ♗xf5 gxf5 32 ♘g5 f6 33 exf6 ♗d8 34 f7+ ♖xf7 35 ♘xf7 ♕d5+ 36 ♔g1 ♔xf7 37 ♕g6+ ♔e7 38 h6 d3 39 h7 ♕d4 40 ♕h5 ♕xb2 41 ♖d1 ♕h8 42 ♖xd3 ♗b6 43 ♕g5+ ♔f8 44 ♖d7 1-0

Game Fifty
Campora – Salgado Gonzalez
Seville Open 2002

1 e4 ♘c6

This is one of Nimzowitsch's less successful opening experiments. It's fine if Black is prepared to transpose back into mainline 1 ... e5 channels, but if he tries to keep it original his position is severely compromised by the premature placement of the c6-knight – in several lines the abscence of a ... c5 break really hurts.

2 d4 d5

2 ... e5 3 ♘f3 is a Scotch.

3 ♘c3

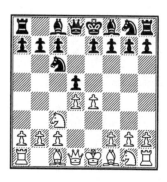

3 ... ♘f6

3 ... e5 is risky: 4 dxe5 d4 5 ♘d5 f5 6 exf6 ♘xf6 7 ♗g5 ♗e6 8 ♗xf6 gxf6 9 ♗c4 ♗b4+ 10 ♘xb4 ♗xc4 11 ♘xc6 bxc6 12 ♕h5+ ♗f7 13 ♕c5 ♕d6 14 ♕xd6 cxd6 15 ♘e2 and it was very surprising that Ponomariov didn't convert against Vlassov in the FIDE Grand Prix 2002.

3 ... dxe4 4 d5 ♘e5 5 ♕d4 ♘g6 6 ♕xe4! is nice for White, for instance 6 ... a6 7 ♘f3 ♘f6 8 ♕a4+ ♗d7 9 ♕b3 ♖b8 10 ♗g5 e5 11 dxe6 ♗xe6 12 ♗c4 ♗xc4 13 ♕xc4 ♗e7 14 0-0 0-0 15 ♖ad1 ♕c8 16 a4 in Zelcic-Rossi, Montecatini Terme 1997.

3 ... e6 4 ♘f3 is good for White – the only example from the past few years is Fercec-Kristovic, Zadar Open 2002, which continued 4 ... h6?! 5 ♗b5 ♘f6 6 ♘e5 ♗d7 7 ♘xd7 ♕xd7 8 e5 ♘g8 9 0-0 with an excellent position.

4 e5 ♘d7

4 ... ♘g8 5 f4 ♘h6 6 ♘f3 ♗g4 7 ♗e3 ♘f5 8 ♗f2 e6 9 ♗b5 ♗b4 10 h3 ♗xf3 11 ♕xf3 ♘h4 12 ♕g3 ♘g6 13 a3 ♗xc3+ 14 ♕xc3 0-0 15 g3 ♕d7 16 0-0 is excellent for White: Moroz-Mikhaletz, Zonal 2000.

5 ♘f3 ♘b6 6 ♗b5 ♗g4 7 h3 ♗xf3 8 ♕xf3 e6 9 0-0 g6 10 ♖d1 ♗g7 11 a4 a5 12 b3!

Again we see that the c6-knight is just a liability.

12 ... 0-0 13 ♗xc6 bxc6 14 ♗a3 ♖e8 15 ♘e2 f6 16 ♕c3 fxe5 17 dxe5 ♘d7 18 f4 g5 19 g3 gxf4 20 gxf4 ♕h4 21 ♖d3 ♕h5 22 ♖e1 ♔h8 23 ♕xc6 ♘xe5 24 fxe5 ♗xe5 25 ♘g3 1-0

Game Fifty-One
Macieja – Vasquez
Curacao Open 2001

1 e4 e5 2 ♘f3 f5

This is known as the Latvian Gambit.

2 ... d5 3 exd5 ♗d6 (*NCO* gives 3 ... e4 4 ♕e2 ♘f6 5 d3! as clearly better for White) 4 d4 e4 5 ♘e5 ♘f6 6 ♘c3 ♘bd7 7 ♗f4 ♕e7 8 ♗b5 0-0 9 ♗xd7 ♘xd7 10 ♘xd7 ♗xd7 11 ♗xd6 ♕xd6 12 0-0 and White was a pawn up for zip in Kotronias-Corbin, Istanbul Olympiad 2000.

2 ... f6?? leads to a king hunt after 3 ♘xe5! fxe5 4 ♕h5+ ♔e7 5 ♕xe5+ ♔f7 6 ♗c4+ – take two minutes and try to force checkmate from here. Your solution should look something like 6 ... ♔g6 (6 ... d5 7 ♗xd5+ ♔g6 8 h4! h5 9 ♗xb7! is equally terminal) 7 ♕f5+ ♔h6 8 h4! when the threat of d4+ leads to mate in 9.

3 ♘xe5 ♕f6

Nunn's analysis has completely destroyed 3 ... ♘c6?: 4 d4! ♕h4 (4 ... fxe4 5 ♘xc6 dxc6 6 ♕h5+ wins) 5 ♘f3! ♕xe4+ 6 ♗e2 with a winning lead in development, when Black's attempt to win material is too compromising after 6 ... ♘b4 7 0-0 ♕xc2 8 ♕e1 ♗e7 9 ♘c3 ♘f6 10 ♘e5.

4 ♘c4 fxe4 5 ♘c3

5 ... ♕f7

5 ... c6 was something of a shock when it landed on my board a few years ago in the Politiken Cup. After 6 ♘xe4 ♕e6 7 ♕e2 d5, however, instead of my 8 ♘ed6+?!, 8 ♘cd6+! wins: 8 ... ♗xd6 (8 ... ♔d8 9 ♘g5! looks good, for instance 9 ... ♕xe2+ 10 ♗xe2 ♗xd6 11 ♘f7+ ♔e7 12 ♘xh8 ♔f8 13 ♗h5 g6 14 ♘xg6+ hxg6 15 ♗xg6 and White is better) 9 ♘xd6+ ♔f8 10 ♕xe6 ♗xe6 11 ♘xb7 and White has two extra pawns for nothing.

6 ♘e3 c6 7 ♘xe4 d5

8 ♘g3

Good enough and leading to an instructive game, but this wouldn't be my choice here.

An even more efficient way is Nunn's 8 ♘g5! ♕f6 9 ♘f3 ♗d6 10 d4 ♘e7 11 c4, when the compensation for Black's f-pawn is simply non-existent.

8 ... h5 9 d4 h4 10 ♘e2 ♗d6 11 ♘g1!

White's inaccuracy on move 8 has led to some awkwardness, but notice how Black can't generate any play even after this.

11 ... ♘f6 12 ♘f3 ♘e4 13 ♗e2 ♘d7 14 h3 ♘df6 15 0-0 ♕c7 16 c4 g5 17 ♘e5!

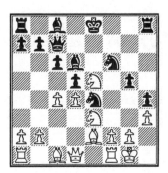

A nice transformation of the advantage.

17 ... ♗xe5 18 dxe5 ♕xe5 19 cxd5 cxd5 20 ♗f3

The threat is ♘xd5.

20 ... ♗e6 21 ♖e1 ♔f7 22 ♘g4 ♘xg4 23 ♗xg4 ♗xg4 24 ♕xg4 ♕d6 25 ♗xg5 ♖ag8 26 ♕f5+ ♔e8 27 ♖ac1 ♖xg5 28 ♖c8+ 1-0

Black drops both rooks.

Index of Variations